AF361270

ETERNAL BONDS, TRUE CONTRACTS

ETERNAL BONDS, TRUE CONTRACTS

Law and Nature in
Shakespeare's Problem Plays

A. G. HARMON

STATE UNIVERSITY OF NEW YORK PRESS

Published by
State University of New York Press, Albany

For information, address State University of New York Press,
90 State Street, Suite 700, Albany, NY 12207

Production by Marilyn P. Semerad
Marketing by Anne M. Valentine

Library of Congress Cataloging-in-Publication Data

Harmon, A. G., 1962–
Eternal bonds, true contracts : law and nature in Shakespeare's problem plays /
A. G. Harmon.
    p. cm.
  Includes bibliographical references and index.
  ISBN 0-7914-6117-3 (acid-free paper)
   1. Shakespeare, William, 1564–1616—Tragicomedies. 2. Shakespeare, William,
1564–1616—Knowledge—Natural history. 3. Shakespeare, William,
1564–1616—Knowledge—Law. 4. Nature in literature. 5. Law in literature.
6. Tragicomedy. I. Title.

PR2981.5.H37 2004
822.3'3—dc22

2003061720

10 9 8 7 6 5 4 3 2 1

Contents

Acknowledgments

Portions of chapter 4 were published in an article entitled "Lawful Deeds": The Entitlements of Marriage in Shakespeare's *All's Well That Ends Well.*" *Logos: A Journal of Catholic Thought and Culture* 4.3 (summer 2001): 115–42.

A version of this book was submitted as a doctoral dissertation to The Catholic University of America, Washington, DC, in May 2000 in partial requirement of the degree of Doctor of Philosophy.

CHAPTER **1**

The Semblance of Virtue

Law, Nature, and Shakespeare

It is a fair generalization of our times to say that the law figures into literature as some type of ordeal the characters must battle through. If it takes the form of a trial, their plight is often unjust; heroes persevere against judicial badgering until they are exonerated. If the law takes the form of rules or imperatives, it often becomes a prohibition the characters labor under, an institutional hindrance they must get past to achieve freedom and happiness. In drama, the law has always provided a certain theatrical tension, but is in itself rather deadly. Few would watch a staged trial for the trial's sake alone. Rather, the dramatic payoff comes in seeing whether the characters will endure. We have come to think that, in art, freedom lies outside the law; indeed, that nature itself lies outside the law. It is a dramatic gauntlet to be run, or a psychological mechanism to be shed.

That this should be so is not without justification in human experience. As Frank Kermode has explained, the discord between what is just and what is real harkens back to one of the first things we learn about the world as children, when we cry that something "isn't fair."[1] When we grow up and experience the law in its more institutional sense, it plagues us with its seeming obtuseness, its capriciousness, its inability to redress the very evils it is supposed to guard against. No wonder then, Kermode continues, the law and the legal profession should be so frequently excoriated in drama:

The animus against the legal profession arose partly . . . because of its habit of obscuring its operations in jargon unintelligible to nonlawyers, but more because of a natural fear of men who, though visibly merely men and theologically sinners, could, by wearing furred gowns and

≺ 1 ≻

other insignia, exercise dreadful powers as the representatives of the great judge, God himself.[2]

To the common man, it frequently seems the lawyer, the judge, and the educated—all those who pronounce the law's shibboleths and make use of its labyrinths—can escape its clutches, while the rest are left to hang. What a relief it is, then, to escape from the "law," if only for a while. The antihero, the confidence man, the rebel without a cause, are only some of the modern protagonists who must (and often do) outwit the law's representative.

As modern as this line of thought may be, there is a long history behind it, at least insofar as law is cast in opposition to pleasure. By the Renaissance, the idea was already old, and Shakespeare made good use of it: revelry in the forest, the midnight carryings-on of confused lovers, the shenanigans of agreeable fools, lost in their cups—all far from the staid and stultifying court. *As You Like It* and *A Midsummer Night's Dream* are chief examples. At the heart of these familiar themes is the whole tradition of topsy-turvy Maytime, boy bishops, and carts put before horses. It is an old, old story.

But it is not the whole story, especially not when it comes to Shakespeare. For alongside the tradition to which I have alluded is another, equally old, and no less dramatic story. It is one in which law is used to actually bring about freedom, happiness, community, and, most important, the dignity of persons and things that comes with sheer, simple integrity. "Integrity" here is meant not only in the sense of honor, but also in the more fundamental and existential sense of something actually being what it says it is, consistent with its nature. In the primary plays under analysis in this book—*Measure for Measure, Troilus and Cressida, The Merchant of Venice,* and *All's Well That Ends Well*—that is precisely the problem: a disjunction of essential proportions; and in these plays, that is a problem the law can help mend. In fact, Shakespeare uses the law and its various instruments as a device to help us through these plays, to bring the events to resolution. Here, law not only "is" something, it also "does" something. It is what makes these works the playwright's most philosophical and most fascinating.

Historically, of course, all except *The Merchant of Venice* have been unpopular works. And all four, from time to time, have been included in a category known as "problem plays." From Ernest Dowden's first accumulation of "dark and bitter" dramas into a separate group, through F. S. Boas's designation of his own grouping as "problem" works to a series of commentators that includes E. M. W. Tillyard, W. W. Lawrence, Ernest Schanzer, William Toole, A. P. Rossiter, Northrop Frye, R. A. Foakes, Peter Ure, Richard Wheeler, Vivian

Thomas, and Richard Hillman, the debate over which plays, and what criteria, should constitute the category has continued.[3] Scholars have struggled to unlock the dramas' unsettling secrets.

Recently, the idea of a separate category for "problematic" works has met with less approval, and the tag has become more convenient than significant. In fact, all of these works have risen greatly in popularity, perhaps due to a modern taste for what seems grim and complex. That is not to say the historical commentators were wrong in suspecting something constitutive in these plays—be it dark, bitter, tragicomic, romantic, satiric, or otherwise. They do resonate with each other, thematically and dramatically. However, my own reason for this focus is not to argue for any particular play's inclusion in, or exclusion from, the old category, or to propose a new definition for constituting the category itself. My assessment starts with certain integrative characteristics among these works: like other Shakespearean comedies, they all involve marriage; but in these plays, there is a marked emphasis on the relationship between marriage and law. Characters either observe marital imperatives or ignore them, and are either aided in marriage by legal instruments or have their marriages frustrated through legal maneuverings. Together, legal marriage can help restore the order and health of the societies portrayed in the action by restoring integrity. When in conflict, marriage and law reflect the disorder of those societies, which worsens as the play progresses.

Scholars have long been aware of the legal aspects in Shakespeare. It has been the subject of various works, especially those concerned with speculation on Shakespeare's legal training. The nineteenth century witnessed a lively debate on the matter. Often conducted by those in the legal field, the analyses centered, predictably, on the plays considered here. Scholars examined the playwright's employment of trial scenes, judges, clerks, and accompanying criminal and judicial systems for clues that might explain or disprove assertions that Shakespeare's "lost years" were spent in the world of the Inns.[4] It is my contention that the extensive use of contractual and transactional terms and concepts in these plays, coupled with Shakespeare's well-recorded legal dealings, is sufficient evidence that the playwright had a working knowledge of the judicial system.

Other early scholarship included taxonomic studies—also conducted by lawyers and judges—that identified the plays' legal terms and maxims, explaining them to lay readers.

Some of these are enlightening, offering insights that reveal details that might otherwise be overlooked. Nevertheless, many legal commentators either submit the plays to the rigors of forensic cross-examination—for example, analyzing the grounds of Portia's case—leave their studies at the level of defining terms, or belabor the complexities of the law in the Renaissance without attempting to explain what their observations mean to the plays as plays; that is, how they help interpret the dramatic events as they unfold.

In the recent past, the study of law and literature has become an independent scholarly enterprise, with Shakespeare as one of its primary interests. The movement's inception can be traced to James Boyd White's *The Legal Imagination*, in which the author proposed that the legal imagination might be defined by comparing it with other types of imagination, such as that of writers and poets.[5] In efforts to illuminate both law and literature, scholars in the area apply legal analysis and perspectives to literary texts, or apply literary analysis to legal texts. In my view, the most valid employment of "law and literature" involves the use of legal insight to help provide an understanding of literary concerns. Otherwise, the literature becomes merely a point of departure, a platform upon which legal points can be made, or political agenda furthered.

In essence, scholarship on the law in Shakespeare's plays has tended to follow two paths. Literary scholars have provided classic treatments of broad themes, such as "mercy" and "justice," and by assuming broad definitions proceed to explain their dramatic significance. However, these assumptions are often without particular reference to the historical meanings and significance of the legal concepts involved in the plays. On the other hand, legal scholars have spotted in Shakespeare's works evidence of positive law in the Renaissance. But rather than explore how the playwright uses these ideas dramatically, they have drawn back to explain and argue over the historical context of legal concepts. Although literary and legal scholars provide important analyses, their approaches can either read too shallowly in the law to fully explain its dramatic consequence, or too deeply in the law to explain that consequence at all. Mine is an integrated approach to Shakespeare's use of the law, an approach that applies a nuanced consideration of legal concepts—here, marriage instruments—to explain the dramatic development of the plays that employ them. It is my contention that Shakespeare's problem plays illuminate meliorative roles that law can play in drama. But before turning to that analysis, it will be helpful to note, briefly, the law as it was understood in Shakespeare's time.[6]

⚜

In Renaissance England, the understanding of the law's philosophical underpinnings was basically that of Thomas Aquinas: law is an ordinance of reason for the common good, promulgated by him who has care of a community.[7] In addition, Aquinas's four types of law were behind what Elizabethan men and women actually meant when they used the term:

Eternal law: the law of God, which exists in his mind and controls the universe.

Natural law: the part of the eternal law discoverable to man.

Human law: the law derived from the operation of human reason and the product of the application of the precepts of natural law to human circumstance. The good ruler carried out this law in harmony with divine and natural law.

Divine Law: the law revealed to man by the Church and Scripture.[8]

Aquinas's thought remained influential in Renaissance England, especially the idea of the law of nature, which both justified and limited man's authority.[9] Richard Hooker's *Of the Laws of Ecclesiastical Polity* (1593) reflects Thomistic thought and testifies to its continued orthodoxy:

> Now that law which, as it is laid up in the bosom of God, they call Eternal, receiveth according unto the different kinds of things which are subject unto it different and sundry kinds of names. That part of it which ordereth natural agents we call usually Nature's law: that which Angels do clearly behold and without any swerving observe is a law celestial and heavenly; the law of Reason that which bindeth creatures reasonable in this world, and with which by reason they may most plainly perceive themselves bound; that which bindeth them, and is not known but by special revelation from God, Divine law; Human law, that which out of the law either of reason or of God men probably gathering to be expedient, they make it a law.[10]

In his study on the natural law in Renaissance literature, R. S. White points out that while there was a tradition of skepticism regarding the natural law model, especially after the Reformation, this alternative revolved around a changed perspective on the natural law itself. Rather than set in the human heart and mind, as Aquinas had held, Calvin and the other "skeptics" placed the natural law in God's will and in the sovereign's fiat.[11] Even so, argues White, the skeptic's model remained that of Aquinas, and though the skeptical model eventually won out during the Enlightenment, it was not yet so in Renaissance England:

> Spenser and Sidney were generally more Calvinist than, for example, Shakespeare, More and Milton, but even they accepted some kind of

Natural Law model, accessible to the reader's understanding as a basis for morally judging characters' actions. The evidence points rather to the anti-Calvinist, Hooker, contemporary of Shakespeare, Webster, and Ford, as the spokesman for the Establishment view.[12]

Although the natural law model might be variously theorized and portrayed, it was still the same basic model.[13] It cannot be proven what Shakespeare knew of these works or those of continental writers on the subject, but his association with the Inns of Court and its members, as well as the use of natural law ideas in his plays, for example, the "law of nations" in *Troilus and Cressida* and *Henry V*, are evidence of his acquaintance with the concepts.

Of course, it is the distance between what is right and what is law, between what is just and what is done in the name of justice, that leaves the playwright room to work; or as Frank Kermode would have it, it is "the gulf that exists between the loftiest representations of Justice as the obedient performance of properly authorized and incorruptible human agents, and things as they inevitably were" that proves rich in dramatic possibility.[14] The conflict between notions of the law provides much tension in Shakespeare's plays. When law is challenged on one level—be it eternal, natural, or positive—the conflict has ramifications on other levels, and in ways that permeate the human psyche. In *Hamlet*'s Denmark, for example, the laws of succession, entitlement to land, adultery, and incest are all at play. They are matched by conflicts that recur in Hamlet himself. In addition to a discord outside, among men, there is a discord inside, within each man. The harmony that man can make of his world, and in himself, when things are ordered—and the disharmony when things are not—is a fact with which Hamlet is all too well acquainted: "how like an angel . . . how like a god" man may be, and yet how like a "quintessence of dust."[15] This awareness of man's potential for both greatness and ruin is part of Hamlet's own greatness; it is also accountable for his woe. For knowledge of the laws of heaven, of nations, and of entitlement does not inevitably result in their observance. Dramatic conflict follows.

Again, it is my contention that the plays discussed here illuminate meliorative roles that law can play in drama. To that end, I will explain what the law, taking the form of legal instruments, does in the four plays considered, and what it means to a literary understanding of these works. These plays are best suited for this analysis, for unlike other comedies, they not only involve a high concentration of societal institutions—governmental, judicial, and ecclesiastical—but also portray these institutions under siege. Disorder reigns at the beginning of these plays, and things must be set to rights.

In other works, notably the festive comedies, conflict resolution comes about during an escape from the court. According to C. L. Barber's highly influential book on those plays, by leaving their "everyday world" for the "holiday world"—a transition that mimics the festive holidays, or "revels," of Renaissance England—the characters and the audience go through "release to clarification."[16] When they return to their everyday lives, having mocked all that is "unnatural," they have a clearer view of where they are in the world, a "heightened awareness of the relation between man and 'nature.'"[17]

That is not the case in the problem plays, as Barber himself notes.[18] There is no release to a holiday world here. With the possible exception of Belmont in *The Merchant of Venice*, the problem plays are set in the everyday world from start to finish. False appearances are especially deceptive in this realm, where vice, corruption, and war disfigure the locales; death looms in the background. Like the festive comedies, a spoiler of some sort works to frustrate the happiness of the protagonists. But here his effects are more far-reaching; the protagonists' society is also at stake, as is the integrity necessary to its preservation.

Although these plays seem unrelated to Barber's ideas regarding nature and the festive comedies, nature does figure into the problem plays, but in conjunction with law, rather than revelry. For in these more sober comedies, it is societal institutions—most prominently, the law—that act as the device to bring about a change vis-à-vis nature. Whereas the main characters in the festive comedies celebrate nature by escaping *to* her, the main characters in the problem comedies run *from* her, or scant her in some fashion. For example, the Duke scolds Angelo in *Measure for Measure* for hoarding the graces nature has lent him, a failure that in turn makes him ignorant of the "nature of the people." But nature must be acknowledged in the everyday world too, and the law, with its ceremonies and duties, is one means to ensure that observance.

A few words of clarification about the meaning of *nature* are in order. Hooker mentions the age-old system of creation based on plenitude (God's desire that the world should be populated), gradation (creation is arranged hierarchically, descending from God), and continuity (the unbroken chain of creation). According to R. S. White, the natural law theory had as its central preoccupation "[t]he survival of humanity effected first through propagation (writers call it love) and secondly through avoidance of killing, which translate into the central subjects of Renaissance imaginative literature, sexuality (comedy) and murder (tragedy)."[19] These ideas are also evident in Shakespeare's plays, where what is meant by nature is the idea of plenitude, abundance, generation—one of the principles in the "great chain of being." From this perspective, the principle is an aspect of man's nature, his raison d'être: to create more "being." In the generative process, to state the obvious, life springs from life; being is multiplied (hence, Benedick in *Much Ado About Nothing*: "the world must be peopled"); when this principle is ignored or frustrated or, worse still, persecuted, then being—reality—is depleted. Another process replaces it, whereby what *is* turns upon itself, consuming its own existence (hence, Ulysses in *Troilus and Cressida*: "Power into will, will into appetite, And appetite, an universal wolfe . . . [at] last eat up himself"[20]) (1.3.120–24). In these four plays, the law plays a crucial role in the unfolding of this dynamic.

By way of explaining dramatic effect, Barber points out connections between nature, holidays, and the festive comedies:

> The underlying movement of attitude and awareness is not adequately expressed by any one thing in the day or the play, but is the day, is the play. Here one cannot say how far analogies between social rituals and dramatic forms show an influence, and how far they reflect the fact that the holiday occasion and the comedy are parallel manifestations of the same pattern of culture, of a way that men can cope with their life.[21]

The same can be said for analogies between the legal rituals and dramatic forms in the problem plays. Here, Shakespeare makes extensive use of the legal culture that was part of everyday Elizabethan life. In particular, legal instruments—contracts, bonds, sureties—are the means that turn the action and transform the characters. On the whole, such instruments secure a changed relationship between parties: Contracts create unions; bonds and sureties engage one person to stand as a guaranty for another. It is important to note that in Shakespeare these terms are nearly always reserved for use in the contexts of marriage and fellowship. Within these contexts he often plays with the double meanings of words—for example, commercial *bonds*, *bonds* of friendship, marriage *bonds*, and even *bonds* of restraint. Far from functioning only in an ancillary capacity, they have both thematic and dramatic purposes. An exploration of the history, nature, and use of these instruments, and their relationship to marriage, will reveal how the playwright employs them to build plots and to create an integrated universe of meaning.

Contracts and marriage have an ancient association, as betrothal agreements between families are some of the earliest known legal arrangements. Such transactions specified not only the parties involved, but also designated other terms. These might include dowries to be paid, properties to be exchanged, and alliances to be formed in support of the new union. To a significant extent, the concepts even overlap semantically. Like *wergild*, the "man-price" paid to ransom a family member from a warring clan, *wed* stems from the Anglo-Saxon word meaning "to wager." Legal historians Sir Frederick Pollock and F. W. Maitland tell us that in early law, the term even acted as a noun; a "wed" was a type of "gage" or pledge, which acted to bind a contract.[22] Somehow, it was this token that accomplished the binding.

Similarly, the notion of "binding" lies within the etymological history of "contract." The word comes from the Latin *contractus*, the past participle of *contrahere* (to draw together). In his plays and sonnets, Shakespeare uses *contract* a few times as a verb, in the sense of "pull together," for example: "Didst contract and purse thy brow together";[23] "aches contract and starve your supple joints;[24] or "to shorten," for example: "to contract the time."[25] However, the term is by and large reserved as a noun, meaning "an agreement to marry," or the marriage itself.[26] It is in this sense that it plays a prominent role in the plays under consideration here.

In many ways, the Renaissance marriage contract resembled the everyday commercial contract between English citizens. Legal historian A. W. B. Simpson explains that the concept of the contract arose from the action of "assumpsit":

> [C]ommon law courts in the early sixteenth century permitted actions to be brought for damages for the breach of parole promises; in the course of the century the action for breach of promise was (according to taste) embellished or marred by the evolution of a doctrine of consideration. At the turn of the century, again after a great deal of dithering, *assumpsit* was allowed to take over the job previously done by the writ of debt *sur contract*. Thereafter the action of *assumpsit* is regarded as *the* contractual action.[27]

Although it did not have to be written, the standard contract required some kind of an agreement between the parties, "agreement" being the central notion behind any contract.[28] In a real sense, the contractual agreement brought two or more people together for a specific purpose, to accomplish a specific end. Simply put, each of the parties sought something, be it money or the performance of some act, from the other party. And each of the parties committed himself or herself in some way to perform that which the other party anticipated under the contract. This exchange, the meeting of the others' expectations, amounted to what the law now calls "consideration."

Consideration may be understood as the conferral of a benefit on the other (e.g., A agrees to paint B's house for a certain amount) or the sufferance of a detriment required by the other (e.g., A promises not to open a business within fifty miles of his former employer, B, in exchange for a certain amount). Scholars argue as to how and from whence the doctrine was originally derived.[29] Simpson observes that in the medieval law from whence assumpsit arose, there was a sense in which the notion of quid pro quo was at root; however, this principle was not well developed in medieval law, and he cautions against a too precise correlation.[30] J. H. Baker traces the first appearance of the clause to 1539. In the King's Bench decision of *Marler v. Wilmer* (1539), KB 7/1111, m. 64, the bench required a connection between a "recited bargain and the undertaking to perform it":

> The local court gave judgment for the plaintiff, upon demurrer, and the defendant brought a writ of error in the King's Bench. One of the points assigned for error was "that it does not appear in the declaration for what cause (*quam ob causam*) he made the aforesaid undertaking, either for money paid beforehand, or receipt of part of the aforesaid good, and so *ex nudo pacto non oritur actio*."[31]

Baker says that some "linking phrase" between the recital and the assumpsit was needed to explain the undertaking.

However, the doctrine actually came about, it was in the late sixteenth century that the term *consideration* came into common use. In the 1587 action of *Manwood and Burstons' Case*, the word was said to signify, among other things, grounds for suits in which a man "is damnified by doing anything or spends his labour at the instance of the promiser," although he receives no benefit in return.[32] Naturally, a party could challenge a contract for failure to receive any value from it. Therefore, the contract anticipated an agreement in which each party received something of value from the other.

Because marriages were typically "contracted," and because dowries were a typical part of any marriage contract, it is not surprising that there was a debate over whether a promise to pay money in respect of a marriage was an actionable claim. The cases of *Joscelin v. Shelton* (1557) and *Hunt v. Bate* (1568) discuss marriage in terms of consideration. Schools of thought differed, says Simpson, as evidenced by the 1566 case of *Sharrington v. Strotten*:

> The first was to explain the rule by saying that (in the standard case of a father's promise on his daughter's marriage) the father derived a benefit or some gain or advantage, from the marriage . . . [the second, pro-

pounded by Plowden] who was concerned to argue in favour of the view that natural parental or family love and affection was a sufficient consideration, [and it] does not stress this idea of benefit; why marriage is a good consideration in the eyes of the law is because nature instils into man a desire to look after his blood, and so marriage as good consideration is not an example of a wider principle about benefit, but instead an example of a wider principle which recognizes natural love and affection as good consideration.[33]

This is important because in the plays to be discussed here, the idea of a "worthy" marriage, that is, one of "true value," and instances of "dowerless" marriages are crucial elements. Therefore, part of the historic background for the dramas is this dimension of the contract that, as has been seen, overlaps with a dimension of marriage.[34]

The ceremonial history of contractual formation also overlaps with that of marriage formation. Pollack and Maitland allude to the ancient hand-clasp as another means by which bargains were historically bound in western European societies:

> It is possible to regard this as a relic of a more elaborate ceremony by which some material "wed" passed from hand to hand; but the mutuality of the hand-grip seems to make against this explanation. We think it more likely that the promisor proffered his hand in the name of himself and for the purpose of devoting himself to the god or the goddess if he broke faith.[35]

The handclasping between the contracting parties is similar to the practice of placing one's folded hands within those of another, in the manner of subjection: "The feudal, or rather the vassalic, contract is a formal contract and its very essence is fides, faith, fealty."[36] The resemblance between the feudal relationship of faith and fealty in this ceremony—with its clasping of hands between parties who receive mutual value from each other—and the ceremony of the marriage contract is even stronger when ceremonial traditions of land transactions are placed alongside each other. Homage, which tied the tenant to the lord, required the tenant to kneel on both knees before his master, with his head uncovered and his hands held between the lord's as he pledged his faith. In addition, the tenant pledged an oath of fealty concerning the lands received of him. P. S. Clarkson and C. T. Warren quote Thomas Littleton's description of the ceremony:

> And when a freeholder . . . [swears] fealty to his lord, he shall hold his
> right hand upon a booke, and shall say thus: Know ye this, my lord, that
> I shall be faithfull and true unto you and faith to you shall bear for the
> lands which I claime to hold of you, and that I shall lawfully doe to you
> the customes and services which I ought to do, at the termes assigned,
> so help me God and his Saints; and he shall kisse the book.[37]

The ceremony is similar to that of "homage," which Clarkson and Warren say
was intended to establish a "strong and intimate relationship" between lord
and freeholder, with duties that arose on both sides.[38] The tenant owed his
livelihood, the fruits of his husbandry, in part to the lord; in exchange, the
lord owed the tenant his protection and providence.

With this background, the unique ceremony by which property passed
from man to man in medieval Europe, and which continued into the Elizabethan era, increases in importance. A written document was not essential to
the conveyance of land, since it was the notoriety of the transaction that testi-
fied to its authenticity.[39] As a result, much attention was paid to the ceremony
of livery. It generally occurred upon the land in question, between the donor
and the donee, but it could also be performed within sight of the land, as long
as the donee "entered" the property, that is, took possession, during the lifetime of the donor. The transaction was known as "livery of seisin," seisin
being, for all intents and purposes, both ownership and possession.[40] Basically, it entailed the delivery of a clod of earth, a twig, a hasp of the door or—
most significantly, for my purposes—its ring, which symbolized the whole of
the land conveyed.[41] The publicly celebrated, publicly witnessed transfer of
property by tokens such as these has obvious parallels with the marriage ceremony. Symbolic transfers in Germany could even take place in a church, so
that any interested third parties could state their objections.[42] The church
played a part in many medieval transfers in England as well; symbols of the exchange—knives, staffs, wands—could be placed on the altar, in front of a full
chapter of monks, as testament to the transfer.[43]

This parallel has more than pure analogical import, and is more than just
evidence of a quaint and colorful past. As S. E. Thorne points out, the public ceremony had a distinctive purpose. In his examination of the equivalent
tradition in German law, he makes a claim that is important here:

> In an age that looked primarily to objective phenomena it was difficult
> to believe a man owner of land unless he actually enjoyed its benefits
> or at least possessed it. No more abstract idea as yet obtained, and to

> make this concept of ownership explicit it was essential not only that the donee enter into possession but that the donor surrender his own possession and enjoyment: a process which took the form of the transfer of material symbols representing the land. . . . But these symbolic acts are not due solely to the incapacity of the primitive mind to conceive of a transfer of things without actual *traditio* [transfer], but owe a substantial part of their continuing importance to the necessity for proof. The Germanic customary law required that transactions not only be capable of being heard and seen but that they be actually heard and seen. Change of ownership must be made publicly and visibly, otherwise it will be unwitnessed and unprovable.[44]

In other words, an objectively verifiable event had to evidence the will of the parties, and act as testament to it. This provided both security against prior claims to title and against claims that the transfer had not occurred. The donor was required to vacate the land, relinquishing all title to it, and the donee was expected to enter and stay there. Seisin came to be closely connected to "enjoyment": "The man who takes and enjoys the fruits of the earth thereby 'exploits' his seisin, that is to say, he makes his seisin 'explicit,' visible to the eyes of his neighbors."[45]

The necessity of proof that the formal livery provided in land law had its formal counterparts in commercial law. Agreements could be oral, but the majority of actions on contracts brought in medieval common law courts were actions of debt *sur* obligation—also known as bonds. To recover, the creditor had to physically produce a sealed bond commemorating the debt in court and even had to aver that he had done so in his complaint. Any failure in this respect, any defacement, loss of seal—let alone loss of the bond itself—resulted in the creditor's loss of right.[46] In the four plays analyzed here, the legitimacy of contracts, and even children born in extracontractual unions, are often spoken of in terms of their being "sealed" or "unsealed," words with multiple meanings in Shakespeare.[47]

As Simpson observes, the instrument itself *was* the obligation; the creditor was strictly required to make proffer of the instrument in court.[48] This quality testifies to an association that we have lost sense of now. The material manifestation of the intangible debt was not so much evidence of a literalist, primitive frame of mind as it was evidence of a different perspective altogether: a fusion of the material and the ideational, not the former as a symbol of the latter. Again, in the four plays considered here, this notion will figure prominently.

Property could also be "gaged" as security for a debt. Pollock and Maitland explain that *gage, engagement, wage, wages, wager, wed, wedding,* and the Scottish *wadset,* all spring from one root: "In particular we must notice that the word 'gage,' in Latin *vadium,* is applied indiscriminately to movables and immovables, to transactions in which a gage is given and to those in which a gage is taken."[49] The "movables" are chattel, or personal property; and the "immovables" are, of course, land and all that is permanently attached to it. The term *gage,* from which *mortgage* is also derived, amounted to what we would now consider security for a debt.[50]

Furthermore, with regard to land transactions, the conveyor could describe the type of estate he was conveying to the purchaser. An estate conveyed "to A and his heirs forever" would transfer an estate "in fee," which amounted to the complete conveyance of the title. Lesser estates might be conveyed in various forms, such as those that retained an interest in the land for the donor. For example, "to A during his lifetime, and the remainder to me and my heirs" would create a "life estate" in the donee, allowing him the use of the land during his lifetime. Upon his death, the estate would revert to the donor and his heirs. In the donor's utterance of these words, legacies for future generations could be provided for or, conversely, denied. These concepts too are prominent in the four plays discussed.

Knowledge of, and experience in, contractual requirements and ceremonies was common in Medieval and Renaissance England. E. W. Ives notes that only the Welsh surpassed the English in Shakespeare's time in resorting to the law courts. The common man knew his recourse at law and had no qualms about availing himself of it. Even those who were not litigants were familiar with the judicial system, as jury duty was a common occurrence in life:

> In Elizabethan society, the law entered into many concerns from which it is now excluded. Estate administration was a matter not of farming, but of court-keeping. How the craftsmen of the towns worked and what the peasants grew was controlled by the gild and the manor court. Law dominated public administration.[51]

Margaret Loftus Ranald uses the term *osmotic knowledge* for this kind of widely understood information: "the moral and behavioral assumptions that a 'reasonable man,' that delightful legal fiction, should somehow have learned, or at least understood."[52] It was the kind of thing people were adequately acquainted with, without having to be formally educated in.

People also saw the courts as a means of recreation, a type of real theater that must have impressed the dramatists of the time. Kermode observes that legal jargon was entertaining in itself, and an easy "target for mockery," as evidenced by the gravedigger who amuses with the niceties and complexities of laws against suicide in *Hamlet*.[53] The double entendres so common in the comedies, often ribald, must have been irresistible when the bench used phrases such as "entry through X, to the benefit of Y."[54] *Troilus and Cressida's* sexual banter using the legal terminology of property transactions is a case in point. While literary critics might hope that the law derived its theatrical tendencies from early modern theater, Luke Wilson cautions that that is rarely so, largely because the two were so closely linked socially and institutionally.[55]

Shakespeare himself was not only a large landholder, and therefore necessarily underwent the formalities and ceremonies of contractual law, but was also a frequent litigant, asserting his rights and titles with zeal. He owned New Place and a total of 127 acres in Stratford, became a tenant of Rowington Manor, and owned the property in Blackfriars, London.

He entered into contracts for the sale of malt, negotiated a dowry for a young couple, and collected tithes owed to Stratford. Also, the Shakespeare family was involved in years-long litigation, stretching into 1597–99, involving a contract that his father had secured with land. Property William Shakespeare would have inherited was never recovered.[56]

The playwright's experience in this area was not uncommon. In his work on legal history, John Maxcy Zane explains that the Medieval England from which this legal process sprung consisted of communities in which business formed a large part of everyday life:

> [T]he main object of litigation was land. Land could not pass without livery of seisen, which was a public act, or by a death which was no less public. The neighborhood knew all about such facts. Legal rules and remedies grow as the intricacy of relations of men in society increases.[57]

Although the litigiousness of English society might imply that the law's ceremonial character made for more problems than it solved, Renaissance England was nonetheless a world in which ceremony, and the utterances pertaining thereto—the deed and the words—formed an inseparable whole. Dispensing of one or the other created problems, which might result in a challenge that the transaction had not occurred at all, or that the parties' relationships had not been altered in any way. By means of the public exchange of words and deeds, this challenge could be met, for the transaction had to be accomplished in full public view, and the relationship toward the object of the transaction—be it land, or chattel, or people—was thereby incontrovertibly changed.

In the plays under consideration here, the difference between the real and the unreal, between appearances and reality, has long been recognized as a central theme. This work will explain the roles that legal instruments play in resolving or complicating this aspect of the dramas. For example, marriages in *Measure for Measure* and *All's Well That Ends Well* are challenged on the grounds of their validity. They *seem* like marriages, but because of one contractual deficiency or another, do not actually amount to marriages. The same may be said for the commercial bond in *The Merchant of Venice*. On its face, it appears to be, and is presented to Antonio as, a simple arrangement for funds. And it is secured—jokingly—by a pound of flesh; or so it seems. In reality, the commercial bond has a much more deadly purpose, which Shylock intends to realize.

The relevance of this history of commercial contracting in England to Shakespeare's problem plays becomes even more clear when it is understood that these works not only contain a concentrated amount of legal instruments—contracts, bonds, wardships, wills, surety arrangements—which in turn play key roles in both the complication and resolution of the plots, but also contain, in reference to marriage and communal relationships, an extensive use of figurative language such as *reversions, remainders, fee, entails, title, deed, use, gage,* and *legacy,* among others. In the same vein, the characters in these plays are not merely betrothed *to* each other, nor are they merely friends *with* each other; instead, they are pledged under contracts of various sorts, bound under commercial obligations in another's behalf, or sworn as sureties for another's promises. Consequently, what might be a commonplace pastoral or agricultural image in the work of another playwright, for example, the sexual conceit of the lover "mowing" the fields of his beloved, "cropping" her flowers, gains a nuance of legality in Shakespeare's problem plays. A girl such as Mariana in *Measure for Measure* is instructed to exercise her "title" to her "husband" by "performing" a "pre-contract," and consummating it with "tilling" and "sewing." More is implied here than by a customary pastoral image of a temporary sexual union; Mariana is to claim exclusive rights to her husband by means of "performing" a marital contract. Later in the same play, Mariana will rely on the elements that constitute this contract—its oaths, its "locked hands," its public nature—in asserting her entitlement to Angelo. Helena in *All's Well That Ends Well* will use the same means to "prove" her contract with Bertram, to whom she has gained "lawful title" by the same means as Mariana to Angelo.

In these plays, the pastoral-agricultural image retains its characteristic qualities: fruitfulness, the tilled and sewn earth. But that imagery is transformed by concepts native to contracts. The tilled, sewn, and fruitful earth signify rights and obligations of contracting parties whose relationship vis-à-vis each other is changed by means of the legal instrument. Nature is still present in the image, but she is not wild, nor is she opposed to the ordering principle of law. Indeed, in the problem plays, a valid legal instrument serves nature's generative ends. When duly performed, it provides integrity, a match between appearances and reality, necessary for nature to flourish. It is the challenge of invalidity—a lack of integrity of some sort, due to some cause—that works as the dramatic complication. In *Troilus and Cressida*, a play in which contracts and their elements are parodied, this lack of integrity is never rectified.

The contracts, bonds, and sureties, when performed properly, work to resolve the disjunctions that plague the societies. In *Measure for Measure*, supplying the missing elements of the marriage contracts remedies the separation between appearances and reality that characterizes Vienna. The valid contracts "contract" the parties, unifying relationships that had heretofore been lacking in either form or substance. In short, the legal instruments act as dramatic conceits, highlighting the theme of integrity.

Another important function of legal instruments in the problem plays is their effect on the community. *Bond* has several meanings: in its participial form, *bound*, it means "secured" or "entrusted." But bond can also signify a relationship between characters, or a legal instrument that secures a debt. *Surety* most often refers to the person who acts as security for an agreement, or the token that binds the transaction. Shakespeare connects both terms with marriage, the most significant instance of which occurs in *The Merchant of Venice*. Two bonds of opposed natures—one, a friendship bond, the other, a commercial bond—act to finance the marriage contract between Portia and Bassanio. Antonio also stands as Bassanio's surety in the match. The same sense of this term occurs in *All's Well That Ends Well*, in which the King of France acts as Helena's surety under her marriage contract with Bertram. The bonds and surety relationships in these plays serve a supporting role to the marriage contract, helping to enable it or, in the case of the commercial bond in *The Merchant of Venice*, threatening to undo it. Those who do not act in good faith can turn the very requirements necessary to effectuate a contract or bond, such as the security in *The Merchant of Venice*, or the contractual consummation in *All's Well That Ends Well*, on their heads. This amounts to the intentional frustration of the contract, or worse still, its perversion. Rather than serving as a means by which a civilized community exchanges needed things or accomplishes self-perpetuation through marriage and fellowship, the instruments are redirected to a private use, serving to satisfy only personal aims of lust, greed, or revenge. Antagonists such as Angelo, Bertram, Shylock, and, to a lesser extent, Pandarus, use legal instruments in this manner.

This threat, the use of legal instruments for other than their intended purposes, and the lack of integrity that results, was recognized in the law of Renaissance marital contracts. And the problem is one of which Shakespeare makes great dramatic use. Before the simplifications of the Marriage Act of 1753, the requirements for marriage were ambiguous in England. Marjorie Garber identifies at least five steps:

1. the written financial contract between the parents;
2. the spousal, or contract—a formal exchange of oral promises;
3. the proclamation of banns three times in the local church of one of the parties;
4. the wedding ceremony in the church;
5. the sexual consummation.[58]

Rings, too, though not required canonically, were a common aspect of matrimonial ritual. As Ranald observes, Shakespeare's lovers use rings, and they signify more than "a mere device of romantic recognition," but act as "a statement that a legal contract has in fact been made, for even in the most secret marriages, a ring was provided, if at all possible."[59] The York marriage service, was typical:

> The bridegroom "takes the ring with his three principal fingers and says after the priest, beginning with the thumb of the bride, *In nominee patris*, at the second finger, *et fillii*, at the third finger, *et spiritus sancti*, at the fourth or middle finger *amen*, and there he leave the ring, because according to the decree, in the middle finger there is a certain vein extending to the heart."[60]

In these four plays, rings and tokens play more than a figurative role; they amount to a kind of fused manifestation of the ideational and the material, like the "bond," or debt *sur* obligation.

The spousals themselves—the oral exchange that bound the two in the eyes of the Church—were of two kinds: *de praesenti* and *de futuro*. The latter was more akin to modern engagement promises, amounting to an intention to marry in the future. The parties did not enjoy a changed relationship with regard to each other, although it may be assumed that their perception in the community was changed. In addition, a *de futuro* contract was considered binding, that is, was transformed into a marriage, in the event the couple consummated their contract prior to the nuptials' public solemnization.

De praesenti contracts were of a different nature altogether. In essence, they amounted to a full-fledged marriage. These contracts involved a promise between the parties made in the present tense—"I take thee as my wife"—constituting what linguists would call a "performative speech act." That is, the act was performed by the very pronunciation of the words. The promise was one with the act, and accomplished the union by virtue of its utterance. Although the vows might be later solemnized publicly, the marriage itself was a foregone conclusion, binding in every way and capable of invalidating a later marriage. Because of their private nature, these marriages became known as "clandestine" or "handfast" marriages; subsequent consummation, or the lack thereof, had no effect on the validity of the *de praesenti* contract. However, the failure to consummate the marriage could be grounds for an annulment, since one of the contracts' purposes, the production of children, would be frustrated.

The difference between the two contracts turned on the expression of the will. R. H. Helmholz sets out the medieval distinction between them, centering on the verb that follows the expression of volition:

> Where that verb denoted the execution of a marriage, the contract was by *verba de presenti*. Where it denoted merely the initiation, the word constituted *verba de futuro*. "I will take you as my wife" therefore constituted only *verba de futuro*, because the verb "to take" refers to the start of a marriage relationship. But "I will have you as my wife" was a present contract since the act of having a woman as a wife denoted the desire to participate in an already existing union. To desire the results of marriage was, according to this view, quite different from desiring the beginning of marriage. He who wills the consequence (having) must already have willed the antecedent (taking).[61]

When it did not spring from intentional deceit, the trouble sprang, says Helmholz, from the apparent distinction that the layman made. To the layman, the formal solemnization and consummation made a marriage; to the Church, the present tense expression of the will to marry did so.[62]

Although recognized ecclesiastically, the *de praesenti* contract caused problems both before and after the Reformation. Since marriage was the province of ecclesiastical concerns, the trouble went to the very nature of the institution. The Church had long conceived marriage as a sacrament that the two parties, husband and wife, conferred upon themselves. It was witnessed by the Church and received her blessing, but she was not central to the contract's validity. The individuals were to become "one flesh," as Scripture commanded, under the contract, and were therefore truly "brought together" whether or not the Church played a part. The free-form nature of this type of contract, and the sole importance of intention, is related in Henry Swinburne's *A Treatise on Spousals.* The contracts could arise by "[w]hatsoever form of words, or by any other means, as Writings, Signs, Tokens &C."[63] Counterintuitive as it may seem, the contract that might justifiably have required a precise form in fact required hardly any.

To address this very issue, dowries, the agreement between the families, were used in the early church by Justinian to change the very basis of the marriage contract. His solution was to require dotal instruments. These written agreements as to the exchange of marital property were meant to act as proof of the valid marriage, and testify to the legitimacy of children produced from it. His idea was ultimately ineffective because of the doubt it cast on older marriages, but though it did not end clandestine marriage, dowry arrangements continued to be supported by the Church as a means of encouraging public marriage.[64]

Of course, Church witness was strongly advised, and grave punishments attached to parties who dispensed with it. Valid though the marriage may have been, the parties often had to do penance for marrying themselves privately. On ideological grounds, the Church could object that a private ceremony excluded a holy witness to the very institution responsible for the growth and vitality, the "fruitful multiplication," of society itself. Scripture used the marriage metaphor to describe the union of Christ and his Church; the Church was Christ's "bride."[65] Making a private affair of the sacrament shortchanged the affirming effects a marriage could have in acknowledging the Church's role in life. As political historians Allan Bloom and Harry Jaffa once remarked, marriage is "a part of political life, of civil society. One cannot purify it of its political element without depriving it of its substance."[66] A private marriage, by definition, excludes society's role, even investment, in the parties.

Moreover, on practical grounds it was nearly impossible for the Church, or anyone else for that matter, to ensure that a marriage had actually taken place. A man could pretend marriage with a woman, then deny the existence of the union after his lust was satisfied. Predictably, the courts were full of men who, having satisfied their lust, subsequently denied their responsibility.[67] If challenged, there was no way to prove that the marriage existed—that the man was now a husband, that the woman was now a wife, or in the event the woman conceived, that a child was their legitimate offspring. Children born of such unions were unprovided for; they had no name and could not inherit.[68] In the case of competing claims to a husband or wife, medieval canon law resulted in gross inequities; for an earlier valid contract would prevail over a subsequent contract, even if the latter was solemnized in church and followed by years of cohabitation and children.[69] A sixteenth-century commentator, Richard Whytford, remarks on the extent of the abuse:

> The ghostly ennemy doth decyve manypsones by ye pretence & colour of matrymony in pryuate & secrete contractes. For many men whan they can not obteyne theyre unclene desyre of the woman wyl promyse marryage, & thervpon make a contracte promyse eche vnto other sayenge, Here I take thee Margery vnto my wyfe, I thereto plyght thee my trouth. And she agayne, vnto him in lyke maner. And after that done, they suppose they maye lawfully vse theyr unclene behauyour, and somtyme the acte and dede doth folow, vnto the great offence of god and theyr owne soules.[70]

Making the marriage public solved these problems; but in England there was no way for the Church to enforce the solution.

The story was different in Rome, at least after 1563. As part of the Council of Trent, called to address the Reformation and reunify the Christian Church, the Roman Catholic hierarchy passed a decree known as "*Tametsi*," on the reformation of Christian marriage.[71] As a result of the decree, no longer would private marriages of consent be considered valid in the eyes of the Catholic Church. Only those marriages celebrated before a priest, and witnessed by at least two people, would be recognized. The Catechism of the Council of Trent, under revisions around the same time as the decree itself, and finally distributed in 1566, conveys the thought behind this monumental change. The drafters say that the apostles "well understood the numerous and important advantages which must flow to Christian society from a knowledge, and an inviolable observance by the faithful of the sanctity of marriage," while ignorance of marriage only brought calamities on the Church. In explaining the nature of marriage, it is said, "Vice not infrequently assumes the semblance of virtue, and hence care must be taken that the faithful be not deceived by a false appearance of marriage, and thus stain their souls with turpitude and wicked lusts."[72] The drafters go on to describe wedlock as the "joining together of lawful wife and husband," "the conjugal union of man and woman," "contracted between two qualified persons," under a "natural contract imposing natural duties."[73] As a final warning, they state:

> But above all, lest young persons, whose period of life is marked by extreme indiscretion, should be deceived by a merely nominal marriage and foolishly rush into sinful love-unions, the pastor cannot too frequently remind them that there can be no true and valid marriage unless it be contracted in the presence of the parish priest, or of some other priest commissioned by him, or by the Ordinary, and that of a certain number of witnesses.[74]

The Catholic Church was not alone in its condemnation of clandestine marriages. Luther, Calvin, and Zwingli required public marriage celebrations with the approval of both sets of parents.[75]

But as commentators have pointed out, particularly in regard to the part these contracts play in *Measure for Measure*, this decree affected all of Christian Europe *except* England.[76] There, clandestine marriage, with its inherent problems, remained valid. The Anglican Church was under no obligation to either Rome or Luther. As a result, for the very same act, a man in France in 1563 would be considered a fornicator, while his counterpart across the channel would be considered a husband, if the Englishman deemed to acknowledge himself as such.[77] This is all the more interesting in light of the fact that Shakespeare's own marriage was hasty, Anne Hathaway being three months pregnant by the time of their nuptials.

Shakespeare did not use, or advocate the use of, one type of law as opposed to another, or condemn any particular legal or ecclesiastical system. Rather, he made dramatic use of what he knew of these and other legal differences. My approach looks to the law in order to deepen Shakespeare's artistic meanings, consulting legal history for elaboration on what Shakespeare's plays are doing *literarily*. Instead of using occurrences of legal terminology as points of excursion into legal minutiae, I will read the terms in context, and in consequence, of the play as a whole. While a legal historian might be interested in defining a word like *reversion* by its legal meaning—and reading the rest of a scene in terms of it—I will explain the legal meaning in hopes of deepening the artistic ideas, images, and themes in that scene. The play, in other words, will rule the law, not the other way around.

There is no doubt these are "knotty" works, complex in more ways than I can go into here, and they may be no less "dark" and "bitter" to those who find

them so after I have made my case. Nonetheless, I believe there *is* a case to be
made about these plays, as a consistent theme runs throughout them. The case
depends on an understanding of several aspects of the law and thought of the
age related to marriage, ceremonies, contracts, property, and nature, all working as a particular vehicle for Shakespeare's artistic powers. Through their in-
terrelation, Shakespeare establishes a norm, to which he returns again and
again, about law and the generative ends of nature—either dramatizing its observance or its frustration. Both made for good drama, so both appealed to
him. In essence, Shakespeare takes the law and makes metaphoric use of it to
achieve his literary ends. To say that something was or was not absolutely necessary to a marriage (e.g., rings, sexual intercourse, and so on), or to a contract
or bond (e.g., a seal)—and therefore Shakespeare could not have used it—is to
object to the imaginative use of something that has an objective, and strict, use
in reality. It was not his aim to use, nor mine to explicate, literary means simply
to dramatize the law.

The use of legal instruments in the dramas under review underscores their
greater themes of integrity and generation/plenitude. In *Measure for Measure*,
Shakespeare uses different types of contracts, their elements and attendant ceremonies, to highlight his main themes, while in *Troilus and Cressida*, he parodies
these same elements and ceremonies, and demonstrates what flows from a perversion of contractual concepts. In *The Merchant of Venice*, there is a connection
among bonds, sureties, and contracts that reveals how the law may be oriented
toward nature, or perverted away from her. *All's Well That Ends Well* emphasizes especially the importance of contractual performance. I will also explain
the significance of agents, who either help nature bring about her generative
ends via legal instruments or work to frustrate nature by perverting those same
instruments. Law and nature may be allies, or they may be enemies; whichever
the case, Shakespeare makes plays from the dynamics of their relationship.

Things Seen and Unseen

The Contracts in Measure for Measure

Of the four plays I discuss in this book, *Measure for Measure* is possibly the last to be composed and contains a particularly high concentration of contracts. Flaws in these contracts, involving two pseudomarriages, help complicate the action of the play, and their eventual correction helps resolve it. An analysis of the contracts in *Measure for Measure* will provide, sometimes by negative example, evidence of what a valid marriage contract means in Shakespeare. It will also provide an overview of the various contractual elements that figure into the other plays.

In act 1, scene 2 of *Measure for Measure*, Claudio enters in chains, having been charged under a seldom-enforced Viennese fornication statute. Lucio begins an exchange:

Lucio: Is lechery so looked after?

Claudio: Thus stands it with me. Upon a true *contract*,
            I got possession of Julietta's bed.
            You know the lady; she is fast my wife,
            Save that we do the denunciation lack
            Of outward order. This we came not to
            Only for propagation of a dower
            Remaining in the coffer of her friends,
            From whom we thought it meet to hide our love
            Till time had made them for us.
            But it chances the stealth of our most mutual entertainment
            With character too gross is writ on Juliet.

Lucio:	With child perhaps?
Claudio:	Unhapp'ly even so. (1.2.133–45; emphasis added)[1]

Literary and legal scholars alike have differed as to the nature of Claudio's "true" contract, and a considerable amount of criticism has centered on the question in the past fifty years. Some have considered it a *de praesenti* contract, some a *de futuro*, and some have objected to the importance of the question altogether.[2]

In a wise cautionary remark, Margaret Scott points out that critics should not forget Shakespeare's law is "story-book law," kept intentionally vague here in a way that the Sallic law in *Henry V* is not.[3] On the face of things, says Scott, the story-book law in *Measure for Measure* is Catholic, consistent with its Viennese setting. She argues that the English knew of the difference between their own more lenient view of marriage as opposed to that of the new, Catholic rule, which insisted on public marriages. The English would be more likely to know this one fact than the intricacies of betrothal contracts. Moreover, they would be more likely to question the fairness of a rule that changed the status of a man from irregular husband to arrant fornicator in one pronouncement.[4]

Scott is correct to say that this is story-book law, and that it is ultimately not about social conflicts arising from different types of spousals. But although the nature of the disputes over the contracts is not the reason for Shakespeare's drama, marriage contracts are central to what he is dramatizing. Storybook law in Shakespeare springs from real law, which both he and his audience knew.

The differences between the contracts are related to deficiencies in their validity, which relate in turn to features—elaborated upon in chapter 1—that constitute all valid contracts: publicity, value, performance, and contractual tokens. These features are the means by which contracts change relationships, and by which they ensure that things are as they say they are. In *Measure for Measure*, Shakespeare uses these contractual elements to highlight greater themes, falling under the general headings of "seeming and being" or "falsehood and integrity"—the distinction between the pseudo, as opposed to the fully realized, state. The full realization of the contract also has a dramatic function. By uniting characters who have been separated, the contract helps establish cohesion in a city where separation has been the norm. From this cohesion, the possibility of societal generation follows. An examination of *Measure for Measure*'s contracts will reveal how Shakespeare uses the elements of publicity, value, performance, and contractual tokens to achieve integrity on personal and societal levels.

Publicity is the central issue in Claudio's "true contract." However Angelo may see the relationship between the two lovers, in Claudio's view, he and Juliet have been married by way of a clandestine ceremony. In Claudio's usage, "contract" is more than just a pledge of an intention to marry, it is the marriage itself—the "drawing together" of two people (1.2.134). Claudio even claims it as a valid defense against the charge of fornication brought by Angelo. In essence, Claudio suggests that he did *not* in fact commit fornication because he was married to Juliet at the time, by means of the true contract.

Despite this fact, there is no evidence that he asserts the validity of this marriage directly to Angelo. Several parties, including Claudio himself, call its very nature into question. Claudio tells Lucio that his "mutual entertainment" with Juliet moved with "stealth" (1.2.143). He also speaks of his restraint as coming from "liberty," "surfeit," and "immoderate use" (1.2.118–20), atypical characterizations for a man who claims lawful access to his wife's bed (1.2.135). The Provost calls Juliet a gentlewoman, "[w]ho, falling in the flaws of her own youth, / Hath blistered her report" (2.3.11–12). Furthermore, Juliet confesses and repents her "sin" as an "evil," and does not object to the Duke's characterization of her and Claudio's actions as "most offenceful" (2.3.26). Finally, the Duke orders Claudio to restore the good name of Juliet, whom he has "wronged," by marrying her (5.1.122), an action hardly necessary if the contract were valid. Therefore, according to the way the play is resolved, the true contract is somehow insufficient.

The most accurate description of Claudio and Juliet's true contract is that it is private; by Claudio's own admission it lacks "outward order," that is, the shape or form of a valid marriage. There has been no publishing of banns, no priest, no public celebration, and so forth. And even were Claudio and Juliet *not* troubled about the nature of their marriage, its secrecy would still cause problems. Being secret, there are no witnesses to confirm its existence, so Juliet's pregnancy leaves them open to a charge under Vienna's fornication statute. Considering the circumstances, the defense of the true contract marriage could be construed as after the fact—a mask for lust, rather than a genuine marriage that brings two people together on a permanent basis. Worse still, the implication prompts Angelo to consider the child of their union illegitimate:

Angelo: Ha! Fie these filthy vices! It were as good
                 To pardon him that hath from nature stolen
                 A man already made, as to remit
                 Their saucy sweetness that do coin heaven's image
                 In stamps that are forbid. 'Tis all as easy

> Falsely to take a way a life true [legitimately] made
> As to put metal in restrained moulds,
> To make a false one. (2.4.42–49)

Although spoken by the hypocritical Angelo, the passage provides further information as to why Claudio's true contract is invalid. For here, Shakespeare extends his use of "seal" imagery, introduced at the beginning of the play when the Duke asks Escalus what "figure of us think you he [Angelo] will bear?" (1.1.16). The child conceived under this true contract is portrayed as a false image, poured from forbidden "moulds."[5] Contracts in the Renaissance carried the extra assurance of authenticity—were "true"—if they were "formalized" with a seal. The misuse of a seal, such as the unauthorized employment of the King's seal, bore dire consequences. But Claudio and Juliet's arrangement, being private, lacks formality. It is subject to Angelo's charge, however unfair, that the marriage does not in fact exist. From the disposition of Claudio's private contract, it appears that a publicly witnessed ceremony is one of the requirements for validity.

Claudio and Juliet's private contract can be contrasted with the other contract in the play, the publicly celebrated "pre-contract" between Angelo and Mariana (4.1.72). The Duke tells Isabella of Mariana's history:

> She should this Angelo have married, was affianced to her oath, and the nuptial appointed; between which time of the *contract* and limit of the solemnity, her brother Frederick was wrecked at sea, having in that perished vessel the dowry of his sister. (3.1.213–18; emphasis added)

The Duke explains that upon Mariana's loss of fortune, Angelo abandoned her, pretending to have discovered that she was unchaste. Nevertheless, the formalities of the marriage ceremony have been observed, publicly.

Like Claudio and Juliet's contract, much has been written on whether this contract is *de praesenti* or *de futuro*.[6] But whatever its nature, what can unequivocally be said is that it has been publicly celebrated; that is its distinguishing feature. Later, when Mariana is called on to prove her contract with Angelo, she uses the public oaths and handclasping as evidence that she has a valid claim to him.

Angelo's objection to marrying Mariana highlights the next element involved in a valid contract: value. Upon her brother Frederick's death, Mariana's dowry was lost at sea. This amounted to what might be called in modern terms a "partial failure of consideration." In Angelo and Mariana's precontract, the dowry and Mariana herself made up the total consideration (on her side) promised in return for Angelo's promise to marry. But Angelo abandons Mariana upon the loss of her dowry. Significantly, Angelo's reason for leaving his contract unrealized is the same as Claudio's reason for bypassing the public formalization of his own. Claudio mentions that one reason he and Juliet did not disclose their marriage was for a lack of dowry:

> This we came not to
> Only for propagation of a dower
> Remaining in the coffer of her friends,
> From whom we thought it meet to hide our love
> Till time had made them for us. (1.2.138–42)

But during the validation of both Claudio and Angelo's contracts at the end of the play, the Duke scolds the men for having "wronged" the women by their pseudomarriages. Objections based on monetary value prove spurious. A lack of monetary dowry is shown as insufficient reason to forego a public contract, as in Claudio's case, and insufficient reason to leave a contract inchoate, as in Angelo's case. In this play, marriage "worth" is larger than monetary worth.[7]

The play's events set up an alternative means of valuation, one that becomes a norm echoed in all the problem plays: "consideration" for the marriage is satisfied not by monetary equivalence, but by the value of the individuals themselves, by their own essential worth. In a similarity with *All's Well That Ends Well*, the Duke appreciates Mariana's worth despite her lack of fortune, just as the King of France appreciates Helena's. She resembles the disinherited but virtuous Cordelia in *King Lear*, who is "herself a dowry."[8] "Good words" go with Mariana's name (3.1.211) and despite Angelo's callous treatment, her love "continues in her first affection" (3.1.239). Mariana proves herself constant, rare for a time in which "novelty is only in request" (3.2.17–18).

As in the debate over value in other plays,[9] Angelo's high worth is assumed, although lacking, and Mariana's is disparaged, although considerable:

> If any in Vienna be of worth
> To undergo such ample grace and honour,
> It is Lord Angelo. (1.1.22–24)

With ironic intent, the Duke asks

> think'st thou thy oaths,
> Though they would swear down each particular saint,
> Were testimonies against his worth and credit

> That's seal'd in approbation? [with the Duke's authority]
>   (5.1.241–44)

Sometimes ironically, sometimes unwittingly, Angelo is called a "worthy" man in the final act. It is the same scene in which he discredits Mariana's worth with false charges of unfaithfulness. He explains that their marriage was broken off

> Partly for that her promised proportions
> Came short of composition [the dowry], but in chief
> For that her reputation was disvalued
> In levity. (5.1.218–21)

His accusations are the mirror of those of Bertram in *All's Well That Ends Well*, who charges Diana with being a camp-follower to discredit her honor. But as in that play, the bed-trick in *Measure for Measure* has been accomplished by the time Angelo appraises Mariana. In addition, the bed-trick is a feat by which Angelo's worth, like Bertram's, has been "scaled" and found wanting (3.1.256). When he orders Claudio to marry Juliet at play's end, the Duke does not even mention the monetary obstacle that Claudio himself found so controlling. Once the marriage is publicly celebrated, the Duke orders Angelo to appreciate Mariana's true value:

> Well, Angelo, your evil quits you well.
> Look that you love your wife, her *worth*, *worth* yours.
>   (5.1.494–95; emphasis added)[10]

This last comment also stresses an awareness of equal value, another constant theme in the play. It is a value that extends further than the marriage partners and has broader import.

The First Gentleman reminds Lucio they are cut from the same cloth: "there went but a pair of sheers" between them (1.2.27). Later, the Provost cautions Abhorson from considering himself superior to Pompey, as a "feather would turn the scale" between the two (4.2.28). Also, the clowns have a discussion on the "mystery" of execution, where equality is again the theme:

> Every true man's apparel fits your thief. If it be
> too little for your thief, your true man thinks it big
> enough. If it be too big for your thief, your thief

> thinks it little enough. So every true man's apparel
> fits your thief. (4.2.41–45)[11]

Along these lines, many have recognized the similarity among the three main characters: Angelo, the Duke, and Isabella all live lives removed from society. They also distance themselves from romantic love: Angelo "rebate[s] and blunt[s] his natural edge" (1.4.60); Isabella, a thing "enskied and sainted," strangely associates sex with masochistic martyrdom, saying she would "strip" herself "to death as to a bed" (2.4.102); and the Duke considers his breast impervious to "the dribbling dart of love" (1.3.2). Perhaps this similarity between the Duke and Angelo explains why the deputy is not the only man affected by Isabella, and can go some way toward justifying his proposal to her, which so many find psychologically unmotivated. The leveling quality of these comparisons works to place all the characters on the same plane, one that the reader is well-advised to remember later, when Angelo alone stands in need of mercy.[12]

Having examined the elements of publicity and value, the next contractual feature of a valid contract is contractual "performance." For a contract to effect the change in relationships that is its purpose, the parties have to perform the obligations contemplated. In the context of marriage, those obligations include conjugal rights. But after the failure of Mariana's dowry, the precontract remains inchoate for five years. Its incompleteness is memorialized in the song to Mariana at the moated grange, which plays upon the notion of "seals":

> *But my kisses bring again,*
> > *bring again,*
> *Seals of love, but seal'd in vain,*
> > *sealed in vain.* (4.1.5–6)

Angelo's abandonment results in an indefinite postponement of consummation, frustrating the contract's purpose. And his refusal to consummate the marriage is only one example of a larger pattern in his life. Whereas Escalus's justice is "pregnant" in the "nature of the people," and thus acquainted with true justice (1.1.9–12), Angelo's "justice" is barren and removed.

Before proceeding to explain how the Duke rectifies the inchoate contract between Angelo and Mariana, it is important to underscore a distinction between this contract and that of Claudio and Juliet. In Claudio and Juliet's situation, the two have engaged in sex as husband and wife, and perhaps consider themselves married—in a way. But there is no "outward form" to their union, no ceremony, as Claudio himself admits (1.2.138). In Angelo and Mariana's situation, on the other hand, some ceremony has taken place—a public denunciation, the appointment of nuptials, the locking of hands over vows—amounting to outward form, but outward form only. Angelo does not treat Mariana as his wife. On the contrary, he banishes her from his company, having not "spake with her, saw her, nor heard from her" in five years (5.1.222). In Claudio and Juliet's case, there is matter without form; in Angelo and Mariana's case, form without matter. And in both cases, supplying the missing elements later validates the invalid contracts. Claudio and Juliet are to be publicly married, thus providing order; Angelo and Mariana consummate their union, thus providing substance. Not only must the marriage contract be *formed* in a certain way—publicly, and with the additional elements of value and ceremony—it must also be *performed*, in order to achieve integrity. The contract must have not only shape, but also substance. It is not only a word, but to have significance, it requires matter. Otherwise, it fails in being what it claims to be. This union of *res* and *verba* is achieved by means of performing the valid contract. Together, the ritual and the performance provide integrity.[13]

The difference in the two contracts contributes to the different treatment they receive from the Duke. The private contract between Claudio and Juliet, though consummated, he casts as a sin (2.3.19). But the Duke takes great pains to assure Mariana that the proposed bed-trick, meant to consummate her union with Angelo, is not wrong: "Nor, gentle daughter, fear you not at all / He is your husband on a pre-contract" (4.1.71–72). According to the Duke's plan, the private rendezvous, born of Angelo's lust, will actually consummate the inchoate contract. It will also preserve Isabella's chastity, accomplish Claudio's salvation, and expose Angelo's corruption—hinging on the potential for public disclosure: "If the encounter *acknowledge* itself hereafter, it may *compel* him to her [Mariana's] *recompense*; and hear, by this is your brother saved, your honour untainted, the poor Mariana advantaged, and the corrupt deputy scaled" (3.1.251–56; emphasis added). An encounter that Angelo has intended as a secret tryst will actually transform his relationship with Mariana. And a public acknowledgment of the consummation will "compel" Angelo to Mariana's "recompense," that is, what she is owed under the contract.[14]

The performance of the contract is brought about inside Angelo's garden, in the "heavy middle of the night," images drawing on the themes of fertility and generation. Importantly, the Duke considers the consummation as a means to realize the long inchoate contract:

> With Angelo tonight shall lie
> His old betrothed but despised.
> So disguise shall, by th'disguised,
> Pay with falsehood false exacting,
> And *perform* an old *contracting*. (3.2.271–75; emphasis
>   added)

The Duke uses a gerund form—"contracting"—that emphasizes not only the contract, but also the process of bringing the two together under the contract, that is, the actual performing of what has remained static. By the sixteenth century, the meaning of *perform* had long included the act of accomplishing the requirements of a legal obligation, and was synonymous with similar constructions, such as to "execute" a contract.[15]

Finally, in addition to the elements of publicity, true value, and performance, contractual tokens and rituals are important in the solemnization of the marriage. Rings, seals, and the clasping of hands figure into the plot development when the characters make claims to authenticity or, conversely, make charges of invalidity. While making a case for the legitimacy of his true contract marriage, Claudio says Juliet is "fast my wife" (except for the public denunciation), with allusions to the handfast portion of the wedding ceremony. And in the judgment scene, Mariana calls Angelo her "husband," and gives reasons for doing so by citing evidence of their bond. She has "locked hands" with him over a vowed contract: "This is the hand which, with a vowed contract, / Was fast belocked in thine" (5.1.208-9). It is also by means of the Duke's handwriting ("hand") and seal that the Provost is brought into the conspiracy to trick Angelo: "Look you, sir, here is the hand and seal of the Duke. You know the character, I doubt not, and the signet is not strange to you?" (4.2.191-93). Without these tokens of legitimacy, the Duke could not win the Provost's confidence and win Claudio's salvation.

Rings, tokens of the marriage bond, are often given, won, lost, stolen, and returned in other plays by Shakespeare. At first reading they appear to be conspicuously absent in *Measure for Measure*, at least in their customary form. But this is appropriate in a play in which the validity of the contracts is so questionable, especially the inchoate contract of Angelo and Mariana. It is only when the "old contract" is in the process of being "performed" that images of rings come into play. Mariana, banished from Angelo, lives at St. Luke's grange, which is *surrounded* by water—a "moated grange" (3.1.265). And it is in Angelo's garden, "*circummur'd* with brick," that is, ringed with a wall, that the unexecuted contract is transformed by the consummation.

"Circummur'd" is Shakespeare's coinage, used here and nowhere else in his plays. Marjorie Garber states that Shakespeare's most traditional symbol of sexual activity is the walled garden, uniting the flower (virginity) with the treasure, casket, or ring. Romeo and Juliet, Troilus and Cressida, Benedick and Beatrice, and Olivia and Sebastian all emerge from or meet in gardens. Garber goes on to describe Domenico Veneziano's painting of *The Annunciation* as illustrative of the iconography: the Virgin stands next to a chest, in a room that opens onto a garden. Before her is a kneeling angel, a cluster of lilies in his hand. Mariana's grange, and Angelo's garden, are symbols of their virginity. Extending this explanation to the contract, the ringed wall here is also emblematic of the consummated, valid marriage itself. That the characters are named Mariana and Angelo, and that Mariana's grange is at St. Luke's, are factors even more suggestive of the Annunciation icon that Garber describes, especially considering the salvation of the characters accomplished by performing the contract.[16]

The most defining action in the play, the hinge upon which all turns and is resolved, occurs in this emblematic, ringed locale. By integrating the marriage contract here, giving it both form and substance, the redemption of the characters at the end of the play can occur. And it is in this act that the significance of the contracts' role is most telling. The particular elements of the contract—a public celebration, bound with rings and hands, between worthy partners, duly executed—come together and form a union. Without them, there is only the pseudomarriage, not the fully realized marriage.

On this important level of individual relationships, the imperfectly realized contracts complicate the plot. But their imperfect realization is also representative of the larger issues that figure into the play, matters related to a dangerous separation between what seems to be and what actually is. At the root of the Viennese problem is a disjunction between the outward and the inward. Thomas Aquinas articulates the nature of the problem: "It belongs to the virtue of truth to show oneself outwardly by outward signs to be such as one is. Now outward signs are not only words but also deeds . . . dissimulation is properly a lie told by the signs of outward deeds."[17] It has been contended that Isabella's theology is based on deeds more than faith, and her impotence in the face of Angelo's evil reveals her mistake.[18] But in this play, and in *All's Well That Ends Well*, "deeds matching words" is not only a central theme, but also a means of solving dilemmas. If anything, Isabella is challenged to go beyond mere talk of mercy.[19]

The disorder caused by "seeming" rather than "being" plagues Vienna on a multitude of levels, not merely the marital. Backing away for an overview of these larger issues will provide a clearer picture of what the play's resolution, via the contracts, actually achieves. For throughout the dialogue, there is mention of disorder in the world. The Duke says that there is a "great fever on goodness" (3.2.216), and Vienna is a place where

> Liberty plucks justice by the nose
> the baby beats the nurse, and quite athwart
> Goes all decorum. (1.3.29–31)

He attributes this sickness in political health to a lack of law enforcement, one that has persisted for fourteen years (1.3.21).[20] The law is variously characterized as unworn armor (1.2.156), a scarecrow (2.1.1), and a barbershop "forfeit" (5.1.318). And the law's ministers, especially Angelo, can be just as empty of integrity. The Duke recognizes this:

> O place and greatness, millions of false eyes
> Are stuck upon thee; volume of report
> Run with their false and most contrarious quest
> Upon thy doings; thousand escapes of wit
> Make thee father of their idle dream
> And rack thee in their fancies. (4.1.60–64)

The conscience-stricken Angelo recognizes it as well:

> O place, O form,
> How often dost thou with thy case, thy habit,
> Wrench awe from fools and tie the wiser souls
> To thy false seeming! (2.4.12–15)

However, Angelo's awareness cannot overcome his swelling appetite. He proceeds in his designs on Isabella with the resignation: "Blood, thou art blood!" (2.4.15). The conflict between what Angelo thought himself to be, and what he actually is, does not find resolution. He pretends to occupy an office that is emptied of real content.

According to Claudio, Angelo's severity in law is meant to establish a reputation, a "name," so that the public can know whether the tyranny is in the office, or in the "eminence that fills it up"—another distinction between form and substance (1.2.152–53). Whatever captures his attention, Angelo seizes on:

> What's open made to justice,
> That justice seizes. What knows the law
> That thieves do pass on thieves. 'Tis very pregnant,
> The jewel that we find, we stoop and take't
> Because we see it, but what we do not see
> We tread upon and never think of it. (2.1.21–26)

And this capriciousness does not go unnoted by Escalus:

> Well, heaven forgive him, and forgive us all!
> Some rise by sin, and some by virtue fall.
> Some run from brakes of vice, and answer none;
> And some condemned for a fault alone. (2.1.37–40)

When asked if he could pardon her brother if he would, Angelo attaches the law to his own will: "Look what I will not; that I cannot do" (2.2.53). Of course, this is the cause of his demeanor toward Isabella. He relies on his "place i'th'state" to overweigh her threats to proclaim his "seeming" (2.4.155). Thwarted, Isabella can only complain:

> O perilous mouths,
> That bear in them one and the self-same tongue
> Either of condemnation or approof,
> Bidding the law make curtsy to their will,
> Hooking both right and wrong to th'appetitie,
> To follow as it draws! (2.4.171–76)

Angelo takes on the form of justice while unable to perform his duties justly; quite the opposite, he perverts the powers of his office and abuses the process entrusted to him.

Like the many other pseudostates in the play, Angelo is the empty "case" he speaks of in his lamentation (2.4.13). To retain his status in the community, he will sacrifice integrity for appearance. To Isabella, smitten with her own integrity, compromise is unthinkable. This provokes another comparison between the two regarding the disjunction between *res* and *verba*. Angelo tells Isabella he is not interested in her soul, but only in her body, which she must yield to his will (2.4.163). Isabella refuses to give up her body for her brother in favor of preserving her soul.[21] This Manichean split, coming from different perspectives, testifies to the siege on integrity in Vienna. Ultimately, it will take the reunification of the outward and the inward to reorder Viennese society, a feat accomplished via the contracts.

By act 5, it appears that the "seemers" have won the day. The lack of integrity typical of Vienna creeps into the aspects of life, even into the characterization of the contractual elements that later help fully realize the marriage contracts. Prior to the last scene, when their meanings are transformed, *publicity, value,* and *execution* are used in perverse ways, and have darker meanings. With regard to publication, things that should be proclaimed are hidden. Claudio and Juliet's union lacks "denunciation," bypassing the public ceremony that requires the proclaiming of banns (1.2.137). Isabella's threat to "proclaim" Angelo's extortion is stifled by blackmail—a threat to proclaim *her* as unchaste (2.4.155-56). On the other hand, Vienna is rife with "proclamations" regarding fornication, prostitutes, and brothels (1.2.73; 1.2.88). And the Duke ironically assures Angelo that his true worth, heretofore hidden, will be "proclaimed" (5.1.16).

Bonds too take on a double meaning and use, the importance of which has even greater significance in *The Merchant of Venice.* In his dire assessment of the world's duplicity, the Duke remarks, "There is scarce truth enough alive to make societies secure, but security enough to make fellowships accursed. Much upon this riddle runs the wisdom of the world" (3.2.220-23). The Duke plays on the double meaning of security: there is so little honesty that there can be no secure bonds of society, but "security"—in the sense of financial bonds, liable to forfeit—enough to make human fellowship a curse. The honest bonds of society, among which marriage and friendship rank, are rare: the Duke is "[b]ound by my charity and my blest order" (2.3.3) and "combined by a sacred vow" (4.3.144); Mariana says she is "always bound" to the Duke as friar (4.1.25); but the "bondage" of human obligation and persecution is plentiful. While bound in chains, Claudio speaks of the immoderate use of "scope" that has turned to his restraint (1.2.120).[22] The chains of restraint and prison cells of Angelo's rule are symbolic of his conception of the judicial system: "the manacles of the all-binding law" (2.4.93-94). Although the law ultimately rectifies the characters' problems, it too begins as part of their dilemma.

Equal worth and value are also shown in a dark light. Near the middle of the play, and in preparation for Claudio's execution, the executioner, Abhorson, and the bawd, Pompey, speak of how the true man's clothes fit the executioner: "Every true man's apparel fits your thief" (4.2.41). Their particular worths having been equated by the Provost (4.2.28), the symbols of unbridled sex, Pompey, and of criminal death, Abhorson ("son of a whore"), are sent off to talk of their "mystery."

This equation of sex with death is all too apt, and Vienna is the worse for it. But rather than draw too great a distinction between the good and the bad, it must be remembered that Angelo is not the only one who has hooked his will to his appetite. The bawd-ridden Vienna suffers from a general "fever on goodness." Isabella betrays a psychological equivalence between sex and death when she "longs" for death and would "strip" herself to embrace it (2.4.101–3). And Claudio characterizes his and Juliet's sexual license as the ravening down of rat poison: "A thirst evil, and when we drink, we die" (1.2.121–22). In these lines is a sketch of a society with unrestrained appetites.[23] The surrender of reason to the will and the disjunction between appearance and reality have led to the association of sex with death, rather than with life. Something is needed to change the situation, some agent who will transform this orientation toward death. That agent takes the form of the Duke, and he accomplishes his feat by ensuring integrity, via the contract.

Fortunately, though he faults himself for being too removed from society, the Duke knows that dissemblance is at the root of Vienna's problems:

> Lord Angelo is precise;
> Stands at a guard with envy;
>
> . . . .
>
> Hence shall we see
> If power change purpose, what our seemers be.
>   (1.3.50–51; 53–54)

As the play progresses, the Duke proceeds to rectify the problems created by the "seemers." His orchestrations have garnered much criticism, but he is nevertheless one who—as the trustworthy Escalus says—always "sought to know himself" (3.2.227). The ancient maxim "know thyself" may entail a broader investigation when the person in question is also the governor. In Ernst Kantorowicz's important work *The King's Two Bodies*, the author explains the theology of kingship and the relationship between the body politic and the kingly body. It seems to me that for the Duke to know himself, he must know his kingdom, and the convention of the player king is an excellent way to accomplish this self-knowledge.[24] The method he employs is the very means by which the world of Vienna operates, under a disguise. But since Vienna is a world riddled with vices, the Duke must disguise virtue.

Tricks are common in Vienna, and the ability of things to achieve ends that seem inconsistent with their natures is also well-known. When Isabella comes with news of Angelo's offer, Claudio begs her to save his life on this basis:

> Sweet sister, let me live.
> What sin you do to save a brother's life,
> Nature dispenses with the deed so far
> That it becomes a virtue. (3.1.132–34)

Another example of this point occurs in *Romeo and Juliet*, when Friar Laurence says "[v]irtue itself turns vice being misapplied / And vice sometimes by action dignified" (2.3.17–18).[25] When the Duke spots his opportunity, he knows his method, and employs it on the same grounds. Proposing the bed-trick to perform the contract, he tells Isabella, "If you think well to carry this, as you may, the doubleness of the benefit defends the deceit from reproof" (3.1.258). And it is the use of a "double," the substitution of Mariana for Isabella, that works the deceit. Doubles are used throughout the Duke's scheme: Mariana for Isabella, Barnardine for Claudio, and even Ragozine for Barnardine. Angelo's crime is even characterized later as a "double violation / Of sacred chastity and of promise-breach"(5.1.402–3).[26] The integrative effect it will have is reflected in Isabella's response to the idea: "The *image* of it gives me *content* already, and I trust I will grow to a most *prosperous perfection*" (3.1.260–61; emphasis added).

The importance of this doubling does not stop at the level of the action, but extends into the level of the language related to consummation. The concentration of meaning in the "ringed-wall garden" is particularly intense, since the equation of sex and death in the clown scene—between the bawd and the executioner—occurs at midnight, the same "heavy middle of the night" when the bed-trick is taking place. At this hour of transformation, the equation of "sex and death" is itself being transformed into one of "sex and life" by the performance of the old contract. As has been mentioned, in the sixteenth century, the "performance" of a contract was one way of expressing its accomplishment, as was "execution" and "satisfaction."[27] All of these words are used at one time or another in the play, but when they are used, and by whom, is particularly telling.

Angelo, having demanded sex from Isabella in return for her brother's life, betrays her, sending instructions to the Provost of what he would have "performed." He orders Claudio's execution. Reading to the Duke from Angelo's letter, the Provost says, "For my better *satisfaction*, let me have Claudio's head sent me by five. Let this be duly *performed*, with a thought that more depends on it than we must deliver" (4.2.120–22; emphasis added). Of course, the Duke has other ways of using the term, and has already provided for their use. In scheming to perform the bed-trick, he tells Isabella, "It lies much in your holding up. Haste you speedily to Angelo: if for this night he entreat you to his bed, give him *promise of satisfaction*" (3.1.262–64; emphasis added). The satisfaction Angelo demands is sexual; and he receives it, but not in the way he intended, nor with the consequences he expected. The event's meaning is greater than he knows. For the "satisfaction" he receives actually ratifies the old contract. As the Duke says in his credo, the old, inchoate contract has been "performed" in the walled garden (3.2.275). Unbeknownst to Angelo, the contract has been "sealed" in this sense, which works to save lives rather than to destroy them. Ultimately, this trumps the kind of "execution" Angelo would have performed. In the last scene, the only thing that is "executed" is the Duke's pleasure:

> Take him [Lucio] to prison,
> And see our pleasure herein executed. (5.1.518–19)

And the pleasure here is merely the marriage of Lucio to Kate Keepdown and the consequent legitimization of their child.

The transformations do not stop there, for a closer look at the place and time of the bed-trick reveal that they too have significance. As part of the Duke and Isabella's own dissembling, he tells her to make certain conditions on her submission to Angelo: "[R]efer yourself to this advantage: first, that your stay with him may not be long; that the time may have all shadow and silence in it; and the place answer to convenience" (3.1.245–49). "Advantage" can denote not only interest, as in *The Merchant of Venice*, but also a condition. Coupled with the time and place conditions of the contract's performance, what will happen in the garden takes on an altogether different nature from what Angelo had planned. The time and place seem characteristic of lust: haste, silence, darkness, and secrecy. But again, this is merely the deception of the deceiver. The ringed-wall garden becomes, instead of a trysting place of sexual satisfaction, an emblematic setting for marital consummation. Under the guise of vice, virtue passes. In so doing, performance accomplishes integrity, unifying the form of the old contract with its substance.

With this understanding of how the Duke's trick performs the old contract, the analysis can turn to the trial scene in the last act. The disjunction of *res* and *verba* in marriage has been quietly remedied, but the disjunction of *res* and *verba* in justice has not. There the consequences of having validated the "old" contract are fully played out.

The Duke, having returned from his "travels," publicly thanks Angelo for his government. The deputy replies: "You make my *bonds* still greater" (5.1.9).

The bonds of duty and friendship are implied, but considering the actual circumstances—what Angelo and the Duke both know of his real deserts—the ideas of punishment and restraint are also at play. The Duke continues, proceeding to expose Angelo while playing on this second meaning of "bondage," associated with locks, prisons, and covert wards, where Claudio is being held:

> O, but your desert speaks loud, and I should wrong it
> To *lock* it in the *wards* of *covert bosom*,
> When it deserves with characters of brass
> A *forted residence* 'gainst the tooth of time
> And razure of oblivion. *Give me your hand*,
> And let the subject see, to make them know
> That outward courtesies would fain *proclaim*
> Favours that keep within. (5.1.10–18; emphasis added)

Considering that "locked hands" and "public proclamations" are the very things that have given substance to the inchoate marriage "bond," the Duke's irony is all the more powerful. Both the "bonds" of human fellowship, said earlier to be rare, and the more common "bonds of persecution and restraint" are present in the image. But the Duke has transformed the secret sexual extortion into a marriage "bond." The disclosure of this transformation will lead to the deputy's unmasking and perhaps to his "bondage" in prison.

Angelo's perversion of the law has been the focus of much critical commentary, particularly regarding justice and mercy, the fitness of the judge, and the hooking of law to the appetite. But Robert Grams Hunter's conception of the play's three "dramatic triangles," which are analogous to the trials in medieval moralities, best illustrates the distortion of the law that results from the triumph of Angelo's will. In typical morality allegories, says Hunter, four characters appear: the *humanum genus* (the "Everyman") as offender, the Virgin Mary as advocate, the devil as prosecutor, and God as judge. In *Measure for Measure*, the judge and prosecutor are combined, leaving only three characters. In the first triangle—before his own temptation—Angelo appears as the prosecutor, Isabella as the advocate, and Claudio as the offender. But in the second triangle—*after* the temptation that causes him to pervert the justice system to his private ends—Angelo appears as a perverse advocate for Claudio's life, forcing Isabella into the perverse position of judge. It is not until the third triangle, after Angelo is exposed, that the deputy switches places with Claudio as the *humanum genus*, and the Duke, having remounted his throne, becomes the judge.[28]

The illustration makes clear that what has always been considered the looming focus of the play—law, and the proper balance of mercy and justice—is actually just as much subject to perversion and distortion as any other institution in Vienna. As Kermode points out, Isabella speaks of human agency's fallibility in, and arrogance toward, justice when it is "dress'd in a little brief authority."[29] The law can be not only flouted, as the bawds show, but also made into a personal tool to accomplish vendetta or satisfaction, as Angelo shows. The Duke transforms that use into a public one, using the marriage contract to bring integrity to what are imperfectly realized unions.

In act 5, Isabella enters calling for "Justice!" and asking to lodge her "complaint" (5.1.21–26). Ironically, the Duke says she must "reveal" herself to Lord Angelo, who is the "justice" (5.1.28–29). Isabella, refusing to seek "redemption from the devil," pleads for the Duke to hear her, on the grounds that appearances are deceiving:

> Make not impossible.
> That which but seems unlike. 'Tis not impossible
> But one, the wicked'st caitiff on the ground,
> May seem as shy, as just, as brave, as absolute,
> As Angelo; Even so may Angelo,
> In all his dressings, caracts, titles, forms
> Be an arch-villain! (5.1.54–60)

When the Duke feigns disbelief as to the likelihood of Isabella's charges against Angelo, she replies: "O, that it were as like as it is true" (5.1.108).

The charade continues. Friar Peter comes in, offering to disprove Isabella's avowals of ruination by presenting a witness to contradict her. The veiled Mariana then answers questions of her identity with paradoxical replies. She is not maid, wife, or widow, but occupies a quasi status:

> My lord, I do confess I ne'er was married
> And I confess besides, I am no maid.
> I have known my husband; yet my husband
> Knows not that ever he knew me. (5.1.185–89)

These words echo those of Helena in *All's Well That Ends Well* who, like Mariana, has accomplished the bed-trick, but says she is wife only in name, until her husband claims her. The same lament can be found in Adriana of *The Comedy of Errors*, and Imogen of *Cymbeline*, with regard to a painful quasi status resulting from their husbands' rejection. Because a marriage is the union of two, making one, they imply that a separation from their husbands makes them in no real sense a wife.[30]

In the process of making claim to the status of wife, Mariana lays claim to Angelo as husband using the terms of the contract. Her unveiling is one of many in the last act, exposing a multitude of hidden truths:

> My husband bids me [to unveil]; now I will unmask.
> This is that face, thou cruel Angelo,
> Which once thou swors'st was worth the looking on.
> This is the hand which, with a vowed contract,
> Was fast belocked in thine. This is the body
> That took away the match from Isabel,
> And did supply thee at thy garden-house
> In her imagined person. (5.1.204–12)

But Angelo denies her claim until the Duke unveils himself. When it becomes apparent that Vincentio has brought about the consummation and that the hidden parts of Angelo are no longer "undiscernible" (5.1.376), even the deputy must drop his charade:

Duke: . . . Say: wast thou e'er contracted to this woman?

Angelo: I was, my lord. (5.1.373–74)

Here again, something significant happens. The consummation of the pre-contract—while serving the Duke's purposes without transgressing holy law—is not entirely sufficient. The Duke orders Friar Peter to marry Angelo and Mariana, telling her he arranged the marriage to prevent public censure from ruining her future:

> Consenting to the safeguard of your honour,
> I thought your marriage fit; else imputation,
> For that he knew you, might reproach your life,
> And choke your good to come. For your possessions,
> Although by confiscation they are ours,
> We do enstate and widow you with all,
> To buy you a better husband. (5.1.417–23)

Again, the public nature of the marriage contract is important as a safeguard of honor. Having proclaimed her night with Angelo, and then having suffered Angelo's public reproof, Mariana is in the position of many compromised

Englishwomen after a clandestine assignation. Despite the five-year-old public ceremony, another ceremony here addresses any possible charge that Mariana has slept with a man who is not her husband. This extra celebration could be evidence for considering the precontract as *de futuro*, needing consummation to be ratified, and solemnization to be sanctified and absolved.[31] But the greater point, which the Duke makes pains to state, is for the celebration to be *seen*, to make sure the status of the two is changed in the public eye.

There is still more accomplished by providing societal witness to this contract. For the play has revolved around Viennese society, sick and dissolute as it is, just as much as it has revolved around its representative characters. And a constant theme throughout the action centers on the characters' complicated, tenuous relationship with their community. They have either removed themselves, or have been removed, from their society: Angelo, by both his early superiority and his late criminal designs; Isabella, by a similar superiority that would fashion a stricter cloister within a cloister; Claudio and Juliet, by their imprisonment; the bawds, by being outlaws; and the Duke, by his "dark-cornered" dereliction. The turning away from society towards the self—a self-lust, as it were—amounts to what Hunter says lies at the heart of these plays: a rejection of love that "results in crimes which, though they do not occur in reality, appear to be serious threats to the existence of an orderly, love-dominated society."[32] R. F. Kaufman provides another instructive elaboration:

> Self-governance, being an individual act by definition is not enough without acceptance of one's social and symbolic role. Not only can man not live alone, he cannot signify alone. The marriages that reform the characters in the play, via the contracts, pay homage to the necessities of the blood, while preserving, if only by its continued existence, the fabric of society.[33]

Proper marriage in Shakespeare is not, and should not be, a private affair, because its consequences are not private. The Duke's assurance of a public witness to the marriage provides a means of ensuring social cohesion.

By providing integrity to the contracts, the Duke helps cure a malady that has plagued Vienna. Earlier in the play, even Angelo bewailed his condition when he spoke of the "unshaping" and stultifying effects his supposed crimes have had on him:

> This deed *unshapes* me quite, makes me unpregnant
> And dull to all proceedings. A deflowered maid, .

> And by an eminent body that enforced
> The law against it! (4.4.19–21; emphasis added)

But now, joined with Mariana in marriage, he is truly her "combinate husband" (3.1.223). This image of "combined souls" is used in other plays, such as the "solemn combination" of souls in *Twelfth Night*.[34] The image is extended here, as the Duke makes a public offer to Isabella: "Give me your hand, and say you will be mine" (5.1.490); and "What's mine is yours, and what is yours is mine" (5.1.534). The idea is somewhat similar to the concept of marriage captured in the metaphysical poem *The Phoenix and Turtle*. There, the relationship of the two birds is said to have been so close that "property was thus appalled" (line 37) as "either was the other's mine" (line 36). The paradox of two separate beings joined in a unique bond is an ideal integrity; the Duke's abundant expression toward Isabella contains a note of the same.

Isabella's silence after the Duke's proposal has been seen as another reason for considering the play problematic.[35] However, to consider her silence as a refusal, or as an open question, is to ignore the many aspects of the play that point toward resolution: Mariana and Angelo, Claudio and Juliet, Lucio and Kate Keepdown, and even Barnardine and the Friar, who will instruct him in how to live a better life. Also, as has often been pointed out, the play works on many levels, naturalistic and fablistic; not only are the characters' individual lives brought to a fuller realization, but also the society as a whole is more fully realized via the resolution of its individual members. Isabella has a societal role as well as an individual one, and the marriage of the "King" with his "Kingdom" is appropriate in a play in which the King and his Kingdom have been separated through self-isolation.

The integrity provided by contractual union is not the final end of the marriage. Rather, integrity here is necessary for a particular goal, stated early in the play and maintained throughout. In *Measure for Measure*, marital disjunction results in a frustration of nature. Bypassing the marriage ceremony in favor of unbridled sex is characteristic of the bawds, and results in their disordered, syphilitic realm. On the other hand, refusal to consummate the marriage is characteristic of Angelo, and results in his frozen, "ungenitured" realm. The world is made diseased and rotten by one group, and barren and starved by the other. Such a society is oriented toward death, and it is that orientation that the bed-trick works to realign. The frigidity and barrenness of those removed from society, as well as the licentiousness and liberality of those who bypass societal institutions, are responsible for denying nature her "due," as the Duke describes it in the play's first scene. The Duke accuses Angelo of hoarding nature's graces as if they were his own:

> Thyself and thy belongings
> Are not thine own so proper as to waste
> thyself upon thy virtues, they on thee. (1.1.29–31)

and

> Nature never lends
> the smallest scruple of her excellence
> But, like a thrifty goddess, she determines
> Herself the glory of a creditor,
> Both thanks and use. (1.1.36–40)

Here, Angelo resembles the young man of the first sonnets, whom the poet scolds for refusing to marry. His injustice is toward both nature and himself, as he cheats both of a child by which a "copy" of his qualities could be left to posterity:

> Nature's bequest gives nothing, but doth lend,
> And being frank, she lends to those are free.
> Then, beauteous niggard, why dost thou abuse
> The bounteous largess given thee to give? (sonnet 4,
>   lines 3–6)

Again, nature is a creditor, whose gifts—"bequests"—are meant to be returned. Her largesse is to be emulated by the recipient. To be niggardly with her graces is to frustrate the purpose of the gift, the production of children. A retirement from nature, and from duty, is a theme throughout the problem plays, and is not limited to Angelo in this one. Isabella seeks a cloistered life, stricter than even the Poor Clares offer, and the Duke faults himself for effectively abdicating his office, having "stolen" from the state by "usurping beggary" (3.2.90). Bertram in *All's Well That Ends Well* and Olivia in *Twelfth Night* fall into a similar category.[36]

    This is Angelo's first fault, as a man whose blood is "snow-broth," who "scarce confesses that his blood flows or that this appetite / Is more to bread than stone" (1.3.51–53). He is said to urinate "congealed ice" (3.2.106); to be "a motion ungenerative" (3.2.108); and an "ungenitured agent" who will "unpeople the province with continency" (3.2.168-69). As his name implies, and conduct suggests, Angelo somehow considers himself above human nature. He floats free of the common desires of man in a type of "angelism."

This rarefied opinion of himself carries over into his idealistic view of justice, so dissociated from the actual world that it becomes pure, rigid form. Angelo's conflation of himself with Justice is so complete that Escalus says he has been forced to call the younger man "Justice" personified (3.2.248). When his appetite is later awakened by Isabella, it is a short step for "Justice" to attach the law to his personal will. His fellow justice, Escalus, proves to be a better governor because he is said, in a generative image, to be "pregnant in the nature of the people" (1.1.9). "Art and practice" as a member of the human community— referred to collectively by the Duke as "yonder generation" (4.3.88)—have enriched Escalus's statecraft, a skill the socially removed Angelo does not possess. Angelo's removal from society echoes his removal from Nature, which results in the frustration of his marriage contract with Mariana. In this light, there is a "multiple harkening" in Mariana's whispered charge to Angelo: "Remember now my brother" (4.1.69). He must not only recall his particular duty regarding the brothers (Mariana's, as well as Isabella's), but also *as* a brother of those to whom he owes his duty. The law, via the contract, effectuates that recall to community here.[37]

But when Isabella awakens his appetite, Angelo slights nature in a different way. Like Claudio, he bypasses the marriage contract by way of indulging his sexual will. And extracontractual sex, with the possibility of resulting pregnancy, is seen in terms of stealing from nature, creating counterfeit images. Claudio's child is considered to have been "stolen" in this way (2.4.43).[38] Theft imagery is common. Immediately preceding the appearance of the prostitute Mistress Overdone and that of the restrained Claudio himself, Lucio and his bawdy companions joke that the commandment "Thou shalt not steal" was rightly "razed from the table of ten" by pirates, a type of thief (1.2.10). Later, when Angelo is tempted by lust for Isabella, he uses the imagery of theft to accuse his own conscience: "Thieves for their robbery have authority / When judges steal themselves" (2.2.176-77). Finally, the law is analogized to a useless scarecrow, unable to protect the crops from thieving crows (2.1.1-4). .

Rather than contribute to societal cohesion, sex outside the contract threatens societal disorder of a kind and degree all too evident in the punks, bawds, bastards, and disease of Vienna. To restore order, the Duke makes sure to legitimize Lucio's bastard with Kate Keepdown, an unacknowledged child whom Mistress Overdone claims to have kept (3.2.196):

> Proclaim it, Provost, round about the city,
> If any woman wrong'd by this lewd fellow,
> As I have heard him swear himself there's one
> Whom he begot with child, let her appear,
> And he shall marry her. (5.1.506–10)

According to Lucio earlier in the play, this would have been the the Duke's approach to the situation. He would have married Lucio to the "wench" for "getting her with child" had Lucio not denied paternity (4.3.170).

The difference between sex within the contract and sex outside it can be seen in the way the two are described vis-à-vis nature. At the beginning of the play, references to sex and nature imply fecundity without order:

Pompey:	You have not heard of the proclamation, have you?
M. Overdone:	What proclamation, man?
Pompey:	All houses [brothels] in the suburbs of Vienna must be plucked down.
M. Overdone:	And what shall become of those in the city?
Pompey:	They shall stand for seed [semen]: (1.2.85–91)

and

> Your brother and his lover have embraced.
> As those that feed grow full, as blossoming time
> That from the seedness the bare fallow brings
> To teeming foison, even so her plenteous womb
> Expresseth his full tilth and husbandry. (1.4.39–43)

Marjorie Garber contends that the prolific agricultural metaphor, the richness of descriptive detail, and even the double meaning of "husbandry," here emphasize the fruitful and productive value of sexuality and childbearing.[39] This is largely so, but when understood in terms of the disjunction of *res* and *verba*, the play Shakespeare makes of legitimate and illegitimate "seals," and the trouble that the private consummation has wrought, it is Claudio's aptitude for plain "husbandry" that takes him afoul of order. The difference in tone can be seen when this passage is laid alongside a later one, concerning the husbandry of Angelo and Mariana:

> Nor, gentle daughter, fear you not at all.
> He is your husband on a pre-contract.
> To bring you thus together 'tis no sin,
> Sith that the justice of your title to him
> Doth flourish the deceit. Come, let us go.
> Our corn's to reap, for yet our tilth's to sow. (4.1.71–76)

Here, order and entitlement are brought to the agricultural images; teeming and blossoming are replaced with the reaping of corn. Rather than an image of people who "feed" to the point of satiation, as in Lucio's passage, we have Mariana, a "constant" girl, being informed that her precontract gives her "just-title" to Angelo. By following the Duke's instructions, Mariana will have an incontrovertible claim to her husband. Further, the similarity between the Duke's depiction and the ceremony by which land was transferred—the livery of seisin—becomes all the stronger. For the commonplace of a husband's duty to "plowe that lande which beyng Tilled, yeldeth children"[40] is seen in terms of a transaction, by which the inchoate marriage will be transformed into Mariana's full, unencumbered possession of her husband.[41] The couple has an obligation, presumably to nature, to consummate the marriage; under the Duke's plan, even the "deceit will flourish."

From these passages a norm arises regarding nature, which the valid marriage contract helps to observe: nature expects generosity from man; he must not hoard the graces that are her gifts. This is Angelo's first fault, as a man whose blood is "snow-broth." He will not confess that he too has a man's desires, and is subject to a man's failings. But neither can man steal from nature—Angelo's second fault, as well as that of Claudio. Both extremes imply an asocial quality that either keeps what nature has given or takes what she has never sanctioned. To return the largess that nature expects, man must indeed be "generative," but this generation must occur within the bounds of legitimacy.

As a marriage brings two people together, it necessarily requires the surrender of the self to the other, a relinquishment of "nature's graces." It also requires that the relinquishment be permanent, not the temporary workings of lust that contribute to the disorder so evident in Vienna.[42] Under these circumstances, legitimate generation takes place, returning nature's graces and providing for society's future.

But the transformation from seeming to being does not necessarily ensure a future for society in *Measure for Measure*. Barnardine, as the ultimate "Everyman" character, is cautioned to take his mercy to "provide for better times to come" (5.1.482–83). The hope for the community, says J. A. Bryant, which is the hope of comedy everywhere, lies in the possibility that a residual charity in some human beings may be appealed to, and that men and women may on occasion give up their charades and accept one another in the kind of love—Mariana's love—of which the human race at its best is capable. Only then has the community a chance of continuing as a civic organism in relative stability and peace.[43]

And that is the largest lesson in the play: society—its individuals and institutions—must be orientated toward preserving what lies at the heart of Mariana's achievement: a largeness of soul, founded in love. This orientation is consistent with the aims of life instead of death, and is aimed toward generation, not destruction.

The law can be geared toward either orientation, a point made with greater force in the two bonds of *The Merchant of Venice.* In this play, the employment of the legal instrument by nature's agent—here, Duke Vincentio—redirects the law toward life. Early on, Angelo's equivalent justice threatens to end the action quite differently. He tells Escalus not to plead for Claudio's life, because

> When I, that censure him, do so offend,
> Let mine own judgment pattern out my death,
> And nothing come in partial. Sir, he must die. (2.1.29–31)

For a moment, it seems as though the Duke is ready to apply this philosophy when calling for Angelo's punishment:

> "An Angelo for Claudio, death or death."
> Haste still pays haste, and leisure answers leisure;
> Like doth quit like, and measure still for measure.
> (5.1.407–9)

But through the validation of the contract, a different pattern emerges. Instead of two like things answering each other "measure for measure," something unusual occurs, especially unusual in a dissolute Vienna: a virtue, though unexpected and disguised, answers vice, thereby integrating things which were only empty pseudostates before. And that virtue is mercy, which Angelo learns that he too needs, and Isabella, that she too must bestow. To extend Hunter's triangles further, Angelo, and the audience, are meant to learn that their natural place in the trial of man is that of the defendant, not the prosecutor, plaintiff, or judge. They learn of their inability to meet a standard of "measure for measure"; they must instead pray for mercy.

It must be noted that the law is not set aside in the play, nor is justice opposed to mercy, as has often been claimed. As C. L. Barber says, Shakespeare is "scrupulously responsible to the principles of social order (however factitious his 'law' may be literally)."[44] There is no reason to doubt the disguised Duke's sincerity when he says to the seated Angelo: "Respect to your great place; and let the devil / Be sometime honour'd for his burning throne" (5.1.290–91).[45] Aquinas relegated a troubled respect for unjust civil laws, because their observance at least showed a respect for the law as an institution. His trouble undoubtedly sprang from the fact that, according to natural law, unjust laws were not laws at all; however, a tension had to be observed between civil disobedience and the overthrow of civility altogether. In fact, even in *Measure for Measure*, it is only the form of punishment that is questioned, not whether the punishment is due. In keeping with his role as agent of nature, the Duke chooses a legal remedy for the disordered Vienna. The contracts provide for life rather than destroy it. It is the ends to which society aims its laws that are productive or destructive; the law reflects and coordinates the achievement of those ends, for good or ill.

This chapter has served to outline Shakespeare's use of the law as a means to achieve his dramatic objectives. As has been discussed, the status of marriages in Elizabethan England, and across the continent for that matter, was highly contentious and sometimes ungracefully resolved. That they were politically charged may also be so. The law as a whole was in a state of change at the time; indeed, the entire sixteenth century was a rolling series of political, theological, and philosophical changes. The Statute of Uses and the Statute of Wills were two large pieces of legislation with political motivations. New laws in contract, let alone in tort and commerce, have been analyzed for causes and effects. Thorough legal histories have been done, and scholarship in this area continues.[46] That Shakespeare, as any other citizen, was aware of these changes is probable, though to what extent we cannot know.

However, Shakespeare is not dramatizing, in Bunyanesque fashion, these legal conflicts in his problems plays. Such readings make too much of the law in Shakespeare by reading too deeply in the law itself. They result in making legal concepts and historical conflicts the sole interest, and elevating those concerns over more important literary themes. That approach cannot reconcile its finding with what happens in the plays, so it finds them more obscure and inexplicable than they need be.

Such a position depends on the assumption that, first, Shakespeare (or any artist for that matter) was artistically strapped by the law of the time, and second, that his purpose was largely to dramatize that law. For example, a historian might hold that Shakespeare could not intend to play Mariana's "worth" against her lost dowry, because marriage contracts at the time did not necessarily require dowries; therefore, Angelo's refusal of the "worthy" Mariana for a lost dowry (replaced by the Duke to make her "worth" match Angelo's) would be simply "mysterious." But this assumes that the artist's goals are partly legal-historical allegory, or that the artist cannot transcend the specifics of the law. Such an approach answers nothing about the play's many other dimensions; instead, it opts for a safer route that does not have to account for consistency with depth of understanding. To say that "overlooking" complexities in the English law oversimplifies the plays is only to overlook thematic parallels, and to contribute to further critical obfuscation.

Surely the point in *Measure for Measure* is that Mariana is "worthy" not for her money, but for her authenticity. In a play in which the false is preferred over the true, and the dissolute over the valuable, this is what Shakespeare is about. For a man to be taught that his affianced is truly worthy, in an essential rather than a mere monetary sense, is indeed a discovery that transcends the law; however, it is a discovery that belongs to the realm of man's history and experience. Whether Mariana and Angelo's contract is of a certain kind is not of supreme importance. What is important is that the Duke supplies the missing contractual elements—consummation and dowry—just as he supplies the elements missing in Juliet and Claudio's contract—publicity in ceremony. The point is not to validate one type of marriage, but to make both marriages, however imperfectly formed, "authentic." Integrity is the aim, not the justification of a legal concept. The vehicle used is the marriage contract, and knowledge of its particulars helps illuminate an artistic understanding of the work.

Finally, among the many causes for consternation the play has fostered is the fact that Angelo's attempted crimes go unpunished. This has been the source of much criticism from those, like Samuel Taylor Coleridge, who would have poetic justice served. But Angelo's crimes are inchoate; attempted, halfhearted (e.g., "Would yet he had lived. Alack" [4.4.30–31]), but ultimately frustrated. Isabella, withstanding her own trial of virtue, becomes his champion, pleading:

> His act did not o'ertake his bad intent
> And must be buried but as intent.
> That perished by the way. Thoughts are no subjects,
> Intents but merely thoughts. (5.1.449–52)

She allows a distinction between attempted and fulfilled crimes, one that the Duke ultimately permits. And the distinction is Isabella's greatest achievement.

For her to deny any difference would be to make the same mistake Angelo does in not distinguishing between the less-than-perfect marriage and fornication. Indeed, the consequences of her failure to make such a distinction would be the same as those that threatened to result from Angelo's failure: execution. In a play concerned with realities and false appearances—and in no small way, with Isabella's education in real mercy as opposed to hollow sanctity—her ability to make this distinction is her triumph. For in this comedy of mercy, it is only un-fulfilled contracts, whose fulfillment can serve nature's generative ends, that must be executed. The disposition of unfulfilled crimes is left for another day, and another play: the Alien Statute in *The Merchant of Venice.*

Before proceeding to that play, with its emphasis on the basis of bonds and contracts and their interrelationship, *Troilus and Cressida* will further illustrate the relationship between law and nature. But in the Trojan play, the contrac-tual elements of publicity, value, performance, and contractual tokens are par-odied, and the contract as an instrument capable of accomplishing union is itself caricatured in a perverse ceremony. *Troilus and Cressida* is an inversion of the scheme worked out in *Measure for Measure.* The order the marriage contract brings to Vienna is contrasted with the disorder the mock contract "celebrates" in Troy.

CHAPTER 3

Perfection in Reversion

The Mock Contract in Troilus and Cressida

Whatever the reason for Shakespeare's parody of Troilus and Cressida's story, it has caused a great deal of consternation among critics.[1] But as is often the case with Shakespearean comedy (if a comedy it is), themes of great weight lie below the surface. Amidst their ribaldry, different characters imply that the laws of the cosmos have slipped. There is not only the disorder of war on the Trojan plain, but also a disorder within the separate camps, and one within the lovers themselves. War is in the background, but the two societies are beset by a still more unsettling disturbance. An organizing principle seems to be missing, and all is the subject of mockery. Because *Measure for Measure* focuses on similar themes, a restatement of how Shakespeare uses the legal instrument in that play will help highlight the use he makes of the mock legal instrument in *Troilus and Cressida*. All that the contract accomplishes in Vienna is, to profound effect, parodied in Troy.

In Vienna, there is a general sickness in society: a "fever on goodness." On both personal and institutional levels, this malady is due to the absence of integrity, a disjunction between "seeming" and "being," between form and substance. In this realm, nature is not given her due. She is bypassed by both the bawds, who steal from her, and by those who remove themselves from society—those who will not "go forth" into the world to prove productive with her gifts. This results in an orientation toward death that must be remedied. In response, the agent of nature, the Duke, achieves this reorientation by substituting the real wife for the "imagined" lover. The substitution brings about the full realization of the marriage contract. Consequently, integrity is achieved, resolving the disjunction between "seeming" and "being."

Likewise, in *Troilus and Cressida*, there is a lack of order, bewailed from the outset. It exists on the societal level, where "checks and disasters" cause plans to go "tortive and errant" (1.3.4–9),[2] as well as on the individual level. Troilus complains about the inward tumult caused by his passion for Cressida: "Why should I war without the walls of Troy / That find such cruel battle here within?" (1.1.2–3). And just as in bawd-ridden Vienna, nature is slighted in syphilis-ridden Troy. But this disdain is not because the characters in *Troilus and Cressida* are unaware of nature's norms, especially concerning marriage. Hector states that awareness during the Trojan council's meeting to discuss Helen's return:

> *Nature craves*
> *All dues be rendered to their owners.* Now,
> What nearer debt in all humanity
> Than wife to husband? If this law
> Of Nature be corrupted through affection [lust]
> And that great minds, of partial indulgence
> To their benumbed wills, resist the same,
> There is a law in each well-ordered nation [3]
> To curb those appetites that are
> Most disobedient and refractory.
> If Helen then be wife to Sparta's king,
> As it is known she is, these moral laws
> Of nature and of nations speak aloud
> To have her back returned. (2.2.173–86; emphasis
>   added)

At the heart of the marriage contract lies the exclusive union to which Hector alludes. As in *Measure for Measure*, in which "counterfeiting" images and "stealing" from nature are deplored, here, nature "craves all *dues* be rendered to their owners." The marriage contract is to be respected. Indeed, the well-ordered laws of nations curb the "disobedient and refractory appetites" of those who indulge their "benumbed wills."

But there the similarity ends between the two plays; for while the performance of the "old contracting" in *Measure for Measure* provides social integrity, which leads to generation and life, the pretend ceremony in *Troilus and Cressida* has no such effect. What lies at the heart of *Troilus and Cressida*, surrounded by all of the aforementioned mockery, is only another illusion: a mock ceremony, which is no ceremony at all, at least not in any real sense of the word. The contractual elements—publicity, value, performance, and contractual tokens, as well as the contractual agent—so central to the theme in *Measure for Measure*, are perverted in this play. This leads to a frustration, rather than a furtherance, of nature's generative ends. The contract's invalidity becomes emblematic of the problems central to both Greeks and Trojans, and the rest of the play depicts a continuous exacerbation of those problems.

As has been seen, the private quality of Claudio and Juliet's contract in *Measure for Measure* accounts for the trouble they encounter. Lacking "outward form," their clandestine "true contract" cannot adequately refute the charge that it is a mask for lust. Indeed, Claudio and Juliet betray their own troubled feelings about the nature of their relationship. A public ceremony at the end of the play not only gives shape to their marriage, but also provides a medium for social cohesion. Public witness to their vows ensures the changed, and exclusive, rights each have to the other.

But all of the efforts taken by the Duke in *Measure for Measure* to publicize the contracts, thereby giving them outward form, are missing in *Troilus and Cressida*. For the couple's purely sexual liaison is accomplished in "secret." The bawd and go-between, Pandarus, brings a "veiled" Cressida to Troilus at nighttime, and the lovers seek to hide from discovery. Cressida "would not for half of Troy" have Troilus seen in her bed (4.2.42). *Secret* is also used in bawdy references to Cressida: she is said to be "a juggling trick to be *secretly* open" (5.2.26); and with regard to herself, she says she relies "upon my *secrecy* [privacy; genitals]⁴ to defend mine honesty" (1.2.252).

Of course, Cressida is only one of many whose purity is in question, and whose private promises later prove untrue. She herself is aware that private vows are not always followed by honorable actions. At her assignation with Troilus, Cressida asserts the common knowledge that lovers' deeds often fail to match their words:

> They say all lovers swear more performance
> than they are able, and yet reserve an ability
> that they never perform . . . (3.2.81–84)

In essence, she questions the good faith of lovers' vows. They are as likely to be fueled by temporary lust as by permanent devotion.

This was behind the general disapproval of clandestine marriages in the Renaissance. By insisting on publicly witnessed vows to an eternal bond, private vows made merely to secure sex were thwarted. The ceremony proves to be the remedy for Claudio and Juliet's pseudocontract, which lacked form. However, in the private assignation between Troilus and Cressida, no real contracting is about to take place, only its parody. Now, although both relationships are initially private, Troilus and Cressida's relationship must be distinguished from that of Claudio and Juliet. The latter's marriage is imperfectly realized, but the two actually consider each other husband and wife. In Claudio and Juliet's case, there is an intention to accomplish a union. There may be a lack of form, ultimately rectified, but there is no lack of substance. A contract requires this material—*res*, matter—as its object. But in *Troilus and Cressida*, there is no real substance to what the couple intend, no union of the two into one. In short, their temporary union lacks both form and substance; it amounts to "nothing," other than as a marker of their shame.

The next contractual element, value, is perhaps the most important in *Troilus and Cressida*. In *Measure for Measure*, the Duke labors to acquaint Angelo with the meaning of true worth, as manifested in the worthy and constant Mariana. And in *All's Well That Ends Well*, similar pains are taken to apprise Bertram of how honor and worth are manifest in Helena. In those plays, worth has a material referent. But in *Troilus and Cressida*, worth is ultimately determined only in terms of other words, or is attributed to individuals who are themselves discounted. Unlike the other plays, in which people of true worth are undervalued, overvaluation and the shifting relativity of value form a common theme in *Troilus and Cressida*.

The repositories of value that the characters choose evidence this relativity. After yet another demand for Helen's return, the Trojans gather to discuss the prudence of a continued fight with her as its object. Thersites rates her as little more than a "placket" (2.3.18), a "whore" for which the war is fought (2.3.69); Cressida says she's a "merry" [wanton] Greek; and considering how many "tithe-souls" have been lost in her defense, Hector says Helen "is not worth what she doth cost the holding" (2.2.51–52). Even Troilus is less convinced of her worth when in private: "I cannot fight upon this argument [Helen] / It is too starved a subject for my sword." (1.1.86–87).

Of course, Troilus's taste runs more to Cressida, and the wars that he fights are against his own raging lust for her. She is the object of his desire and causes his personal disruption. This is evidenced by his first complaint regarding the "cruel battle" that goes on inside his own "walls" (1.1.3); Cressida is the theme of Troilus's particular war. But the theme of Troilus's private war is no more noble than the larger Trojan conflict; Cressida's honor is no better than Helen's. Diomedes says he will answer to his own lust for Cressida, "prizing her at her worth" (4.4.132–33). And after she allows herself to be passed around the Greek camp, Ulysses says, "There's language in her eye, her cheek, her lip; / Nay, her foot speaks" (4.5.56–57).

The Greeks show how very similar they are to the Trojans by also discounting Helen's value. Diomedes indicts Helen and all who fight for her, suggesting
an equality of worthlessness, not worth, between the Greeks and Trojans:

> He merits well to have her that doth seek her,
> Not making any scruple of her soilure,
> With such a hell of pain and world of charge;
> And you as well to keep her that defend her,
> Not palating the taste of her dishonour,
> With such a costly loss of wealth and friends.
> He like a puling cuckold would drink up
> The lees and dregs of a flat tamed piece;
> You like a lecher out of whorish loins
> Are pleased to breed out your inheritors.
> *Both merits poised, each weighs nor less nor more,*
> *But he as he; which heavier for a whore?* (4.1.58–68; em-
>   phasis added)

Later, when Diomedes fights Troilus over Cressida, and over Troilus's stolen
"horse," Diomedes himself is the subject of a similar observation by Thersites:
"Hold thy whore, Grecian! Now for thy whore, Trojan!" (5.4.23–24). In the
end, the Greek's knowledge of worthlessness of the fight does not lessen his
zeal to fight for a worthless cause.

When she appears with Paris and Pandarus, Helen only reinforces what has
been said of her. She tickles and strokes Pandarus and begs for his lusty song of
a "shaft" confounding a "wound" (3.1.109–21). His song of love, says Helen,
in unintentional prophecy, will "undo us all" (3.1.104). Yet Helen is the very
"theme of honour and renown," and a spur to valiant deeds (2.2.198–99; emphasis added). Despite their high rhetoric, the idea of what Helen is does not match
the reality; honor's theme is a whore. It is a distinction driven home with all
the greater force when the bawd Pandarus, sick with venereal disease, claims,
"'Honour' and 'lordship' are my titles" (3.1.15–16). Titles themselves lose value
when attached to so unworthy a referent.

The consequences of value having such lecherous referents are grave.
Thersites, after escaping death, loses sight of the fighting Diomedes and
Troilus: "What's become of the wenching rogues? I think they have swal-
lowed one another; I would laugh at that miracle; Yet, in a sort, lechery eats
itself" (5.4.31–32). The play's disease-ridden lechers, rotting toward hol-
lowness and extinction, symbolize this idea of self-cannibalization. It is yet
another role that emptiness takes in the play.

Rene Girard's comments regarding illusory worth in *Troilus and Cressida* are particularly informative. Girard considers the play the finest example of "mimetic desire," a phenomenon in which individuals imitate each others' desires, not because of the intrinsic worth of the desired object, but simply because the object is desired by another.[5] "Nothing incites desire like desire itself," says Girard, and "as a magnet for countless desires, Helen is matchless."[6] The Greeks want Helen back because the Trojans want to keep her. The Trojans want to keep her because the Greeks want her back. Similarly, the war is fought for Helen, not because she is worthy, but because she is honor's theme; she is honor's theme, not because she is worthy, but because the war is being fought for her. All mimetic circles are vicious circles, says Girard, which Hector proves when he agrees to continue the destructive and perfectly insignificant war. This confusion also leads to a circularity that sometimes shows in the character's logic, as in Paris's speech: "He eats nothing but doves [symbols of love], love, and that breeds hot blood, and hot blood begets hot thoughts, and hot thoughts beget hot deeds, and hot deeds is love" (3.1.123-25).

Perhaps the most profound example of relative value in the play occurs in the midst of the Trojan council. In debating whether to return or keep Menelaus's wife, Hector contends she is not worth the years of war and death she has cost. In his epigrammatic reply, Troilus sums up all that has been spoken regarding the relativity of value: "What's aught but as 'tis valued?" (2.2.52). This view attaches worth to the will, which in this play is drawn about by the appetite. The will can only select among the objects that are presented to it, but the objects presented to the will in this play are worthless or hollow, however attractive in appearance. Helen, Cressida, the passing glory and titles won in battle—personified by the "botchy-cored" golden warrior killed at play's end—are without value.

Hector answers Troilus's assertion of relative value with a different standard: "But value dwells not in particular will" (2.2.53). For Hector, worth has a referent that lies outside the fickle estimation of men's taste, or "will." Attaching value to the appetite rather than to the nature of the thing prized is unreasonable, and Hector characterizes it as "mad idolatry" (2.2.56). Troilus's mistake is that of Angelo, Bertram, and all the others who devalue the worthy and overvalue the worthless.

Troilus then retorts with an example. A "wife" taken—chosen by the will— cannot subsequently be dispraised and returned, at least not in a way consistent with honor (2.2.61-70). A. P. Rossiter says Troilus's analogy to a marriage contract shows that Shakespeare was writing for legal-minded law students: "Carrying off Helen established no contract; the analogy of marriage is therefore totally spurious."[7] Rossiter's remark reveals what a contract can achieve in terms of what the lack of a contract fails to achieve. There are simply no rights to Helen; her taking was a "rape." Even Paris admits the defilement. He would prefer to have the "soil of her fair rape wiped off in the honourable keeping her" (2.2.147-48).[8]

What follows Troilus's and Paris's argument is another sally in favor of reason. Hector says his brothers argue "superficially," like men too young to hear moral philosophy, and too hot-tempered to make a "free determination" based on sound judgment (2.2.164-70). He then articulates the norm that nature is said to "crave," regarding the dues owed a husband and wife based on their marriage contract. That Hector speaks this also carries weight, for among the proud, lecherous, and vacuous cast of characters, he alone is said to possess "patience as a virtue fixed" (1.2.5). It is all the more devastating when Hector chooses, freely, to reject this well-reasoned norm immediately after expressing it:

> —yet ne'ertheless
> My sprightly brethren, I propend to you
> In resolution to keep Helen still;
> For 'tis a cause that hath no mean dependence
> Upon our joint and several dignities. (2.2.189-93)

In his pause "—yet ne'ertheless," Hector makes a choice in favor of honor, which seals his fate and that of all the Trojans.[9] He knows of nature's law regarding the marriage contract and understands where true value lies. Still, he consciously abandons reason. As a consequence, he abandons both what reason tells him is valuable and what reason tells him is right in favor of the Trojans' "joint and several dignities."

Just as now, land in Renaissance England could be held by tenancy in common, "jointly and severally." This is a kind of legal fiction in which each tenant is held to own a separate estate in an undivided portion of the whole.[10] When taken in conjunction with Helen's "common ownership," the Trojan dignity does not fare well. A. W. B. Simpson describes areas held "in common" as tracts of uncultivated wasteland: "Of the land which was cultivated some parts would always be lying fallow, or be temporarily unused after the harvest had been gathered. On such land the villagers as a community would pasture their beasts and from it they would gather wood and turf and so forth."[11] Rights that should be exclusive, such as those of marriage, are held "jointly and severally" in this play. All is held in common, and all is debased—and made "common"—in the process.

In recounting the perversion of the contractual elements, thus far I have mentioned the replacement of publicity with secrecy, and the replacement of the truly valuable with the truly worthless. Before proceeding to a discussion of the elements of performance and contractual tokens, it is important to restate the root problem in the Greek and Trojan system of valuation. For the repositories of value in the play have no objective merit, but are objects of the appetite. The will is given free reign in the play, and it triumphs over reason. What is presented for the will to choose among is always an apparent good, based on appearances, not a substantive good, based on true worth. There is no real reason for the war; no real reason for stealing a man's wife; no real reason to seek honor. In such a state, reason is the stuff of sport.

On the Greek side, Achilles makes reason the theme of his "pageants." In fact, the two great heroes on whom the Greeks pin their fortunes, Achilles and Ajax, not only scoff at reason, but are also deficient in it. Thersites mocks that Hector shall have "a great catch an a'knock out either of your brains" (2.1.97–98). Achilles's brains are said to be "barren" (1.3.328), his wit lying in his sinews (2.1.97). Similarly, Ajax's "*pia mater* is not worth the ninth part of a sparrow," he wears his "guts in his head" (2.1.69–71), and the whole of his intelligence would not "stop the eye [vagina] of Helen's needle, for whom he comes to fight" (2.1.78–79).

This link between the lack of "reason" and the reason for the war, Helen's "nothing," shows how slightly reason is valued among them. The association is echoed in Diomedes's charge for Cressida to "let your mind be *coupled* with your words" (5.2.16), and in Cressida's punning self-characterization: "Ah, poor our sex! This fault in us I find: / The error of our eye [vagina] directs our mind" (5.2.115–16). Thersites replies she could not prove her point better unless she said "*My mind is now turned whore*" (5.2.120; emphasis added).

As in other cases, the Greeks' scoffing at reason has its Trojan counterpart. When Helenus objects to continuing the war, since there is no good reason for it, Troilus replies:

> You are for dreams and slumbers, brother priest.
> You fur your gloves with "reason."
> . . . Reason and respect
> Make livers pale and lustihood deject. (2.2.37–38;
>   49–50)

The danger of such a choice is that, without reason, the choice falls to the appetite. And the appetite in this play chooses the illusory delights of the imagination. The appetite is intent on its own satisfaction, not with the rights, duties, and obligations that concern a marriage contract.

This preoccupation with satisfying the appetite is Troilus's problem, and is related to the contractual element of "performance." Awaiting Cressida's arrival for their night together, Troilus says he is "sick" with "imaginary relish" of Cressida's delights (3.2.16-18) He stalks about her orchard, enthralled, anticipating how "wat'ry palates taste" of the "thrice-repured nectar" (3.2.19-20). But the images he uses regarding sex—like those of Angelo, Isabella, and Claudio before the contractual resolution—are laced with death. He compares himself to a soul wandering about the Stygian banks, waiting for Charon—here, Pandarus—to bring him to the lily-beds where he may "wallow" (3.2.7-14).[12] Moreover, he fears that "[d]eath . . . Swooning Destruction" will be the result of his acutely felt joys (3.2.20). While the association of the orgasm with death was a Renaissance commonplace, the link here goes further. For the same orientation of sex and death occurs in *Measure for Measure*, just before the "old contract" is performed and integrity restored. As a result of that integrity, the orientation is changed from "sex and death" to "sex and life." But the "performance" that follows Troilus's imaginings is purely sexual, as revealed in the group's multitude of puns.

Troilus, Cressida, and Pandarus also use the same agricultural and transactional metaphors when speaking of the "performance" about to take place. But whereas the Duke portrays Mariana as having "just title" to her "husband" Angelo under a precontract, and instructs her to "sow corn" in tithe to nature, Pandarus's agricultural and transactional puns are bawdy, revolving around sexual foreplay: "How now, a kiss *in fee farm*! Build there, carpenter, the air is sweet. Nay you shall fight your hearts out ere I part you" (3.2.48-50; emphasis added) and "*Words pay no debts*; give her *deeds*. But she'll bereave you o'th'*deeds* too, if she call your activity in question. [*they kiss*] What, billing again? *Here's 'In witness whereof the parties interchangeably.*' Come in, come in. I'll go get a fire" (3.2.54-58; emphasis added). A "deed," of course, is the instrument by which a conveyance is made. "Fee farm" was a term that gave a tenant unencumbered rights to his estate, in exchange for perpetual rent, replacing the knight service previously required of the tenant holder.[13] The kiss granted is of this dual nature: freely held, but held at a price. There is also the irony of applying metaphors referring to instruments of *permanent* transfer to sexual conquests, or "deeds," *temporary* in nature. Troilus, as "carpenter," is to "build" (achieve an erection) on Cressida's "farm." Also, formulaic legal terminology—"in witness whereof"—was commonly used in legal documents to commemorate public witness to a mutual—"interchangeable"—transfer.[14] But this standard language is also meaningless, since the public witness that such words are meant to denote is lacking. Theirs is a private affair, and the witness, Pandarus, is a mock witness, a mere bawd who has actually arranged this secret liaison. Further, the "interchangeability" of the parties has its own ribald significance as it precedes an act of brokered sex. Finally, the use of "fee" in this context must be seen next to its other uses in the play; Thersites will use "fee-simple" to describe the entirety of Patroclus's syphilis (5.1.22).

The distinction between the two "performances" in *Measure for Measure* and *Troilus and Cressida* lies in what the first contract achieves, and what this mock contract fails to achieve. The performance of the "old contract" in *Measure for Measure* functions to transform the nature of the sexual acts. Reflecting this transformation, agricultural metaphors built around a wild, "teeming foisome" are brought within the order of "just title" and contract. The poetic idea of the wife gaining legal interest in her husband, and his "husbanding" the soil of his wife's womb, has a meliorative, generative quality in that play.

But in *Troilus and Cressida*, the same language takes a commodified quality when uttered by the bawd Pandarus; the bargain-and-sale nature of what transpires stains the meanings. Troilus refers to Pandarus as a "merchant," who is the "only way" that he may "come to" Cressida's bed (1.1.91–100). And Pandarus speaks of Cressida as though she were a "horse" that must be hobbled from backing away from her mate (3.2.43). When she later pulls back from Troilus's embrace, his high-blown remark contains allusions to sexual interruption: "What makes this pretty abruption?" (3.2.62–63).[15]

Following Pandarus's association of legal terminology with the sexual act, Troilus assures Cressida that there is nothing "monstrous" in love, except that "the will is infinite and the execution confined" (3.2.77–80). There is also something of Claudio's lament in Troilus's claim. But while Claudio bemoans that appetite from "too much scope" leads to restraint, Troilus bemoans the restraint of a boundless desire. He contemplates nothing sinister in this excessive liberty, and thus lacks the awareness that Claudio, however torn he may be, possesses. Enslavement to the appetite sits more easily with Troilus than it does with Claudio.

Cressida then picks up the legal strain by using "performance," which may be withheld, or "reserved," though due; as well as "perfection," the achievement of title to property; and "discharging," a means of achieving perfect title by eliminating its debt through discharge. "Performance" is again tinged with sexual implications: "They say all lovers swear more *performance* than they are able, and yet *reserve* an ability that they never *perform*; vowing more than the *perfection* of ten, and *discharging* less than the tenth part of one" (3.2.81–84; emphasis added).

"Performance" and "discharge" remain purely sexual terms—Troilus's sexual prowess and potency. They are unrelated to the union of form and substance that the contractual "performance" in *Measure for Measure* brings.

Next, Troilus reassures Cressida with sexual innuendo, this time interspersed with the language of legal estates *in futuro*: "Praise us as we are tasted; allow us as we prove. Our head shall go bare till merit crown it. *No perfection in reversion* shall have a praise in present. We will not name desert before his birth, and being born, his addition shall be humble" (3.2.87–91; emphasis added). "Perfection in reversion" is a right to enjoy unencumbered title to property in the future, upon the reversion of rights temporarily invested in another for a certain time.[16] But in Troilus's usage, the performance that prompts his reply is sexual; he declines praise until his own "performance" is "tasted."[17] The disdain for any future estate also has significance, for it belies the insistent concern, by Troilus and others, for only that which is immediate.

Ironically, Troilus makes a boast for constancy, the opposite of the raging lust he has complained about. He says that the worst "Envy" will be able to say of him is that he is altogether "too constant" (3.2.94). Intentionally or not, Pandarus deflates this claim with a similar boast about his kinswoman Cressida: "Our kindred, though they be long ere they are wooed, they are constant being won. They are burrs, I can tell you: they'll stick where they are *thrown*" (3.2.105–8; emphasis added). They go through the motions of swearing fidelity, a marital feature that is particularly ironic considering the reason they have come together. Upon promising to "war" with each other in constancy, they go on to make their famous pledges, he praising his potential faith with rising, positive claims: "as sun to day, as turtle to her mate";[18] "as true as Troilus" (3.2.167–77); and she, condemning her potential falsehood with falling, negative ones, "as fox to lamb, or wolf to heifer's calf"; "as false as Cressid" (3.2.178–90). Within this context occurs the mock marriage contract, with the traditional elements—including performance—stood on their heads:

Pandarus: Go to, a *bargain* made. *Seal it, seal it.* I'll be the *witness.* Here I hold your *hand*; here my cousin's. If ever you prove false one to another, since I have taken such pains to bring you together, let all pitiful goers-between be called to the world's end after my name: call them all panders. Let all constant men be Troiluses, all false women, Cressids, and all brokers between, panders. *Say Amen.*

Troilus: *Amen.*

Cressida:	*Amen.*
Pandarus:	*Amen. Whereupon I will show you a chamber with a bed . . .*
	(3.2.192–203; emphasis added)

But their pledges seal nothing, because there is nothing of substance for them to seal. Instead, the clandestine ceremony is characterized as a bargain, "solemnized" by a sexual broker, pertaining to a temporary coupling, born of lust. Rather than being contracted to each other, all that the ceremony contracts is the trio to their dubious names in history.

The final element, contractual tokens, figures into the many separations featured in the play. At their parting, the two exchange remembrances, just as the other lovers in Shakespeare do. But rather than swap rings, Troilus and Cressida swap a sleeve and a glove. The symbol of virginity and fidelity is replaced by a token that, elsewhere in the play, is lewdly associated with Helen—"Venus glove" (4.5.180), and a sleeve that, though a common love token in courtly tradition, carries its own sexual connotations in this context.

Contractual tokens are evidence of the exclusive rights one party has to the other and to the "binding" that has occurred. Their worth, even their sacrality in medieval times, was sometimes evidenced by their being placed on the church altar in order to effectuate the transfer of property.[19] They could also be used as proof of the union, as evidenced by Helena in *All's Well That Ends Well*. Commensurate with the marriage bond are rights to object when one's partner attempts to "bind" with a third party. This is the objection of Mariana in *Measure for Measure* (5.1.201–8), of Diana on Helena's behalf in *All's Well That Ends Well* (5.3.170–76), of Adriana in *The Comedy of Errors* (2.1.110–46), and of Albany in *King Lear* (5.3.84–89). But in *Troilus and Cressida*, the mock contract has given no permanence to the union, and certainly no exclusivity. As a result, a perverse transformation takes place with the pairs' tokens. Troilus's sleeve, meant to strengthen and seal the "bond" between him and Cressida, is transformed into a pledge—*surety*—to perform sex. The surety becomes a down payment, as it were, to guarantee future sexual performance. For Cressida's coyness with Troilus is repeated with Diomedes; the pledges, vows, and exchange of tokens that she gives and takes from Troilus are trotted out in the Greek camp and given to Diomedes. Thersites, who rails truths with impunity against both Greeks and Trojans, comments as Cressida angles for the Greek:

Thersites	
[*aside*]:	How the devil Luxury with his fat rump and potato finger,
	tickles these together. Fry, lechery fry . . .

Diomedes
  [*to Cressida*]:   Give me some token for the *surety* of it [sex].

Cressida: I'll fetch you one . . .   *Exit*

Thersites
  [*aside*]:   Now the *pledge*! Now, now, now!

  Enter Cressida [*with Troilus's sleeve*].

Cressida: Here Diomed, keep this sleeve. (5.2.57–68)

Although a "false-hearted rogue" (5.1.86), Diomedes drives a shrewder bargain than Troilus. He makes no pledges of love, but only secures a pledge of sexual performance. Troilus's naiveté is all the more striking in this scene when he witnesses, clandestinely, a second clandestine pledge between his supposed partner and another man.

The impermanence of the relationship between Troilus and Cressida is a problem that the marriage contract is capable of addressing. By binding the parties permanently, it provides for their rights in the future, long after the celebration has past. In this way, the contract respects time in all its aspects and provides for the future of the parties drawn together. In contrast, there is no respect for time in this play, or for constancy. The characters demand the present in all things, sex and honor, and make no allowance for all that time is: past, present, and future.

Unlike other plays in which time is "redeemed," "freed," or "marked," in *Troilus and Cressida*, time is vilified. Ulysses says time eats all (3.3.146–51), and portrays it as a "fashionable host" that pushes past a parting guest to welcome the newest comer (3.3.166). It is "envious and calumniating," paying nothing to past virtues of "beauty, wit, high birth, vigour of bone, desert in service, love, friendship, or charity" (3.3.172–74). And it is not only the past aspect of time that suffers in the play; as has been seen, Troilus scoffs at "perfections in reversion," interests that come to bear in the future, in favor of present "performance" (3.2.90). Time is often out of joint in Shakespeare, but here it is a villain.

With Time in such a role, the character's logic calls for immediacy, not patience. Ajax, anxious to gain honor against Hector, arrives early: "Anticipating time with starting courage" (4.5.2). And it is with great irony that after Cressida's night with Troilus, the bawd Pandarus counsels her to "[b]e moderate, be moderate" (4.4.1), although her trade for Antenor is imminent.

As for Troilus, although Ulysses says he is reported to be a balanced, temperate young man (4.5.97–110), he has proven, and will yet prove himself, otherwise. Upon witnessing Cressida's betrayal, he fights with his warring emotions, calling seven times on a patience he has not practiced in the play, toward either women or honor, for example, "I will be *patient*; outwardly I will" (5.2.72). Defeated, he admits the war of passions that he is subject to: "O madness of discourse / That cause sets up with and against itself!" (5.2.149–50).

Using a trial metaphor, Troilus speaks of being at war with himself, as both Plaintiff and Defendant. But the "outward" patience he claims is a contradiction in terms, as patience is an inward virtue. Indeed, though Troilus has claimed to be patient from the beginning of the work, "Patience herself, what Goddess e'er she be, / Doth lesser blench at suffrance than I do—" (1.1.25), the impatience of his lust for Cressida is his most characteristic feature. Of course, in this he is not alone; the entire Trojan War is being fought over the whorish Helen and Paris's lust for her.

In *Measure for Measure*, following the resolution of all the contractual elements, there is unity for both the marriage partners and the Viennese society. But perversion of the contractual elements—publicity, value, performance, and tokens—is further underscored by the fact that this mock contract has failed to unify the two. Claudio and Juliet, and Angelo and Mariana, are matched in an "eternal bond," but Troilus and Cressida's temporary union does not "entitle" them to each other. Consequently, their temporal "performance" is followed by a series of separations, an aggravation of the disjunction that exemplifies the play. The separations start almost immediately after the mock contract. In fact, a mock "alba" scene, suggestive of *Romeo and Juliet*, finds Troilus slipping away from Cressida's bed, rather than leaving it reluctantly (as in Romeo's case):

Troilus:	Dear, trouble not yourself. The morn is cold.
Cressida:	Then, sweet my lord, I'll call mine uncle down. He shall unbolt the gates.
Troilus:	Trouble him not. To bed, to bed! . . .
Cressida:	Good morrow, then.
Troilus:	I prithee now, to bed.
Cressida:	Are you aweary of me?
Troilus:	O Cressida! But that the busy day, Waked by the lark, hath roused the ribald crows, And dreaming night will hide our joys no longer, I would not from thee. . . .

Cressida:	Prithee tarry. You men will never tarry.
	O foolish Cressid! I might have still held off,
	And then you would have tarried . . . (4.2.1–19)

Just as the Nurse interrupts the "alba" scene in *Romeo and Juliet*, Pandarus enters the room to mock Cressida about her night of sport. He even calls her "capocchia" [foreskin] (4.2.32).[20]

The next event in the plot involves another separation, Cressida being sent from Troy. As the couple's night consisted only of physical acts, the reversal of those acts characterizes the end of the relationship. Troilus makes a catalog of his losses as Cressida departs:

> And suddenly—where injury of chance
> Puts back leave-taking, jostles roughly by
> all time of pause, rudely beguiles our lips
> Of all rejoindure, forcibly prevents
> Our locked embrasure, strangles our dear vows
> Even in the birth of our own labouring breath.
> We two, that with so many thousand sighs
> Did buy each other, must poorly sell ourselves
> With the rude brevity and discharge of one. (4.4.32–40)

Lips, embraces, vows are all forced apart, and the result is lamented in a telling metaphor of frustration: their vows are like a stillborn child, strangled "even in the birth of our own labouring breath." But even the poetry of this passage is strung with the language of "buy" and "sell" and with rude interruptions that cause the "discharge of one." After this speech, Cressida is swapped for Antenor, then is swapped among the Greeks. Finally, she swaps herself to Diomedes.

Separation, instead of union, is one of the hallmarks of the play. The mock contract's celebration in Cressida's orchard is emblematic of the disjunction that plagues *Troilus and Cressida*, just as the old contract's realization in Angelo's circummur'd garden is emblematic of the reunion in *Measure for Measure*. Whereas the latter brings *res* and *verba* together, establishing a much-needed integrity in Vienna, the former brings no such integrity to Troy. Indeed, the mock "form" is matched by a lack of substance—or "matter"—mentioned throughout the drama. The characters are constantly looking for it, asking about it, and finding only emptiness or rot in its place.[21]

An exchange between Achilles, Ajax, and Thersites is representative:

Achilles:	How now, Thersites? what's the *matter*, man?
Thersites:	You see him there? Do You?
Achilles:	Ay. What's the *matter*?
Thersites:	Nay look upon him.
Achilles:	So I do. What's the *matter*?
Thersites:	Nay, but regard him well.
Achilles:	Well? Why I do so.
Thersites:	But yet you look not well upon him. For whosoever you take him to be, he is Ajax [a jakes].
Achilles:	I know that, fool,
Thersites:	Ay, but that fool knows not himself. (2.1.54–64; emphasis added)

Thersites, the fool and "knower" of the other characters, also labels Ajax a "thing of no bowels," a "sodden-witted lord," who has in his skull "no more brain than I have in mine elbows," and like Cressida, is "bought and sold among those of any wit like a barbarian slave" (2.1.45). Nestor concludes that Ajax lacks "*matter*, if he have lost his argument" (2.3.92; emphasis added).

A lack of substance is hardly limited to Ajax. Agamemnon, for all his being the "nerve and bone of Greece" and "heart" of their numbers (1.3.54–56), considers the Greeks' failure a result of the god's testing, not his own shortcomings. He equates matter with "bulk," and an ability to persist that Distinction will reward: "And what hath mass or *matter*, by itself / Lies rich in virtue and unmingled" (1.3.29–30). In Thersites's estimation, such a leader is no more than a "botchy core" (2.1.6), and the only "matter" that could be found in him is the "matter" that might run from his boils (2.1.8).

Neither does Achilles fare well. Ulysses says he "never suffers matter of the world" to enter his thoughts (2.3.183). And Thersites tells the great hero, "A great deal of your wit, too, lies in your sinews, or else there be liars. Hector shall have a great catch an a' knock out either of your brains. 'A were as good crack a fusty nut with no kernel" (2.1.96–99). Similarly, Patroclus is "a gilt counterfeit," so insubstantial he slips from Thersites contemplation, and deserves no better curse than "no *matter*; thyself on thyself" (emphasis mine; 2.3.24–25). The Greeks as a whole fare poorly. Their tents stand on a "hollow" plain and amount to "so many hollow factions" (1.3.79–80). Ulysses, though the Greeks doubt that any needless "matter" of importless burden should divide his lips, proves in fact to be full of fraudulent tricks (1.3.70–74). Considering his references to "policy" and his various stratagems, the charge of Machiavellianism is more justified when made against Ulysses than it is against the Duke in *Measure for Measure*. The Duke's plots are for the best interest of the characters.[22]

The Trojans sum each other up in the same fashion and ask the same questions. Cressida and Pandarus often remark that events have "no *matter*" (1.2.86), or ask "what's the *matter?*" (4.2.44; 4.2.89). Of Pandarus, Cressida says: "If you love an addle [rotten] egg as well as you love an idle head, you would eat chickens i'th'shell" (1.2.128–29). Helenus says it is no marvel that his brother Troilus "bite so sharp at reasons / You are so empty of them" (2.2.33–34). The "shapes and forms" that prove substantial come by way of a dream, sent from heaven as a warning. Andromache's vision, seconded by Cassandra, is prophetic:

> For I have dreamt
> Of bloody turbulence, and this whole night
> Hath nothing been but *shapes and forms* of slaughter.
>   (5.3.10–12; emphasis added)

That which truly takes shape and acquires meaning in the play is the death to come. Finally, upon reading Cressida's letter sent to him from the Greek camp, Troilus scoffs at his betrayer's promises, empty of content:

> *Words, words, mere words, no matter from the heart.*
> Th'effect doth operate another way.
> [He tears the letter and tosses it away.]
> Go, wind, to wind! there turn and change together.
> My love with words and errors still she feeds,
> But edifies another with her deeds. (5.3.107–11;
>   emphasis added)

Having bargained to fulfill his lust, then having confronted its image in Cressida and Diomedes, Troilus is no longer fooled by words passing for substance. There is no *res*, no matter from the heart, under which the *verba* may rightfully pass.

But then, this division in form and substance is like that of the mock contract: a pretense in form and substance. And Troilus's complaint is not all that different from Cressida's. Before their night together, she worries about the difference between what lovers swear and what they perform, and then admits that she herself has only been hard to "seem won" (3.2.113):

> I have a kind of self resides with you [Troilus]—
> But an unkind self, that itself will leave
> To be another's fool. (3.2.143-45)

The difference in "seeming" and "being" becomes the norm for the lovers in this play, who employ more "craft than love" (3.2.148).

The parody of the contractual elements, the failure of the mock contract to form union, and the separation and disjunction that characterize the drama, prove to be an inversion of the same features in *Measure for Measure*. Instead of the integrity that comes to that play through the contracts—"seeming" matching "being"—this play illustrates the triumph of appearances over reality. "Seeming" instead of "being" becomes the standard for *Troilus and Cressida*.

Whereas the mock contract is the strongest example of this standard, instances of mockery and imitation can be found throughout the drama. Even as the play begins, Ajax imitates Achilles's refusal to fight (1.3.185), and Achilles mocks the Greeks with his pageants:

> Having his ear full of his airy fame
> Grows dainty of his worth, and in his tent
> Lies *mocking* our designs. (1.3.144-46; emphasis added)[23]

In the pageants, Patroclus pretends to be Agamemnon, "seeming" like "a strutting player," with his wooden dialogue, and joys at the sound of his own foot on the scaffold (1.3.153-60).

On the Trojan side, Pandarus and Cressida alternate mocking the pageant of Trojan warriors as they pass beneath the walls. Cressida also takes the occasion to mock Pandarus with bawdy misrepresentations of his meanings, a favor he returns after her night with Troilus: "Now will he [Pandarus] be *mocking*. I shall have such a life" (4.2.22–23).

Once she has been traded for Antenor, Cressida mocks Menelaus with his cuckoldry (4.5.45), and Hector does the same:

> Mock not that I affect th'untraded oath.
> Your quondam wife swears still by Venus' glove.
> She's well, but bade me not commend her to you.
> (4.5.179-81)

Not all of the characters accept this mockery, however. Diomedes, much more realistic than Troilus, will not permit Cressida to make him the same kind of fool. Impatient with her teasing, he calls it just that:

Diomedes: Why then, farewell. Thou never shalt *mock* Diomed again.

Cressida: You shall not go. One cannot speak a word
                 But it straight starts you.

Diomedes: I do not like this fooling. (5.2.105–7; emphasis added)

Here, the mockery that preceded the ceremony, and which the ceremony commemorated, picks up again on the Greek side of the wall. Eventually, after he loses Cressida to the Greeks, Troilus bewails "How my achievements mock me" (4.2.71), and tells Ulysses, "O sir, to such as boasting show their scars / A mock is due" (4.5.290–91).

The quotations establish a mocking disposition toward things ordinarily revered, things that provide some type of order to the appetite—in war, degree; in love, marriage. Institutions such as these channel the appetite, guiding it toward a health beneficial for all of society, rather than toward a satisfaction pleasing only to the self. But in *Troilus and Cressida*, the opposite is preferred; pride and lust give the appetite full rein.

Another difference between the contracts in *Measure for Measure* and the mock contract in *Troilus and Cressida* lies in their alignment of society with nature. In Vienna, the dissemblance that oriented things toward barrenness and death, cheating nature of the generous return she is due, is realigned toward life. But in *Troilus and Cressida*, though nature "craves that all dues be rendered to their owners," nature is slighted, constantly. What is stolen is never returned, and the orientation toward death is never overcome. Hector's rejection of the order that he knows—the law of all nations, respecting the marital contract—flies in the face of nature. It is further evidence of the disorder and chaos in nature described in Ulysses's famous soliloquy on order and degree:

> Take but degree away, untune that string,
> And hark what discord follows. Each thing meets
> In mere oppognancy.
> . . . .
> Then everything includes itself in power,
> Power into will, will into appetite;
> And appetite, an universal wolf
> So doubly seconded with will and power,

> Must make perforce an universal prey,
> And last eat up himself. (1.3.109-24)

The self-annihilation manifests itself in a collapse of power into will, and will into appetite, with appetite's own eventual destruction. When Cressida likens the "strong base and building" of her love—which proves as false as her famous similes—to "the very center of the earth," the analogy is apt; the center of the Trojan world is just as unstable as her faith (4.2.104-5).

By the end of the play, the battle scenes show a pattern of destruction leading away from nature and life and toward negation. As Diomedes and Troilus fight for the return of Troilus's "horse," Thersites mocks that "lechery eats itself" (5.4.34). Self-destruction, born of the appetite, appears again a few scenes later. When the once noble Hector chases the golden-armored soldier to win glory, he discovers the armor is filled only with a "putrefied core." In a fateful irony, Hector tells the soldier that the armor has cost him his life, words that redound to Hector (5.9.2). In his discovery of the putrefied core, he disarms himself, and the brutish Achilles sweeps down upon him.

The death that comes to Hector as a result of his quest for what proves to be only a "botchy core" is symbolic of the orientation toward disease and death. The negation continues, even in the language, as Troilus performs great deeds of "execution" while "engaging and redeeming" himself with "careless force and forceless care"—all images of cancellation (5.5.39-40). "Execution" here takes the sense of exacting death, but it is followed by another transactional metaphor. He risks and saves himself by engaging and redeeming; but an engagement also means a type of pledge, such as a mortgage, which is canceled upon its redemption. That death from "execution" should be followed by this image of self-cancellation, and then by the inverse syntax of "careless force" and "forceless care," underscores the theme. The canceling-out quality of the characters' speech, on both sides, is further evidence of the trend toward negation:

Menelaus: An odd man, lady? Every man is odd.

Cressida: No, Paris is not; for you know 'tis true,
                   That you are odd, and he is even with you; (4.5.44-45)

and

Aeneas: If not Achilles, sir, What is your name?

Achilles: If not Achilles, nothing.

Aeneas: Therefore Achilles. (4.5.77-79)

And most famous of all is Troilus's impassioned denial of the reality that stares him in the face, Cressida's pledging herself to another man: "This is and is not Cressid" (5.2.153).

Again, Girard is helpful in distinguishing exactly what is at stake when the culture trades order for appetite:

> "Degree," or *gradus*, is the underlying principle of all order, natural and cultural. It permits individuals to find a place for themselves in society; it lends a meaning to things, arranges them in proper sequence within a hierarchy . . .
>
> . . . As in Greek tragedy and primitive religion, it is not the differences but the loss of them that gives rise to violence and chaos, and that inspires Ulysses's plaint.[24]

When there is no distinction in value or worth, and when all is common property, rivalry proliferates. When there is no private right to a thing, it is the public claim of all. That is the case at the play's outset with Helen, whose worth and status are debased. It also proves to be the case with Cressida by the play's close. The contract, uncelebrated in this play, would provide distinction, an ordering principle that is missing from this world.

After analyzing the parody of the contractual elements in the mock contract, their failure to bring meaning to the union, and the disjunction, separation, and mockery that fill the play, it is possible to trace a trajectory of the Trojan–Greek problem: there is no marriage contract because there is no substance; there is no substance because there is no repository of true worth; and there is no repository of true worth because the characters choose their appetites over reason and order. This results in a flouting of nature's laws, leaving the world with no standard and resigning it to a state of inconstancy and turmoil. As O. J. Campbell observes, when reason abdicates as prince of the microcosm, men follow the usurping passions, and divide and dissipate his authority.[25] The disordered, inconstant universe that results should be no surprise. Nevertheless, it proves so to Troilus when he witnesses Cressida's betrayal:

> The *bonds* of heaven are slipped, dissolved, and loosed,
> And with another *knot five-finger-tied*
> The fractions of her faith, orts of her love
> The fragments, scraps, the bits an greasy relics
> Of her o'er-eaten faith, are *bound* to Diomed.
> (5.2.163–67; emphasis added).

The image is laced with parts of the marriage contract that have been paro-died. Cressida does not acknowledge the "bonds" of heaven, ceremonialized by handclasping. Order has slipped, and she is tied, by virtue of the grossly imagined appetite, to Diomedes instead. However, since the mock contract is indeed a mockery, Troilus's objections are without foundation. He has no real right to Cressida.

The characters are caught in a world of imitation, mockery, and mirrors, to which they constantly refer. It is what is most characteristic of that world, just as dissemblance is most characteristic of Vienna in *Measure for Measure*. And just as the agent of nature in the latter play—the Duke—uses what is most characteristic of his society in order to perform his transformational trick, the agent of war in this play, Ulysses, takes advantage of the imitation and mock-ery that beset his world to perform another kind of trick. It is a final point of comparison between the plays, and a final point of distinction. For the bed-trick in *Measure for Measure*, which establishes integrity and a reorientation to-ward nature, is itself parodied in *Troilus and Cressida*. In the Trojan play, the trick is used for the ends of war and death. There is no agent of nature to see that she is given her "due." Instead, there are only the agents of lust: Pandarus, who trades on images of Cressida to entice Troilus; and war: Ulysses, who trades on the images of reputation to entice Achilles.

The widespread self-deception in the play finds a particular manifestation in Achilles. He is "caught" in his own image of self-worth, and so prideful that he would rather bask in his tent than serve the Greek cause. When Hector sub-mits a challenge to any Greek who will fight for the honor of his lady, Ulysses works to bring about a substitution. Rather than choose Achilles as their cham-pion, the Greeks will pretend to prefer Ajax. Ajax will be "dressed in our voices" and given "allowance as the worthier man" (1.3.377–85). If he wins the battle with Hector, all is well; if he loses, they can claim that they have a better man still: Achilles. The scheme relies on pretense, the "shape" of an idea that has no real substance. The Greeks put on a "form of strangeness" toward Achilles, not genuine aloofness (3.3.51).

The difference between the "bed trick" in the other late comedies, and the "battle trick" in this one, is revealing. In *Measure for Measure* and *All's Well That Ends Well*, the substitution that achieves marital integrity involves the re-placement of the object of lust with the wife. Here, the substitution has a dif-ferent goal. The Greeks "seem" to prefer one warrior for another, not in order to deflate Achilles's reputation, but to incite his zeal for it. A kind of integrity is hoped for by this substitution, but it is not aimed at furthering nature's gen-erative ends, but in bringing the warrior onto the battlefield. And at the play's close, the trick only succeeds in this end, not in the means. Achilles does not actually fight; he does not become a warrior in name and deeds. He remains one only in name. Neither does he observe authority and degree, the subject of the early Greek council. He merely finds a way to achieve his ends—to "seem" Hector's slayer—and thereby maintain the name of a great warrior. Whereas the real replaces the illusory in *Measure for Measure*, in *Troilus and Cressida*, one illusion simply replaces another.

The power of the scheme lies in what Girard calls the "interdividual mechanism," an inability to enjoy what one possesses—mistress, military power, or political glory—except by reflection.[26] Achilles, who had been the center of attention, is given a mimetic rival, Ajax. Each warrior then maneuvers for the chance to fight Hector, to increase his reputation.[27] And the mimetic quality of reputation is, according to the exchange between Ulysses and Achilles, dependent solely on the appraisal of others. Using allusions to mirrors, which reflect a man's worth, each ties value to "th'applause" of other men (3.3.120). In fact, honor has no particular nature, says Ulysses, but simply depends on deeds. The impermanence of honor is reflected in Ulysses's assessment: "The present eye praises the present object" (3.3.181).

That it is not a wife substituted in Ulysses trick, but a warrior, has another significance related to a perversion of the marriage contract. It is also a warrior, Antenor, who is traded for Cressida. The swapping and substitutions of a genuine character in the other problem plays is missing in this one.

In stating that the Trojans will assume the Greek champion is "distilled out of our virtues" (1.3.351), Nestor uses imagery similar to that of giving birth to an "ideal man." If the designated hero "miscarries," he will lead to the downfall of the Greek cause (1.3.352). Ulysses uses the same image in his answer to Nestor:

Ulysses:	I have a young conception in my brain;
	Be you my time to bring it to some shape.
	. . . .
	Blunt wedges rive hard knots; the seeded pride
	That hath to this maturity blown up
	In rank Achilles must or now be cropped
	Or, shedding, breed a nursery of like evil
	To overbulk us all. (1.3.12–13; 316–20)

Similar to the generative imagery discussed earlier, the imagery here relates to warriors, and schemes to generate them. There is also the threat of miscarriage, a frustration of nature, lurking within the image. Troilus uses the same idea when he talks of vows being strangled "[e]ven in the birth of our own labouring breath" (4.4.37).[28]

A perversion of nature continues in the linking of sex and war. The lust that has raged in Troilus's head, and has played out in the Troilus/Cressida–Paris/Helen plot, carries over into images of battle lust. Ulysses, in a role perversely similar to that of Pandarus's, tempts Achilles back to the field by suggesting: "And better would it fit Achilles much / To throw down Hector than Polyxena" (3.3.209–10). Patroclus, thought to be Achilles's "male varlet" or "masculine whore" (5.1.15–17), urges him to "rouse" himself to war by shaking off the "weak and wanton cupid," a suggestion that, considering the context, amounts to little more than shifting from one type of lust to another (3.3.218–27). Aroused, Achilles responds:

> I have a woman's longing,
> An appetite that I am sick withal,
> To see great Hector in his weeds of peace,
> To talk with him and to behold his visage
> Even to my full of view. (3.3.239–43)

When Hector comes to the Greek camp, Achilles's newly stirred battle lust appears in the way he addresses the Trojan. Hector answers him in the same fashion:

Achilles: Now, Hector, I have fed mine eyes on thee;

             . . . .

Hector: Stand fair, I pray thee, let me look on thee.

             . . . .

Achilles: Tell me, you heavens, in which part of his body
                Shall I destroy him? Whether there, or there, or there?
                That I may give the local wound a name.
                And make distinct the very breach whereout
                Hector's great spirit flew. Answer me, heavens!

             . . . .

Hector: For I'll not kill thee there, nor there, nor there,
                But by the forge that stithied Mars his helm
                I'll kill thee everywhere, yea, o'er and o'er. (4.5.231; 235;
                242–46; 254–56)[29]

The men's delight in naming the ways that they will kill each other is echoed in the rhetoric that passes between Aeneas and Diomedes. Aeneas says, "No man alive can love in such a sort / The thing he means to kill more excellently" (4.1.25–26). He tells Diomedes that they "know" each other well, to which Diomedes replies, "We do, and long to know each other worse" (4.1.33). Paris sums up the paradox of sex and war: "This is the most despitefull'st gentle greeting / The noblest hateful love, that e'er I heard of" (4.1.34–35). As Rene Girard points out, the hatred of the warriors for one another is "suffused with eroticism."[30]

There is no greater example than the perverse marriage imagery used in reference to the meetings of Ajax, Hector, and Achilles. Ajax arrives in "appointment fresh and fair / Anticipating time with starting courage" (4.5.1–2). After a trumpet call to summon Hector, they await an answer from the "Trojans' *trumpet*" [strumpet]. When Hector does arrive, he and Ajax engage in a "maiden battle" (4.5.88), with Hector praising Ajax's "lusty arms" he would have "fall on him thus" (4.5.137–38).

In the Achilles/Hector match, elements of the marriage contract can be seen:

Achilles: Dost thou *entreat* me, Hector?
                   Tomorrow do I meet thee, fell as death;
                   Tonight all friends.

Hector: *Thy hand upon that match.* (4.5.267–70; emphasis added)

Achilles has cast himself as holding a "woman's longing" to meet Hector in battle, and the opposite role is confirmed in Aeneas's charge to the Trojans: "With a *bridegroom's* fresh alacrity / Let us address to tend on Hector's heels" (4.4.144–45; emphasis added). Hector himself says of his appointment, to his own wife Andromache, no less, "I must not break my faith / You know me dutiful" (5.3.71–75). He is "engaged " to many Greeks, he says, and begs his father's "consent" to meet them (5.3.67; 74).[31] The bonds of the marital tie with his wife are forsaken in favor of this sworn, and strangely conceived, pledge to the warrior.

The supreme instance of parody lies in this "war contract" between Achilles and Hector. The warriors take great pains to observe its formalities—making vowed pledges, clasping hands, preparing for their "morning" engagement, where they will "know" each other in a battle that will end in death. Of course, the ends of this perverse contract are death's, not life's. By way of contrast, in *Measure for Measure*, it is when sex and death are coupled most strongly, and "execution" for Angelo's "satisfaction" seems most imminent, that things are transformed, unified, and reoriented toward life. But in *Troilus and Cressida*, the insubstantial and discordant only continue, and worsen.

The pattern of destruction of "measure for measure," transcended in the play of that title, ironically becomes the standard for this one: Helen, a Greek whore, is stolen by the Trojan Paris; Cressida, a Trojan whore, is stolen by the Greek Diomedes. The Greek cuckold, Menelaus, is matched by the Trojan cuckold, Troilus; the Greek hero Achilles is fooled into war by pride, and the Trojan hero Hector is fooled into death by honor. When considered alongside what the contract in *Measure for Measure* accomplishes—the full integration of things that had been only partially realized, in furtherance of nature's generative goals—the lack of integration in *Troilus and Cressida* is all the more striking. Rather than act as an instrument to sustain and perpetuate society, here the contract is mocked. In its absence, a disordered, unprincipled society lies on either side of the Trojan wall, and each is consumed by appetite. The bedtrick substitution, the marriage contract, and the emblems of permanence in the other play are perverted in this one, with disastrous effects. All ends in "wars and lechery," as Thersites predicts, and all in the play, Trojans and Greeks, are indicted. The indictment may have been intended more widely still, for the closing leaves the syphilis-ridden Pandarus on the stage, bequeathing his diseases to the audience.[32] Presumably they clapped, delighted at their inheritance. And by the late 1580s, "clap" had already acquired a dual significance, appropriate to end such a play: "a) to applaud; to show approval b) venereal disease."[33]

In *Measure for Measure*, the legal instrument, once fully realized, enables marriage and is consistent with Nature's generative ends. In *Troilus and Cressida*, on the other hand, the mock legal instrument parodies marital concerns, and the "war contract," so faithfully observed by the heroes, proves inconsistent with Nature's ends; it is oriented toward death. These same two orientations are present in the bonds that figure into *The Merchant of Venice*, the friendship bond and the commercial bond. One of the bonds enables a marriage, the other threatens to undo its happiness.

CHAPTER 4

Matching Meanings

Contracts, Bonds, and Sureties
in The Merchant of Venice

Measure for Measure and *Troilus and Cressida* reflect the two orientations toward nature that run throughout the plays under consideration here. They also demonstrate the different uses Shakespeare makes of the law, and particularly of the legal instrument. In *Measure for Measure*, those who cheat nature also bypass integrity, creating a disjunction between seeming and being. Nature's agent rectifies this state of affairs by means of the marriage contracts, providing a solution that returns nature's largesse. But while similar problems exist in *Troilus and Cressida*, there is no similar resolution. The agents of lust and war in that play further exacerbate a disorder stemming from the preference of appetite and illusion over reason and reality. The contractual elements that bring about marital realization in *Measure for Measure* are mocked in *Troilus and Cressida*, ending in a frustration of nature's goals. In short, one play resolves disorder, reorienting society toward life by virtue of the contract; the other portrays the absence of order, which the contract can supply, and illustrates the disorienting and deadly effects that result from that disorder.

In *The Merchant of Venice*, both orientations are again present. And again they are related to legal instruments—this time, to bonds. One exists in the "friendship bond" between Antonio and Bassanio, based on love. It promotes nature's goals by enabling the marriage contract between Bassanio and Portia. The other exists in the "commercial bond" between Antonio and Shylock, based on the famous "pound of flesh." At first blush, it also seems intended to enable the marriage contract. But in the course of the play, Shylock's true motives, and the true basis of the commercial bond, are revealed. In the end, this bond actually threatens the burgeoning society that the friendship bond has generated.

The play opens on the relationship between the merchant Antonio and his friend Bassanio. Bassanio has wasted his "faint means," and his "something too prodigal" youth has left him financially "gaged" (pledged) (1.1.122-30).[1] Bassanio divulges his plan to come clear of his debts to Antonio, to whom he owes the most "in money and in love" (1.1.131). Even Bassanio's plan to enter the lottery of the caskets stems from a "warranty," both a sanction and a guarantee, of Antonio's affection (1.1.132). The friendship between the two men is depicted throughout the play, by Bassanio and others, as a bond: Bassanio introduces him to Portia with "This is the man, this is Antonio / To whom I am so infinitely bound" (5.1.134-35); and Portia returns "You should in all sense be much bound *to* him / For, as I hear, he was much bound *for* you" (5.1.136-37; emphasis added). Well before the commercial bond between Shylock and Antonio, Shakespeare develops an association between "means" and "love" under a bond, here nominated as a pledge (gage). Importantly, this bond is also forfeit. Bassanio, "like a wilful youth," has entirely lost the means that Antonio has previously afforded him (1.1.146).

Forfeiture notwithstanding, Antonio insists that Bassanio's promises to repay this new debt are unnecessary. Between them there is no need to "wind about" love with explanations and oaths (1.1.153-55), an image that relates the friendship bond with freedom, and opposes it to the slavery images later associated with the commercial bond. Indeed, Antonio says his "uttermost" would be available to Bassanio even if he had wasted all (1.1.157). The "hazard," or risk, of his money is lent with one condition, that it stand within the "eye of honour" in the same way that Bassanio himself does. In that event, says Antonio:

> be assured
> My purse, my person, my extremest means
> Lie all unlocked to your occasions. (1.1.137-39)

The friendship bond, of course, costs Antonio greatly, for he pledges his flesh under the commercial bond to finance his friend's venture. The ship that will repay that bond is "wrecked" (3.1.3) at a place called the "Goodwins," meaning "friendship" (3.1.4). This pun on "racked" evokes an image of suffering quite common in the play and illustrates the lengths to which Antonio will extend himself for his friend.

It is important to understand the basis, or "consideration," for the friendship bond. Although Bassanio receives material benefit from the bond—consideration in the form of money—the consideration passing to Antonio is no more than the happiness of his friend. Bassanio assures Antonio that repayment of the bond is forthcoming, but this is clearly not Antonio's motive for undertaking the obligation. The assurance in the bond between them is in the nature of "love and affection," a type of consideration based on moral obligation.

This type of consideration was recognized in the English courts of Chancery, though refused in the Courts of Common Law around 1600.[2] As Baker reports, it was rejected only after some debate:

> At the beginning, the word "consideration" was closely associated with the context of marriage (See Yorke's reports, B.L. harg. MS 388, fol. 180 (1530); and in 1549 a surety launched an action on an undertaking given "in consideration of friendship and good will" [*Rent v. Danyell* (1549) KB 27/1150, m. 104].[3]

In this type of consideration, which supported "uses" (trusts), parents might make bequests to their children, or a husband to his wife. As an aspect of the friendship bond, the consideration helps develop an outline of its nature: based on love (1.1.154), conditioned upon honor (1.1.137), and freely given in spite of forfeiture (1.1.146).

The friendship bond between the two is further characterized by what it does, or rather, by what it enables Bassanio to do. By virtue of the "means" provided by Antonio, Bassanio may travel to Belmont and enter the lottery for Portia's hand. As a result, the friendship bond gives life to Bassanio's chances to form yet another bond, with Portia, under a marriage contract. By analyzing this contract, and the conditions that attach to it by way of Portia's father's will, the difference between the natures of the friendship and commercial bonds becomes more apparent, and more important.

To win Portia, Bassanio must eschew the temptations of his will, which can be deceived by false appearances. Further, he must "hazard all he hath": that is, risk self-sacrifice by forswearing marriage to any woman in order to succeed. A willingness to sacrifice one's self *for* another is the condition to the marriage contract, just as it was the basis of the friendship bond. The commercial bond, on the other hand, is adversarial; it requires the sacrifice of one party *to* the other—in that case, Antonio to Shylock.

Portia herself is called fair, virtuous, and as constant as Cato's daughter of the same name (1.1.166). Constancy is a virtue she has in common with Mariana in *Measure for Measure*, Helena in *All's Well That Ends Well*, and other heroines who play crucial roles in plot resolutions. Bassanio claims that no one in the "wide world" is ignorant of her worth (1.1.167). But whether it is her virtue or her monetary value they are so knowledgeable of is not entirely clear. Considering the group of suitors who precede Bassanio, ignorance of her true value is more likely the case. And as has been seen in the plays discussed so far, a crucial element in a valid contract is the appreciation of real worth.

Portia's father, said to be "holy" and "ever virtuous" (1.2.24), has provided conditions to Portia's marriage that will ensure a worthy suitor. According to its terms, Portia may marry only the man who guesses which of three caskets—gold, silver, and lead—contains her picture. The three caskets bear riddles as to their contents: "Who chooseth me shall gain what many men desire" (gold); "Who chooseth me shall get as much as he deserves" (silver); and "Who chooseth me must give and hazard all he hath" (lead). Portia may not disclose the secret, and any failed suitor must leave Belmont, vowing never to woo Portia or any other lady in way of marriage. The will protects not only Portia, but also all of womankind, testifying to the father's good intentions.

In Shakespeare, such contractual conditions are not always instituted in such good faith. Similar restrictions are placed on marriages in *A Midsummer Night's Dream* and *Pericles*. But in the former, Hermia's father seeks her death under Athenian law if she will not marry the inconstant Demetrius;[4] in the latter, King Antiochus employs a perverse riddle as a condition to his daughter's hand, intending to keep her for incestuous purposes.[5] Bad faith conditions also occur in *All's Well That Ends Well*, when Bertram tries to foil his marriage with seemingly impossible stipulations. In these cases, Shakespeare uses contractual conditions to work against union, providing a threat to marriage that must be eventually overcome. This reveals that the conditions to the marriage contract require something of the "legislator/judge." He must act in good faith with regard to those impacted by the conditions. Hermia's father does not appreciate, and Antiochus is not interested in, the worth of the suitors. Considering his arrangement of the lottery, Portia's father proves he understands the meaning of true worth. He will only surrender his daughter to a proper man. Glossing Mark Van Doren's comment that there is no incompatibility in Belmont between love and money, C. L. Barber adds that there is no conflict between enjoying Portia's beauty and her wealth.[6] To extend these observations to my topic, the play shows there need be no conflict between law and love either; the will serves romance well in Belmont. It is in Venice that the law turns threatening, due to its vengeful application.

In effect, it is proper to speak of the will as both conditional contract and legislation, as it functions as a type of law. Although not a formal declaration or statute, its rules are universally accepted, binding, and prescriptive. And in acquiescing to her father's will—however begrudging that acquiescence may be—Portia implicitly accepts the idea that the law can limit freedoms when to do so is in the best interest of its subjects. In her case, Portia's will to marry a man of her own choosing is "hedged" and "scanted" (2.1.17–18). Her father seems to know what the Viennese in *Measure for Measure*, the Trojans and the Greeks of *Troilus and Cressida*, and most of the characters in *The Merchant of Venice*, learn only at great cost: appearances can deceive, and steps must be taken to assure that the contract is among only the worthiest parties. According to Barber, the lottery of Portia's father points in the direction of a mystery, that "love is not altogether a matter of the will, however willing"; and faith in the law, however reluctant, causes Portia to censor her desires.

In this way, faith exists as a crucial factor in the relationship between the law and its subjects, as well as between the lovers in the play. Portia must surrender her will to her father, in faith. Without the consent to be governed—a basic and fundamental trust—the law cannot perform its function. This surrender of the will is painful in any context: to both the highborn Portia, regarding her marriage:

> O me, the word "choose!" I may neither
> choose whom I would nor refuse whom I dislike; so is
> the will of a living daughter curbed by the will of a dead
>   father:
> is it not hard, Nerissa, that I cannot choose one nor
>   refuse none? (1.2.23–26)

and to the low born Launcelot, regarding his service: "My conscience, hanging about the neck of my heart, says 'My honest friend Launcelot' . . . my conscience is but a kind of hard conscience, to offer to counsel me to stay with the Jew; . . . I [Ay] will run" (2.2.13; 28; 30).[7] Rather than fashion the will to the law, the law is often "hooked to the appetite," as in the case of Angelo in *Measure for Measure*, and in the case of Shylock in *The Merchant of Venice*.

While Portia bewails her inability to choose her own fate, the will actually protects her from the various unsuitable men who come to claim her. The litany of Portia's suitors shows them to be: deficient in substance, such as the Frenchman, who is "everyman in no man" (1.2.57); deficient in words, such as the Englishman, who cannot communicate (1.2.65); laboring under some great excess, such as the horse-mad Neopolitan (1.2.38) or the drunken German (1.2.73); or some great deficiency, such as the melancholic Palatine (1.2.45). None is worthy of Portia; in the end, none hazards to venture for her.

The unsuitable are disqualified because the conditions are based on one of the elements so central to marriage contracts in the problem plays, an understanding of true worth. For in attempting to solve the riddles, the men incidentally reveal their own value. The lottery requires them to betray their understanding—or as it proves, misunderstanding—of true worth's meaning. The winning suitor's meaning must match that of Portia's father. Nerissa explains:

> Your father was ever virtuous; and holy men at their
> death have good inspirations,—therefore the lott'ry,
> that he hath devised in these three chests of gold,
> silver, and lead, whereof *who chooses his meaning*
> chooses you, will, no doubt, never be chosen by any
> rightly, but one who you shall rightly love. (1.2.27–32;
> emphasis added)

The importance of the "matching" of "meanings" is key not only in the casket lottery, but also prefigures the same concern dramatized in the trial scene of act 4.

Of course, Morocco's and Arragon's meanings of worth do not match those of Portia's father, and for telling reasons. Morocco, while cautioning Portia not to "mislike" him for his "complexion" (2.1.1), goes on to make his choice based solely on the appearances of the caskets—their "complexions"—preferring gold because of its monetary value: "A golden mind stoops not to shows of dross; / I'll then nor give nor hazard aught for lead" (2.7.20–21). He compares himself to Hercules (2.1.32), and claims he "deserves" the lady Portia on grounds of fortunes, graces, breeding, and love (2.7.31–34). He likens her to the image of gold coins, bringing into question what is the true object of his affection, Portia or her wealth:

> They have in England
> A coin that bears the figure of an angel
> Stamped in gold, but that's insculp'd upon;
> But here an angel in a golden bed
> Lies all within. (2.7.55–59)

The inscription accompanying the gold casket's skull berates this kind of reasoning:

Gilded tombs do worms infold.
Had you been as wise as bold,
Young in limbs, in judgment old,
Your answer had not been inscroll'd. (2.7.69–72)

Arragon's choice is no more sound, or humble, than Morocco's. While he steers clear of gold's inscription—"what many men desire"—he does so on the grounds that he will not "jump with common spirits / And rank me with the barbarous multitudes" (2.9.32–33). After a discourse on how few deserve the "stamp of merit" and "clear honour," he vainly claims as much for himself in choosing the silver casket: "I will assume desert / Give me a key for this" (2.9.51). He receives a fool's head as his prize, and like Morocco, also receives a schedule that berates his judgment:

The fire seven times tried this:
Seven times tried that judgment is
That did never choose amiss.
Some there be that shadows kiss,
Such have but a shadow's bliss.
There be fools alive [iwis]
Silvered o'er, and so was this. (2.9. 63–69)

As a final blow to their reasoning, Portia says "O these deliberate fools! when they do choose, / They have the wisdom by their wit to lose" (2.9.80–81).[8]

Both men fail because their choices are rooted not in good judgment, but in insubstantial, and deceiving appearances. As in *Troilus and Cressida*, the greed and pride that foster bad choices is born of the appetite, which is precisely what Portia's father's will sets out to curtail. Portia characterizes the will as a "curb" on her own "will." It is a "cold decree"—born of the "brain," meant for the "blood"—and over which her hot temper wishes to leap (1.2.15–22). The depiction of her father's "will" as a "curb" (the bridle chain that works in conjunction with the bit) to the appetite echoes Duke Vincentio's portrayal of laws as "needful bits and curbs to headstrong weeds."[9] Both draw on Plato's famous analogy of the soul in the *Phaedrus*. There, Plato describes the rational element of the soul as a charioteer, who must skillfully control his two steeds, one representing irrational desire, the other, spiritual yearning.[10] Portia's father's "decree" tempers hot blood, which might choose rashly, and orders it in a way that protects her interests.

The only way to satisfy the condition to the contract lies in a choice based on good judgment, born of reason—not based on appearances, born of appetite. It is significant that prior to Bassanio's choice, Portia tells him to "pause before you hazard," the very thing required of him by the lead casket: "give and hazard." She also commands her servants to sing a song that associates "fancy"—the bait to which the will often succumbs—with appetite.

> Tell me where is fancy bred,
> Or in the heart, or in the head?
> How begot, how nourished?
> Reply, reply.
> It is *engender'd in the eyes*,
> With gazing *fed*; and fancy *dies*
> *In the cradle where it lies.*
> Let us all ring fancy's knell
> I'll begin it,—Ding, dong, bell.
> Ding, dong, bell. (3.2.63–72; emphasis added)

Fancy is born from appearances, in the eyes; feeds itself by the indulgence of the appetite, by gazing; and quickly dies, in its cradle. Bassanio apparently grasps the clue, for his speech on the deception of "outward shows" and "ornament" follows.

Of course, the endings of the first three stanzas all rhyme with "lead," and whether the song is a clue or not is the subject of debate. Bloom and Jaffa see Portia as having a great respect for the forms of law, if not the substance. She observes her traditional duty, working within the law's conventions, not outside them.[11]

Bassanio derides religious error, which may be blessed with the gloss of a text (3.2.77–80). Presaging the abuse of process to come, he also derides the law:

> What plea so tainted and corrupt
> But, being seasoned with a gracious voice,
> Obscures the show of evil? (3.2.75–77)

He goes on to speak to the flaws that Morocco and Arragon exhibit. With relation to Morocco, who bragged of his courage and compared himself to Hercules, he says:

> How many cowards . . .
> . . . wear yet upon their chins

> The beards of Hercules . . .
> Who, inward searched, have livers white as milk?
> (3.2.83–86)

With relation to the vain Arragon, who came to Belmont with "one fool's *head*" and left "with two" (2.9.75–76; emphasis added), Bassanio says, "Look on beauty / And you shall see 'tis purchased by the weight," its golden locks "often known to be the dowry of a second *head* / The skull that bred them in the sepulchre" (3.2.88–96; emphasis added). His own choice, "meagre lead / Which rather threatenst than dost promise aught" (3.2.104–5), is the only one that demands something of the suitor, a complete surrender and a "hazarding of all he hath." Like the trust required of Portia vis-à-vis her father's law, the winning suitor must also trust in order to satisfy the contractual condition. In so doing, he both proves his own worth, and "chooses his [Portia's father's] meaning" (1.2.30):

> You that choose not by the view
> Chance as fair and choose as true.
> Since this fortune falls to you,
> Be *content* and seek no new. (3.2.131–34; emphasis
> added)

The reward goes to the judgment that surrenders to faith. This is similar to what Bassanio must do in "choosing" Portia's father's "meaning," which is achieved only in "a hazard of faith." The result is "contentment," the state of integration.

Evidencing an orientation toward life, Christian imagery of faith and trust surrounds the lottery of the caskets, the friendship bond, and the marriage contract.[12] Like Christ, Antonio is the "'tainted wether of the flock'" who will lay down his life for Bassanio's debt (4.1.114). That Bassanio is a profligate whose debts Antonio has paid many times before, places Bassanio in the position of "everyman," or *humanum genus*, as Robert Grams Hunter would have it.[13] Bassanio makes a "pilgrimage" to Belmont to win Portia (1.1.120), who "stands for sacrifice" during his trial (3.2.57). Portia not only identifies with the Christian-type sacrifice Bassanio is willing to make in her behalf, but also identifies herself as a sacrifice. Portia too is at stake in the wager. Each offers himself/herself for the other in the lottery, a disposition at odds with the self-interest of Shylock's demands in "I stand for judgment" (4.1.103) and "I stand here for the law" (4.1.142). And similar to the anticipation of the resurrection, Portia's "form" is ribbed in "cerecloth in the obscure grave" (2.7.51); before she can be freed from that grave to work the redemption of Antonio (whose own sacrifice has worked to free her), she must be chosen by one who risks all in a hazard of faith.

As has been seen, the idea of risk is found in the root of the word *wed* itself, which means "to wager or "to stake." The risks that those in the friendship bond and marriage contract take for each other are opposed to the risks demanded by the commercial bond's wager of flesh. Portia sums up the idea best when she says that the basis of Bassanio's being bound *to* Angelo is because Angelo has been bound *for* him (5.1.136–37). Questioned by Portia, Bassanio's uncertainty causes a doubt that can be offset only by a promise of life (3.2.34). Portia, in keeping with the religious tone, answers, "Well then, confess and live," to which Bassanio responds that "confess and love" was the answer needed for his "deliverance" (3.2.24–38). His response is among the many religious images of suffering and love; Antonio's credit will be "racked" to the uttermost for Bassanio (1.1.181), and he offers to be "prest unto" Bassanio's bidding (1.1.160). Later, the note commending "Balthazar" states that his worth will be shown through the "trial" (4.1.162), and when Bassanio pleads with the disguised Portia, he asks her to

> grant me two things, I pray you,—
> Not to deny me, and to pardon me.

Portia: You *press* me far, and therefore I will yield,—(4.1.419–21; emphasis added)

These images of sacrifice, suffering, and surrender, all in hopes of winning life and love, surround both the friendship bond and the marriage contract that it makes possible. They also underscore the subplot of Lorenzo and Jessica.

Lorenzo and Jessica's love is mocked by the coarse Salerio and Solanio for not "seeming" like other "bonds new-made," in that it is not impatient, having no "keen appetite" (2.6.5–9). But in the problem plays, impatience is the hallmark of lust, not love; witness Troilus and Cressida. Instead, Lorenzo and Jessica's love is both patient and trusting. Their first scene occurs on a darkened balcony, but though Jessica cannot see Lorenzo, she knows his "tongue" (2.6.27) and blindly casts down her fortune for him to catch.[14] The strength of their union allows them to mock themselves with a litany of false lovers, including Troilus and Cressida, while turning toward a "gilded heaven" that reflects the same reasoned order as the music to which they listen.

Like the other unions created by legal instruments in the problem plays, Portia and Bassanio's is laden with legal metaphors. Bassanio, having received his fortune from the scroll, comes to Portia "by *note*, to give and to receive" (3.2.140). A note is an instrument commemorating both indebtedness and the receipt of consideration for which the indebtedness has been incurred. Synonymous here with a bond, the note also requires marks to confirm its transaction. Bassanio, distrusting his eyes—a distrust favored in a play in which appearances are discouraged, and blind faith encouraged—remains doubtful of his fortunes until they are "confirmed, sign'd, ratified" by Portia (3.2.148).[15] Portia picks up the imagery with claims that, for Bassanio's benefit, her virtues would bear interest:

> I would be trebled twenty times myself;
> A thousand times more fair, ten thousand times more
>   rich;
> That only to stand high in your account,
> I might in virtue, beauties, livings, friends,
> Exceed account. (3.2.153–57)

Although she says the full "sum" of her, which she "terms in gross," amounts to no more than a girl, she proceeds to employ a metaphor that builds upon itself, rising in quality:

> *Happy* in this, she is not yet so old
> But she may learn; *happier* than this,
> She is not bred so dull but she can learn;
> *Happiest* of all is that her gentle spirit
> Commits itself to yours to be directed
> As from her lord, her governor, her king. (3.2.160–63;
>   emphasis added)

Bassanio and Portia play on the terms of *sum*, *something*, and *nothing*, which in Shakespeare have both metaphysical and sexual connotations. Bassanio speaks at 3.2.181–82 of every "something" being "blent" together into a wild "nothing" of joy. In sacrificing all for each other, their "nothing" turns to "something," an example of the metaphysical conceits in the plays.

In addition, Gratiano later wishes to marry when Bassanio and Portia "solemnize the *bargain*" of their faith, and Bassanio speaks to Lorenzo of his "new interest" in Belmont (3.2.220; emphasis added). The image is monetary, but here it is associated with a fruitful growth in love, as opposed to the barren growth of Shylock's usury.

But most important, Portia achieves a transfer of herself. Although publicly made and followed by a solemn church ceremony (3.2.302)—and therefore not lacking in the form that causes problems in *Measure for Measure*—the transfer has the stamp of the clandestine marriage: a first-person, present intention to marry:

> Myself and what is mine to you and yours
> *Is now converted:* but now I was the lord
> Of this fair mansion, master of my servants,
> Queen o'er myself: and even now, but now,
> This house, these servants and this same myself
> Are yours, my lord: *I give them with this ring;*
> Which when you part from, lose, or give away,
> Let it presage the ruin of your love
> And be my vantage to exclaim on you. (3.2.167–69;
>   emphasis added)

This transfer of self and possessions, realized in the language of transaction and secured with a ring, accomplishes the kind of integrated union eventually achieved by the contracts of *Measure for Measure* and *All's Well That Ends Well*, and never achieved by the mock contract in *Troilus and Cressida*. The significance of the contractual token, the ring, is more than symbolic in these terms. It becomes a requirement to the contract's solemnization. Similar to English land transactions of Medieval and Renaissance times, the ring takes on a decided weight, and performs a role that is not optional.

The agricultural and transactional metaphors that Shakespeare employs with regard to marriage help explain the gravity of the marriage ring. It not only binds the transaction, but also fuses with the transaction. This significance causes the problems when it is lost in act 5:

> To part so slightly with your wife's first gift
> A thing stuck on with oaths upon your finger
> And so riveted with faith unto your flesh. (5.1.166–69)

Despite Portia's apparent coaching in the casket scene, it seems Bassanio's appreciation of marriage is not as profound as hers. She must give him additional lessons at the play's end.

Finally, like the integrated unions of the other plays, Portia and Bassanio's marriage is oriented toward generation. Immediately following the exchange of the ring, Bassanio plans the *double* marriage feast, and Gratiano tells Nerissa, "We'll play with them the first boy for a thousand ducats" (3.2.213-14). When Lorenzo and Jessica arrive with news of Antonio's plight under the commercial bond, Portia adds:

> When it is paid, bring your true friend along.
> My maid Nerissa and myself meantime
> Will live as maids and widows. (3.2.307-9)

The Belmont "bond" gains "interest," yielding a larger community: first Gratiano and Nerissa, then Lorenzo and Jessica, and in the end, Antonio. Even Launcelot is brought within the fold.

The association of marriage and generation, turning on the conceit of "interest," is the same as that employed by the Duke in *Measure for Measure*. He portrays nature as a "thrifty goddess" who never lends her excellence without demanding a return, determining "herself the glory of a creditor / Both thanks and use [interest]."[16] These two images are similar to the sonnet's charges to the Young man, regarding marriage and children:

> *Nature's* bequest gives nothing, but doth *lend*,
> And being frank, she lends to those are free.
>
> . . . .
>
> Then how when *nature* calls thee to be gone:
> What acceptable *audit* canst thou leave? (Sonnet 4, lines
>   3-4, 11-12; emphasis added)

and

> Ten times thyself were happier than thou art,
> If ten of thine ten times refigured thee. (Sonnet 6,
>   lines 9-10)

In contrast to this fruitful union is Sonnet 134, which also deals with "bonds" and "sureties" between the poet, the Young Man, and the Dark Lady. But there, rather than the bond of love yielding fruit, the bond "fast-binds" both the poet and his "surety"—the young man—to the "will" of the dark lady. The poet is "mortgaged" and "forfeit," the dark lady is a "usurer" who takes all for "use" (sex), while the young man "pays the whole" (hole) without winning his freedom. As will be seen, the linking of illicit sex, usury, and enslavement in this sonnet is similar to the unnatural qualities of Shylock's commercial bond, with which he "fast-binds" Antonio.

The community-expanding generation that flows from the friendship bond and the marriage contract has another effect. Upon receiving the news of Antonio's trials, Portia articulates a transformation achieved by her new bond:

> I am half yourself,
> And I must freely have the half of anything
> That this same paper brings you. (3.2.247–49)

Clarkson and Warren explain that deeds were also known as "indentures" in Shakespeare's day, their name derived from the precautions taken against fraud: "As many copies were made on one sheet of parchment as there were parties, the copies then being cut apart in an indented, or saw-toothed, fashion across some such word as 'Chirograph,' so that forgery was very difficult."[17] Like Helena, Mariana, Adriana, and other comic heroines, Portia conceives of herself as so completely integrated with her husband by their contract that his suffering is "half" hers, and hers, his. She anticipates this metaphysical union when she laments, prior to Bassanio's success, that they are separated by the times:

> One half of me is yours, the other half yours,—
> Mine own, I would say; but if mine, then yours,
> And so all yours. O, these naughty times
> Put bars between the owners and their rights!
> And so, though yours, not yours,— (3.2.16–20)

Again, like Helena, Mariana, and Adriana, the separation causes a painful "half-state" that is rectified only by reunion. In light of this, keener still is her reflection on the motives for saving her husband's friend:

> For in companions
> That do converse and waste the time together,
> Whose souls do bear an equal yoke of love,
> There must be needs a like proportion
> Of lineaments, of manners and of spirit;
> *Which makes me think that this Antonio,*
> *Being the bosom lover of my lord,*

> *Must needs be like my lord. If it be so,*
> *How little is the cost I have bestow'd*
> *In purchasing the semblance of my soul*
> From out the state of hellish misery!
> *This comes too near the praising of myself.* (3.4.11–22;
>   emphasis added)

The contractual bond has worked a union between Portia and her husband, combining them. The same idea is present when Duke Vincentio tells Mariana that Angelo is her "combinate husband." But the friendship bond in *The Merchant of Venice* has done the same thing. Antonio, as surety for Bassanio, has taken his place in the commercial bond with Shylock. He has, for all intents and purposes, *become* Bassanio, so much so that his own body will pay his friend's price. As Bassanio and Antonio are joined through this bond, so are Bassanio and Portia by their contract; therefore, Portia and Antonio are united through Bassanio. The connected relationship becomes startling even to Portia, whose comment that this "comes too near the praising" of *herself*, is true in more ways than one. Recognizing others' flesh and blood as one's own, one's "kind"—as Old Gobbo does, and as Shylock must learn to do—becomes a startling revelation for the characters.[18]

In light of these considerations, the transformative union accomplished by the friendship bond, and the marriage contract it enables, follows a certain trajectory, familiar in the plays discussed thus far. Good judgment controls the will, avoiding the deceptive appearances that appeal to the appetite. An integrated union based on true value results and natural generation follows. In a recent work, Frederic Turner has made a distinction between the nature of "bonds" that is in line with my view. He speaks with regard to *King Lear*, but the point is applicable to *The Merchant of Venice*:

For expedient Machiavellians in the play [*King Lear*], bonds are either literal bonds—ropes to tie up a prisoner for torture—or mere social conventions maintained by the weak-minded and credulous to be broken by the stern and realistic when the right moment comes. Such social bonds are for them the tissue of foolish trust that binds the wealthy in their illusions. . . . But for the more humane characters in the play, bonds, while not promising the infinite wonders of unconditional love, are the humble but trustworthy assurances of real human caring. Such bond relationships as daughter to father, husband to wife, master to faithful retainer, because they are mutual and loop back reciprocally upon themselves, contain within them the same mysteries of unpredictable growth and profit that we have already found in the natural processes Shakespeare celebrates in the sonnets and *The Winter's Tale*.[19]

The friendship bond brings about this mysterious "growth and profit in the natural process," while the commercial bond leads to prison and—almost—death.

An analysis of the commercial bond's nature, with its metaphors of appetite, enslavement ("bondage"), and perverse marriage, will divulge an orientation opposed to the friendship bond. However, the two bonds are never far from each other in the impact they have on the characters' lives. For the friendship bond and its resultant marriage is always intertwined with, and threatened by, the commercial bond. Indeed, although the friendship bond has enabled the valid marriage contract at this point, with the elements of publicity, value, and tokens all observed, the consummation, or "performance," of the contract must be delayed. News of Shylock's threat under the commercial bond interrupts the completion of the marriage contracts, and the ensuing events menace their happiness. They also reveal a disparity between the worlds of Venice and Belmont.

As in *Measure for Measure*, *Cymbeline*, *The Winter's Tale*, *Romeo and Juliet*, and *Twelfth Night*, secret marriages—even those solemnly celebrated between worthy parties—cause problems. Here, it provides Shylock with an ostensible justification for carrying out his plans regarding the commercial bond. Shylock has sworn "he would rather have Antonio's flesh / Than twenty times the value of the sum" (3.2.285-86), so Lorenzo and Jessica's secret marriage (and their looting of the house) is not his only grounds for retaliation. He also claims that "were he [Antonio] out of Venice I can make what merchandise I will" (3.1.117-18). However just Shylock's anger for the suffering of his tribe, and however eloquent his soliloquy on the Jews' humanity, his motives for enforcing the commercial bond cannot be explained completely on those grounds.

While the friendship bond enables the publicly celebrated contract of Bassanio and Portia, the secretly celebrated marriage of Lorenzo and Jessica provokes Shylock's "execution" on the commercial bond, in all its ferocity. The pattern of the friendship bond leading to Portia and Bassanio's fruitful, public marriage is reversed here, with Jessica and Lorenzo's secret marriage leading to Antonio's persecution under the commercial bond. Shylock takes the Duke of Venice to search Bassanio's ship for the couple. The commercial bond has financed the ship, and Shylock blames Antonio for his loss, though the merchant certifies that the two were not aboard (2.8.4-10). Even the raucous

Solanio and Salerio appreciate the gravity of the situation: "Let good Antonio look he keep his day / Or he shall pay for this" (2.8.25–29). But Antonio cannot "keep his day," and the bond that has financed the marriage venture falls forfeit. In fact, the news of Antonio's "not keeping his day" reaches Belmont at the very moment Bassanio is keeping, and celebrating, his own. The difficulty of keeping "obliged [pledged] faith unforfeited" is mentioned in terms of "love bonds" earlier (2.6.7), and recurs here in regard to the commercial bond. As with the "war contract" in *Troilus and Cressida*, in *The Merchant of Venice* there is a perverse similarity between the commercial bond and the marriage contract.

Early in the play, Bassanio says he is "gaged" to Antonio for the debts of his prodigal youth (1.1.130). And when the bond is forfeit, Bassanio uses the same term with regard to Antonio and Shylock:

> I have *engaged* myself to a dear friend,
> *Engaged* my friend to his mere enemy,
> To feed my means. (3.2.260–61; emphasis added)

More marriage imagery occurs in the language Shylock and Antonio use in their bargain:

Shylock: Go with me to a *notary, seal me there*
       Your single bond; and, in a *merry* sport,
       If you *repay* me not *on such a day*,
       In *such a place*, such sum or sums as are
       Express'd in the condition, let the forfeit
       Be nominated for an equal pound
       Of your fair flesh, to be cut off and taken
       In what part of your body pleaseth me.

Antonio: Content, i' faith: *I'll seal to such a bond*
       And say there is much kindness in the Jew. (1.3.140–49;
       emphasis added)

The *merry bond*—as Shylock refers to it, with a pun on "marry"—is due three months from the day it is sealed. But three months after the "bond" is sealed, when Antonio does not keep his day, Shylock refers to their bond as a "bad *match*" (3.1.39). He insists on the bond despite what he deems to be Antonio's "broken faith":

> I'll have my *bond*; speak not against my *bond*:
> *I have sworn an oath* that I will have my *bond*. (3.3.4–5;
>   emphasis added)

and

> *An oath, an oath, I have an oath in heaven:*
> Shall I lay perjury upon my soul?
> No, not for Venice. (4.1.224–26; emphasis added)

Like Bassanio, who must "confess and love," Antonio is told he must "confess the bond" between Shylock and himself (4.1.177).[20] Shylock also swears, with perverse double entendre, that upon Antonio's forfeiture he will "have the heart of him" (3.1.117). If the trial scene later in the play is indeed a "love-test" for Shylock, as Wallace Kerrigan claims, he does indeed fail it.[21]

The ferocity of Shylock's irascible appetite manifests in these distorted marital images. The "strange nature" of his "suit," as Portia describes it (4.1.173), also shows up in the many appetitive metaphors he uses. Upon meeting Antonio, he says he "will feed fat the ancient grudge" (1.3.42) he bears him, and tells the merchant that he was "the last man in our [his and Bassanio's] mouths" (1.3.55). He also goes to supper with Antonio "in hate, to *feed* upon / The prodigal Christian" (2.5.14–15).

Whereas honor is the sole condition Antonio insists on in the friendship bond, in the commercial bond, Shylock insists on the sole condition of "an equal pound" of Antonio's flesh. And whereas love and affection are consideration for Antonio's pledge, for Shylock the repayment of the indebtedness is really no consideration at all. He tells Jessica that he would prefer Antonio's flesh to twenty times the sum owed (3.2.286). The real consideration is the forfeiture of the "carrion flesh" (4.1.41), and when questioned what such a thing is good for, Shylock's answer has the same voracious property: "To bait fish withal: if it will feed nothing else, it will feed my revenge" (3.1.47–48).[22] This hatred underlies his "craving" for the law (4.1.203), and leaves little doubt that Shylock seeks not the rule of law, but its penalties; only they will serve his ends.

Another distinction between the friendship bond and the commercial bond is their respective dispositions toward generation. For Shylock's commercial bond, generation is tied to the material. He uses the story of Laban's sheep, whose "work of generation" Jacob multiplied, in order to make a point about "advantage" (usury). Countering that it was the hand of heaven that worked Jacob's blessing, not his thrift, Antonio objects to Shylock's depiction:

Antonio:	Was this inserted to make interest good?
	Or is your gold and silver ewes and rams?
Shylock:	I cannot tell, I make it breed as fast,— (1.3.89–91)

Material worth, which acts as a "means" to afford the ultimate ends of love and life in the friendship bond, is elevated to the "meaning" of the ultimate end in Shylock's world. Seeing the natural world in terms of its effects on material wealth is a perspective repeated in Launcelot's jokes: "This making of Christians will raise the price of hogs" (3.5.21); and in Salerio's jests:

> My wind cooling my broth
> Would blow me to an ague when I thought
> What harm a wind too great might do at sea.
> (1.1.22–24)

But when asked if financial risks do not cause his sadness, Antonio's answer is no; his "means" are not his ends. He makes a clear distinction between friendship and the unnatural "generation" that results from usury:

> When did friendship take
> *A breed for barren metal* of his friend?
> But lend it rather to thine enemy,
> Who, if he break, thou mayst with better face
> Exact the penalty. (1.3.128–32; emphasis added)[23]

And in the commercial bond, that penalty is death.

Like the images of natural generation that correspond to those in the sonnets, this unnatural generation also corresponds to the scoldings of the Young Man. There, the sonneteer associates "interest" (usury) with barrenness, futility, and death: "Profitless *usurer*, why dost thou use / So great a sum of sums yet *canst not live?*" (Sonnet 4, lines 7–8; emphasis added); and

> That use is not forbidden *usury*
> Which happies those that pay the willing loan;
> . . . .
> Be not self-willed, for thou art much too fair
> To be *death's conquest* and make worms thine heir.
> (Sonnet 6, lines 5–6, 13–14; emphasis added)

The "self-will" the sonneteer speaks of is added to the group of images—appetite, appearances, and unnatural generation in the form of usury.[24] Contrasted to Portia's father's "will," which acts as a kind of reason, curbing appetites and fostering right judgment, Shylock uses the commercial bond to feed his irascible appetite and satisfy his "self-will."

Without question, the consideration for the commerical bond provides one of the richest moments in all of literature, and it is one legal history can help enlarge. Shylock asks Antonio to enter a "single" bond, apparently meaning an agreement without condition.[25] However, what actually transpires in the play is most productively looked at through the history of instruments known as "penal bonds with conditional defeasance." Under these arrangements, a crippling amount could be exacted from a forfeitor who did not strictly meet—down to the letter of date, time, and manner—the requirements of the bond. Simpson provides an example:

> Let us take first what was called the common money bond. Suppose Hugo proposes to lend Robert 100 pounds. Robert will execute a bond in favor of Hugo for a larger sum, normally twice the sum lent, thus binding himself to pay Hugo 200 pounds on a fixed day; the bond will be made subject to a condition of defeasance, which provided that if he pays 100 pounds before the day the bond is to be void. This condition will normally be indorsed on (i.e. written on the back of) the bond. What is essentially the same technique could be employed in the case of a contract for the sale of land, or indeed in the case of any agreement where what was desired was the performance of some act, or the granting of some forbearance.[26]

No alteration was to be countenanced, despite the fact that the bondholder would suffer no real loss in consequence. Parole evidence was forbidden to vary the terms, so when Shylock refuses to have "speaking" against his bond, he is not only well within his legal rights, but is consistent in his refusal to hear any but his own voice. Earlier, he has "shut up the ears" to his house against the music of the revelers.

The courts eventually relaxed this legalistic perspective. In Elizabeth I's reign, petitions for relief from unreasonable hardships were commonly granted.[27] But Shakespeare does not let things develop that way. One reason may be that penal bonds with conditional defeasance were arguably usurious. There was a debate on their nature in this respect. One school held that they were in fact licit, since the bondholder was not assured of getting anything back but his agreed-upon sum. Nor was the higher payment, however stiff, forced on the debtor.[28] These arguments notwithstanding, the penal bond could truly act as mask for usury. If the bondholder actually lent less money than recited in the bond, then the holder could rely on the fact that parole evidence could not contradict what the bond said. In the event of prompt payment, he got his usurious sum, and in the event of forfeiture, he got his penal sum.

It is this aspect of the penal bond that makes the debate at the heart of act 2 between Antonio and Shylock of greater interest, especially when viewed in light of the moral judgment of usury as, in Aristotelian/Thomistic terms, "dead" and "barren." For Shylock takes his "merry" single bond and, as a champion of usury, turns it into a disguise for a deadly, exacting penalty.[29]

Illustrated here, the dimensions of contractual consideration—specifically, its sometimes dubious nature—is a prominent subject for ethical reflection. The consideration is sometimes referred to as the "motivating cause," that is, that which "moves" each party to perform.[30] Since in Elizabethan England the ethical analysis of commercial propriety was generally that of Aristotle, as developed by Aquinas and then Hooker, it can be used to tease out problems modernity faces in the commercial setting.

There are four Aristotelian "causes," or ends, associated with any enterprise—for example, the making of a chair:

Material (that out of which the chair is made):	Wood and nails
Efficient (that by which the chair is made):	Carpenter
Formal (that into which the chair is made):	The form of a chair
Final (that for the sake of which the chair is made):	To be sat in

But in the commercial enterprise, the maker and his final cause are separated. Instead of making a chair for himself—to be used for his comfort and ease—the final cause becomes monetary: to be sold for a profit. That is, the final cause becomes the consideration or value he expects to get under the contract. The step from the "unnaturalness" of usury (i.e., money making money, dissociated from any edifying labor) and the sale of one's labor, or its fruits, is not really a very large one. Under this paradigm, the commercial contract, bound by valuable consideration, shows it is worthy of a sharp eye when examined for its relationship to the "natural."

Of course, arguments can be made: in one way, the chair can still be considered the final end of the maker, rather than the cash it will eventually be sold for. In another way, other important societal ends, such as the communal interdependence that commerce maintains, must be taken into account. And then there is the practical concern: human beings cannot possibly fulfill all of their own needs and must trade and barter for them as a consequence. But the dimension is worth noting, and from the Thomistic ideal, worth watching carefully, lest the bargain's final cause degenerate into materialism, rather than the inherent good of the material thing. There is much beneath Shylock and Antonio's "merry bond."

Having distinguished the natures—and orientations toward "nature"—of the two bonds in the play, it is clear that by act 4, once again the alignment away from nature has the whip hand. Attempts to reason with Shylock about his bond are fruitless in the face of his will's demands. Antonio resigns himself to his fate, and asks the others to do so:

> Therefore (I do beseech you)
> Make no moe offers, use no farther means,
> But with all brief and plain conveniency
> Let me have judgment and the Jew his will. (4.1.80–83)

The bond marrying society with death is stronger than that marrying it with life. As at similar points in the other plays, something must be done to transform the meaning of the commercial bond to reorient events toward life. Bassanio suggests one way to accomplish this, and it involves a certain disposition toward the law. Pleading that he would pay Antonio's debt with his own life, Bassanio asks the disguised Portia:

> Wrest once the law to your authority
> To do a great right, do a little wrong,
> And curb this cruel devil of his will. (4.1.211–13)

The suggestion, understandable in light of the circumstances, nevertheless reveals that Shylock is not alone in desiring to "hook the law" to his appetite. Here, he and Bassanio resemble each other—in method, if not in intention. For Bassanio suggests that Portia set aside the law, reason's curb on the appetite, in order to frustrate Shylock's will. In effect, Bassanio asks her to hook the law to *his* will, rather than to Shylock's. This she cannot do; the law's stability is necessary for Venetian society, and errors could "rush into the state" through such a precedent (4.1.214–18). It is true that Shylock abuses legal process by perverting a social institution to personal aims, aims of hate and vengeance at that. In his hands, the law actually becomes a weapon, and lies as an object to his will: "I crave the law" (4.1.202). Moreover, he revels in his aboveboard manipulation: "What judgment shall I dread, doing no wrong?" (4.1.89). It is also true that this is merely a mask for his real intentions—a "tainted plea" seasoned with "a gracious voice, obscuring the show of evil" (3.2.75–77). As in the other plays, dissemblance is a successful tactic.

But Shylock's perversion of the law cannot be met with another perversion. To do so would make the law ultimately irrelevant, only a point of departure.[31] Shylock knows this, and threatens with real consequences: "If you deny it [the forfeit], let the danger light / Upon your charter and your city's freedom" (4.1.38–40); and "[i]f you deny me, then fie upon your law / There is no force in the decrees of Venice" (4.1.101–2). Bassanio's suggestion is an error that Portia must correct, and one that signals other lessons he must learn.

However, the method that Bassanio suggests is the one by which Portia ultimately triumphs: he wants her to answer Shylock "in kind." This Portia does, but within the law, rather than outside it, transforming the meaning of the bond rather than discarding it altogether. Like the Duke in *Measure for Measure* and Helena in *All's Well That Ends Well*, she does this by means of a trick, the terms of which have been introduced by her opponent. But before analyzing Portia's trick, and as a means of fully understanding its nature, it will be helpful to analyze what lies behind Shylock's own trick.

The freedom of the friendship bond, and the productivity it brings about, is overshadowed by the "strange nature" of the enslaving commercial bond.[32] In fact, enslavement has been Shylock's conception of their bond all along; his first words in the play are of having Antonio "bound" for three months, an idea that he enjoys repeating—"Antonio bound" (1.3.4; 9–8). In his defense, he compares the merchant to Venetian slaves, who labor under their master's burdens without the inequity being challenged (4.1.89–97).

Shylock's trick is all the more powerful because he denies any obligation to explain himself. The matter, like the law, is subject to his caprice:

> You'll ask me, why I rather choose to have
> A weight of carrion flesh than to receive
> Three thousand ducats: I'll not answer that!
> But say it is my *humour*: is it answer'd?
> What if my house be troubled with a rat,
> and I be pleased to give ten thousand ducats

> To have it baned? What, are you answered yet?
> *. . . So can I give no reason, nor I will not.* (4.1.40–46; 59;
> emphasis added)

In essence, the nature of the Venetians' pleas are for Shylock to be "reasonable"; and in answer, he is just that. He responds to them with "reasons," but ones that are in service to his will. Of course, this is a deceptive method. He claims that he asks for only his due under the bond, but what Shylock truly wants is his will. And the horrible strength of his case reveals that, even within institutions based on reason and meant for the public good, the individual will can have its way, using reason as a disguise. If it succeeds, then the instruments of the law, and the law itself, can be redirected toward the will's use. Without submission of the will to the reason, reason is used to accomplish the will, and the very instruments meant to curb the will can be employed to a distorted advantage. This usurping of a public good for a private end is characteristic of Shylock's method, and it is best demonstrated in the way he uses language.

In Belmont, the law curbs the appetite, and the friendship bond provides for the integrated union of the marriage contract, which in turn breeds a natural generation and an exponential expansion of the community. This is all accomplished by Bassanio's proper choice: matching Portia's father's "will" in a shared meaning of true worth. Shylock, on the other hand, uses the law in a capricious fashion, employing it to satisfy his own will. He does not employ shared meanings, only private ones. In his use, words are fashioned to individual purposes. The law becomes a matter of "cleverness," a means to trick one's enemies. Having Antonio "bound" means abjection to him, not merely an expression of obligation. His meaning of "kindness" (1.3.139) is "in kind," while it means largesse and generosity to Bassanio and Antonio (1.3.138; 174). He assures the two that the "merry bond" is made in "sport" and meant to "buy" Antonio's "favour" (1.3.164), dispelling Bassanio's fears. In truth, Shylock uses the bond to "purchase" Antonio's "semblance" (favor). There is further evidence in the way he assesses the merchant:

Shylock: Antonio is a good man.

Bassanio: Have you heard any imputation to the contrary?

Shylock: Oh, no, no, no, no: my meaning in saying he is a good
                man is to have you understand me that he is sufficient [of
                adequate worth]. (1.3.11–15)

The way he uses words is part of a plan to "catch him [Antonio] once upon the hip" (1.3.41), a wrestling metaphor that, to Shylock, signifies advantage, itself synonymous with "interest."

Shylock's tactics with language are the same as Launcelot's, although the clown's sport has less dire implications. While at Belmont, Launcelot intentionally takes commonly understood words and turns them to his private purposes. The exasperated Lorenzo comments that "every fool can *play* upon a *word*" (3.5.40; emphasis added) and asks Launcelot to "understand a *plain* man in his *plain meaning*" (3.5.51–52; emphasis added). Lorenzo could just as easily be speaking of Shylock when he says:

> O dear discretion, *how his words are suited!*
> The fool hath planted in his memory
> An army of good *words*; and I do know
> A many fools, that stand in better place,
> Garnish'd like him, that for a *tricksy word*
> *Defy the matter*: (3.5.59–64; emphasis added)

"Tricksy" words, ornaments to shifty meanings, "defy matter." Once again, the *res/verba* problem so prevalent in the problem plays arises. Not only is reality impossible when they are separated, but society is impossible as well, since "tricksy" words defy shared meaning. The disorder and death threatened in *Troilus and Cressida* by "[w]ords, words, mere words, no matter from the heart," threatens yet.[33] For without the coupling of words and matter, providing integrity, neither words nor matter have meaning.

Indulging in this process is not exclusive to Shylock, which Shakespeare underscores in the "trial" of conscience that Launcelot conducts in act 2, scene 2. The "servant" goes to elaborate lengths—using bold legal metaphors—to make his "conscience *serve* his will."[34] Through this rationalizing process he convinces himself to leave Shylock's employ for Bassanio's, his main objective being the appetitive objects of more and better food and a fancy livery. This comic scene acts as a lens through which Shylock's more serious rationalizing can be seen. Together with Shylock's famous speech on Jewish/Christian similarity, Portia's pregnant inquiry—"Which is the Merchant here? and which the Jew?"—and Bassanio and Gratiano's desire to hook the law to their own wills, Launcelot's trial of conscience draws yet another likeness between Christian and Jew.

Also, Shylock's literal, legalistic approach to words has a material quality. He insists on only those words that physically appear in the commercial bond;

those words and those words only. He will "tear the bond," as he is bid, only "when it is paid according to the tenor" (4.1.231), and will only allow what "*appeareth* due upon the bond":

> So says the bond, doth it not, noble judge:
> 'Nearest his heart'— those are the *very* words.
> (4.1.249–50; emphasis added)

His first mention of the bargain requires an "equal" [exact] measure (1.3.145), and the scales he brings to weigh the flesh grimly underscore the materiality of his meanings (4.1.251–52).

This approach to words leaves no room for a larger concept, no semantic extension that would incorporate any meaning but his own; certainly none large enough to contain, as has often been pointed out, the law's spirit. His particularity, a literalist interpretation taken to a deadly extreme, makes justice equal only to the sum of its parts. For Shylock, the bond has terms: an amount certain, due on a date certain, and at a place certain. If the particular terms are in default, the penalty follows, with no need for further consideration of the law's intent. Justice is no greater than, and need concern itself with no more than, the *particular* terms of the bond.

Here, although similar in their rigid approach to justice, Shylock differs from Angelo in *Measure for Measure*. For Angelo takes a *general* approach to the law, one that neglects what justice consists of in favor of its title. He is called "Justice" incarnate,[35] and seeks that "name" without concerning himself with the particulars of Claudio's case. Indeed, Angelo often comforts himself that no one would believe his accusers, since no one would believe such things of a "Justice."[36] So while Angelo's justice becomes the empty form, Shylock's justice becomes a checklist of particular offenses. Although true justice is more than the sum of its parts, as *The Merchant of Venice* shows, it *is* made up of its parts, as *Measure for Measure* shows. This understanding results in the judicial integrity, what judges must do and be, soliloquized in Duke Vincentio's credo.[37]

With this understanding of the nature of Shylock's trick, the brilliance of Portia's own trick can be demonstrated more clearly. The power of her accomplishments in transforming the meaning of the bond lies in the fact that she does so on Shylock's terms. Just as Vincentio in *Measure for Measure* uses Angelo's dissemblance to overcome the deputy, and just as Ulysses in *Troilus and Cressida* uses Achilles's vanity to the same effect, Portia uses Shylock's penchant for particular, literalist interpretations against him. Indeed, part of her method involves allowing him as much leeway as he wants, committing himself to a position he will later regret.

Portia introduces something greater than what the bond requires before proceeding to judgment, the quality of mercy. But Shylock will not be compelled to it (4.1.179), and as is his way, he immediately turns her idealistic concept, "deeds of mercy," into one of retribution: "My deeds upon my head" (4.1.203). Their positions established, the struggle begins over the largeness, or smallness, of the bond itself.[38]

Having awarded him the forfeit, Portia picks up on his precision:

Portia:	—are there balance here to weigh The flesh?
Shylock:	I have them ready. (4.1.251–52)

This allows Shylock to define the scope of the bond's interpretation; once more, it is rigidly fixed. In answer, Portia again tries to introduce a certain "largeness" to the meaning of the bond. Shylock's answer not only betrays his motives, but also further betrays him of, and commits him to, his chosen method:

Portia:	Have by some surgeon, Shylock, on your charge To stop his wounds, lest he do bleed to death.
Shylock:	Is it so nominated in the bond?
Portia:	It is not so expressed, but what of that? 'Twere good you do so much for charity.
Shylock:	I cannot find it. 'Tis not in the bond. (4.1.253–58)

As this passage illustrates, Shylock accepts only the narrowest context, which satisfies his will. Any context large enough to be within the realm of "charity," which would amount to life for Antonio, he disallows.

Linguist Charles J. Fillmore explains that words are associated with "semantic frames," a context of related words that goes along with them. The meaning of *cut*, for example, implies not only a wound in flesh, but a knife (or some other instrument), a cutter, blood, pain, and so forth. Shared meaning, which makes communication between speakers possible, requires some cooperation as to what that context is: how broad or how narrow.[39] Shylock is intentionally uncooperative, and Portia follows suit, to his regret. Once Shylock commits himself to so small a frame, Portia proceeds "in kind." He would bait a fishhook with Antonio's flesh (3.1.47), and now Portia baits Shylock with his own meaning of the same:

> Tarry a little. There is something else.
> This bond doth give thee here no jot of blood.
> The words expressly are 'a pound of flesh.'
> But in the cutting it, if thou dost shed
> One drop of Christian blood, thy lands and goods
> Are by the laws of Venice confiscate
> Unto the state of Venice. (4.1.301–7)

With the frame now shrunk to a point beyond his advantage—indeed, to his disadvantage—Shylock wants to enlarge it: "I take this offer, then. Pay the bond thrice / And let the Christian go" (4.1.313-14). But Portia will not allow him to change the terms he has defined himself. Earlier, he has even disallowed options that would fulfill the terms of the bond, at twice its face value, in favor of what he truly wants, the "penalty and forfeit" (4.1.85-87; 203).

The enlarging and shrinking of semantic frames in *The Merchant of Venice* brings out another similarity with *Measure for Measure*, and another similarity between the literalists, Shylock and Angelo. For in the Viennese play, once he has gotten Isabella to admit she is a frail woman, the image of a corrupt man, Angelo "arrests" her words (2.4.133). With meanings where he wants them, Angelo will allow her to go no further, insisting she submit to his will. Isabella pleads for an enlargement—a return to "the former language"—one whose topic is charity and mercy (2.4.139). But Angelo will not have it, and like Shylock, must be tricked into a place where he stands in danger of the "smallness" of his own meanings.

In a comment on the law's appeal to dramatists, Richard Posner says that technicalities, such as Portia's, are based in the general fear that law can "trick" us. It also explains why readers should not bring high hopes of finding "legal meat," which is often sacrificed for dramatic exigencies.[40] Still, many legal critics have not been able to resist criticizing the play on legal grounds, and have offered "better" cases for both Antonio and Shylock.[41] But this loses sight of the fact that the trial is, in the end, part of a play that has its own dramatic purposes. Portia will not let Shylock have what he has refused, and takes his own precision to its absurd conclusion:

> If thou tak'st more
> Or less than a *just* pound, be it but so much

> As makes it light or heavy in the *substance*
> Or the division of the twentieth part
> Of one poor scruple—nay, if the scale do turn
> But in the estimation of a hair
> Thou diest, and all thy goods are confiscate.
> (4.1.322–28; emphasis added)

Now Shylock lies "within the danger" of his own meaning. The consequences of his will have turned upon him, indiscriminately, and have made him his own victim.

Robert Grams Hunter's "triangles"[42] can be applied here in the same way they are in *Measure for Measure*: Antonio, in keeping with his sacrificial role, stands in the place of Bassanio as *humanum genus*. Shylock acts as the prosecutor, and Portia as both the Virgin/Advocate and Judge. Because of Portia's trick, Shylock's role is conflated with Antonio's. He stays in the position of Antonio's prosecutor, but also joins Antonio as *humanum genus*. Whatever he exacts upon Antonio he will also exact upon himself. This situation underscores not only the old law, *lex talionis*—an eye for an eye and measure for measure—but also the changed relationship that the new law brings—one in which each man stands in the place of his brother and must recognize him as such.

At this point in the play, Shylock's defeat is assured. As in *Measure for Measure*, where the Duke transforms Angelo's deadly meanings of *execute* and *satisfy* in order to "perform" the old contract, Portia has transformed the meanings of a bond bent on death in order to achieve freedom for Antonio. Shylock, who uses law and language as a snare for his enemies, the private meaning of which he only reveals when they are caught, is now faced with the consequences of his method.

But Portia's work is not complete. Although defeated, Shylock wants to retain what he has brought with him: "Give me my principal and let me go" (4.1.332). Like so many words with double meanings in the play, his principal signifies both his material wealth and his old standards, the ones with which he has approached and ordered his life, his "principle." It is at this point—just as Gratiano gloats of having Shylock "on the hip," and reveals himself to be no more charitable, or less vengeful than Shylock—that a further transformation takes place, which denies the old man the possibility of his old "principal."

As it comes to pass, Shylock cannot retain both his "principle" and his life. Just as Antonio could not fulfill his bond, Portia has created a situation in which Shylock's deeds cannot match his promise. No matter what the words of the bond require, it is impossible to cut the flesh without the blood, or to be so exact that a hair will not turn the scale. This re-creates Antonio's failure under the bond, but with Shylock in his place. The failure is so complete that only an interpretation under a new principle, one with a context large enough to include charity, will save the forfeiture. So it is in law; so it is in society. And with regard to society, Portia accomplishes much.

Under the Venetian "Alien" Statute, inchoate crimes against a citizen are punished in Venice. It is an opposite position to that championed by Isabella in *Measure for Measure*. But as in the Venetian play, the price of death is not exacted, and the punishment actually takes the form of a provision for Shylock's child. Half of his estate will go to his intended victim, half to the state, and "the offender's life lies in the mercy / Of the Duke only, 'gainst all other voice" (4.1.351–52). The only way around the statute is mercy, which the Duke grants as to his life, but not as to his property.

Shylock's objections are strongest here; it is not his child that is the "prop" of his life, as is the case for Old Gobbo (2.2.64), nor is it, most surprisingly, his faith—but rather his "means," which he would rather keep than his life (4.1.371). But Antonio is willing to relent in part, based on Shylock meeting a condition corresponding to life, not death. Shylock must no longer be an "alien," but come within the Christian fold (4.1.383). His acceptance is a change from the old principle to the new. And with that acceptance, the community again grows at an exponential rate, just as it did at Belmont when Bassanio "hazarded" all he had. Half of the funds, Antonio—the other agent of nature in the play—allows to Shylock, provided that he leaves all to Lorenzo and Jessica at his death (4.1.378–80). This amounts to a life estate, an estate limited by the life of the recipient and inherited by whomever the testator designates. The designees are Lorenzo and Jessica, who receive "deeds of gift" after the life estate. These "deeds of gift," says Lorenzo, are like "manna in the way of starved people" (5.1.293). The other half of the funds Antonio will hold in "use" for Jessica and Lorenzo.[43]

Of course, Shylock's treatment is as controversial as it is famous. It caused A. D. Moody to contend that the play was ironic, satirizing the Christians for their lack of mercy.[44] In line with this ironic reading, recent scholarship often finds Portia, like Duke Vincentio in *Measure for Measure*, to be a negative figure.[45] But these interpretations stem from an exclusive emphasis on Shylock's eloquence and predicament that overlooks evidence of both Shylock's intrigues and Portia's generosity. Troublesome as the conversion is to modern sensibilities, that Shylock and Antonio come to share the same faith is consistent with the transformation of their bond. The commercial bond of slavery and death becomes a new bond between them, granting life to both Shylock and his child. It also relates them further in a play filled with references to equality, not only in wealth, but also in similarities that even Shylock notes between Christians and Jews (3.1.52–60). That the title to the play offers an alternative, "*The Merchant of Venice* or *The Jew of Venice*," strengthens this equality, which also surfaces in Portia's inability to distinguish between the men when she first enters the courtroom: "Which is the merchant here, and which the Jew?" (4.1.170).[46]

The play's ending returns to the marriage contract. After the threat of the commercial bond has ended, the "performance" of the marriages, which it interrupted, can take place. Interestingly, the characters argue over the meaning of a bond again, but this time it is the marriage bond, and the significance of the contractual token, the marriage ring. The ring, of course, means both fidelity and integrity, and a full appreciation of that fact is the final lesson of the play. At the end of the trial scene in act 4, the disguised Portia tells Bassanio he must "know her" the next time they meet (4.1.415), revealing that lessons are yet to be learned, and that truth must constantly be maintained.

Upon their marriages, Bassanio and Gratiano vowed never to part with their rings:

> but when this ring
> Parts from this finger, then parts life from hence,—
> O, then be bold to say Bassanio's dead! (3.2.183–85)[47]

But the rings are won from them when their disguised wives seek tokens for their service. When the wives pretend to discover this for the first time, the play's themes are revisited. In the ensuing debate, true value is at issue: "What talk you of the posy or the value? / You swore to me" (5.1.151–52); as is the *res/verba* disjunction and the void created when words have no meaning:

> Even so void is your false heart of truth.
> By heaven, I will ne'er come in your bed
> Until I see the ring! (5.1.189–91).[48]

Portia alludes to the duplicity of appearances: "In both my eyes he doubly sees himself / In each eye one" (5.1.244–45), and describes the combination that the rings should have already effected between the husbands and their wives:

> You were to blame, I must be plain with you.
> To part so slightly with your wife's first gift,

> A thing *stuck on with oaths* upon your finger,
> And *so riveted with faith unto your flesh*. (5.1.166-69; emphasis added)

She equates the ring with the ceremony itself—"the thing held as a ceremony" (5.1.206)—not merely with a *part* of the ceremony. Like the law, the union is not separable from its oaths or its parts, but is a full integration of both. It is not to be worn lightly, nor bargained with lightly.[49]

Of course, they are arguing about the same person's worth, Portia's, and at bottom they are in agreement as to her value. But the dilemma serves to repeat that of Antonio and Shylock, both laboring under a commitment to a law, and yet falling short in its observance. Again, an intercessor must step forward, here in the form of Antonio. He once more becomes "surety" for Antonio, but this time for a bond conditioned on love:

Antonio:	*I once did lend my body for his wealth;* Which, but for him that had your husband's ring, Had quite miscarried: I dare be *bound again*, My soul upon the forfeit, that your lord Will never more *break faith* advisedly.
Portia:	Then you shall be his *surety*. Give him this And bid him keep it better than the other. (5.1.249-55; emphasis added)

That it is "faith" promised here returns that virtue to the prominence it played in the venturing scene. And as in the trial scene, it is mercy in the face of forfeiture that steps in to restore the union, a response that lies within the context of charity. The community also grows larger with the inclusion of Antonio, who says Portia has given him "life and living" (5.1.286).

Finally, the characters return to speaking of the impending consummation of their union in metaphors that are both legal and generative:

Portia:	It is almost morning, And yet I am sure you are not *satisfied* Of these events at full. Let us go in, And charge us there upon *inter'gatories* [questions posed to a witness], And we will answer all things faithfully.

Gratiano: Let it be so: the first *inter'gatory*
That my Nerissa shall be sworn on is,
Whether till the next night she had rather stay,
Or go to bed now, being two hours to day:
But were the day come, I should wish it dark,
That I were couching with the doctor's clerk.
Well, while I live, I'll fear no other thing
So sore, as keeping safe Nerissa's ring. (5.1.295–307; emphasis added)

In the final ring scene the parties share an understanding of true worth. This harkens back to the shared meanings of worth so important in the casket scene, where the winner had to choose Portia's father's meaning—to "match" in a marriage of minds. A shared understanding of worth, goals, and the proper means of achieving them results in such a match. Under this union, society can flourish. Without this union, there is an asocial, adversarial relationship established by unshared meanings; existence can be as dangerous as the trial scene depicts.

The orientation toward life finds expression in this last scene. As Lorenzo and Jessica discuss the "gilded" heaven and the harmony of the spheres, Portia and Nerissa return from Venice. They spot a candle glowing in the window, giving great light. "So shines a good deed in a naughty world" (5.1.91), remarks Portia. When Nerissa questions why they could not see it when the moon shone, Portia answers that the "greater glory" dims the less, making her point against the larger context; she elaborates with regard to the music they hear, which sounds sweeter in the night than it has by day: "Nothing is good, I see, without respect [context]" (5.1.97–99). Following the trial scene, in which the commercial bond falls outside the realm of charity and becomes the deciding factor, it seems this comment on "context" relates to the instruments of the law, as well; for they too require a context large enough to achieve the aims of life. Otherwise, they are small enough only to achieve the aims of bondage and death.

The many legal instruments in *The Merchant of Venice* illustrate the two perspectives on the law's capability. It is true that the friendship bond, Portia's father's will, and the marriage contract create restrictions and obligations. The law here sets perimeters; it acts as a "fence," as it were, to appetites. But the play also shows that the law can act as an ordering principle, serving meliorative ends; it can act as a "road," leading to generative goals for self and society. The commercial bond shows a third possibility, a perversion of the law—the law as "knife"—aimed toward a personal and destructive end.

Bloom and Jaffa suggest that the play shows laws in themselves as insufficient in ordering society: "They must be accompanied by good dispositions on the parts of those who live under them."[50] To analogize, the bonds in the play also must be accompanied by the good faith of the parties who employ them. As a general concept, positive law, that is, law made by human beings, is neutral here. The goal toward which the characters direct it, whether to exact revenge for personal satisfaction or to order life and provide for societal productivity, reveals something about the characters themselves. They must decide whether the law will fall "within the realm of charity." In *The Merchant of Venice*, owing to Portia's trick, the characters' good faith is ultimately triumphant.

Echoes of this same achievement, and of the achievements in the other plays, resound in *All's Well That Ends Well*, with particular emphasis on contractual performance. But there, Helena has a dual role, as both agent of nature and as party to an inchoate marriage contract.

CHAPTER 5

Lawful Title

Contractual Performance in
All's Well That Ends Well

The folkloristic elements of *All's Well That Ends Well* that W. W. Lawrence identifies as "the healing of the king" and the "fulfillment of the task,"[1] have accounted for some of its specific unpopularity.[2] But although there is a mixture of the realistic and the fairy-tale worlds, this quality exists in all of the dramas discussed here, and I consider it one of the groups' virtues. Their existing in two worlds, hanging between them, keeps the reader unsure if this is a fantastic, folklore-inspired world, or a realistic, psychologically complex one. This is particularly appropriate for plays in which metaphysical concerns—the disjunction and reunification of appearance and reality—are so prominent.

In his introduction to the Arden edition of *All's Well That Ends Well*, G. K. Hunter says that critics have failed to apply a context by which the virtues of the play may be appreciated.[3] Perhaps viewing the play with an eye toward the metaphysical issues involved, and the way that those issues are resolved via contractual performance, can provide one such context. With this perspective, the play can be understood in light of the works discussed so far. *All's Well That Ends Well* resembles all three of these plays. With its underlying tension between the relationships of war, lust, and love, it is most like *Troilus and Cressida*; in its quests, riddles, pilgrimages, and bargains, it is most like *The Merchant of Venice*; and in its theme of a contract left inchoate due to questions of true worth, it is most like the "pre-contract" in *Measure for Measure*. But in *All's Well That Ends Well*, the way that contracts are brought to performance, and the particular purposes for doing so, finds its most complete expression. In this play, the fulfillment of the contract is made one with its purpose.

Like *Measure for Measure*, which opens on a society gone "athwart," and like *Troilus and Cressida*, which starts with wars of blood and lust, *All's Well That Ends Well* begins with a bleak picture. Death has won both the Old Count of Rossillion, Bertram's father, and Gerard de Narbonne, Helena's father. It is also in the process of claiming the King of France, whose physicians have abandoned him to "the losing of hope by time" (1.1.15). Moreover, the Countess of Rossillion is about to lose her son and heir, Bertram, to a position at court. She expresses her loss in an image epitomizing the tone at the play's start: "In delivering my son from me, I bury a second husband" (1.1.1–2).

The idea of birth and immediate death resonates with similar associations regarding "fancy" in *The Merchant of Venice*, which dies in its cradle,[4] and the empty vows of *Troilus and Cressida*, which are strangled even as they come into being.[5] These losses testify to the insubstantiality of the things in question and, like the loss expressed by the Countess, evoke an atmosphere of frustration and lost purpose that must be counteracted. In *All's Well That Ends Well*, this dilemma arises at the outset, and is not fully overcome until the play's end.

Bertram, the young heir to the duchy, sets out to find honor at the Parisian court. He is "unseasoned," says his mother, and she solicits counsel from the old retainer LaFew (1.1.63). Her own advice at their parting seems as much intended to address Bertram's present deficiencies as to mold his future conduct:

> *Succeed* thy father
> In manners as in shape. Thy *blood* and *virtue*
> *Contend for empire in thee*, and thy goodness
> Share with thy birthright! (1.1.57–60; emphasis added)

Quite the opposite of his son, the Old Count's integrity—the union of his "manners" and his "shape"—are a standard for true worth in the play. The honor that flows from that worth does so rightfully. The King describes the man:

> So like a courtier, contempt nor bitterness
> Were in his pride or sharpness; if they were
> His equal had awak'd them, and his honour,
> Clock to itself, knew the true minute when
> Exception bid him speak, and at this time
> His tongue obeyed his hand. Who were below him

> He us'd as creatures of another place,
> And bow'd his eminent top to their low ranks,
> Making them proud of his humility,
> In their poor praise he humbled. Such a man
> Might be a copy to these younger times;
> Which, followed well, would demonstrate them now
> But goers-backward. (1.2.36–48)

The man's decorum, a "clock to itself," was manifest in his reserve and humility, which the King offers as a model for present-day youth. Moreover, Bertram's father did not "scatter" his words in people's ears, but "grafted them / To grow there and to bear" (1.2.54–55). As in the other problem plays, the image of integrity here revolves around nature: the Old Count's "plausive" words are fruitful, as opposed to the wasteful "scattering" of empty speech. The mere memory of the man's virtue is restorative: "It much repairs me / To talk of your good father," says the dying King (1.2.30–31). The influence of the honorable Old Count, whose deeds matched his words, extends beyond his death. In this way he is similar to Helena's father, a physician whose "skill was almost as great as his honesty" (1.1.17–18). Gerard de Narbonne's reputation for virtue precedes him with the King, and is so self-evident that Helena declines the opportunity to praise him further: "Knowing him is enough" (2.1.103). To this pair, whose honor has a productive influence, the King himself is added: "whose worthiness would stir it [worth] up where it wanted" (1.1.8–9).

The integrity for which these men stand resounds with the theme of *res* and *verba* in the other plays—form matching substance, word matching deed—but with a different emphasis. In *All's Well That Ends Well*, the much-heralded integrity of the Old Count and the physician is spoken of in terms of *descent*, an uninterrupted legacy passing from father to child, and uniting past, present, and future. For example, along with the Countess' hopes that Bertram will succeed his father in integrity, the King hopes he will have inherited his father's "moral parts" (1.2.21). This concept of succession implies a perpetuation of integrity.

Because this idea is established before Helena's venture for the marriage contract in act 2, in which she hopes to "propagate" her "humble name" (2.1.196), a special importance attaches to it. Helena early laments that only her wishes have a "body" in them, "which might be felt" (1.1.177–78). The rest of the play has her rectifying this situation, as she works to incorporate her hopes and consign her integrity to yet another generation. Like Bertram,

Helena is charged to "hold the credit" of her father (1.1.75–76), a duty that she fulfills by all accounts. Honor in terms of testamentary inheritance is an idea that extends throughout the play. When the action moves to Florence, Diana is told "the honour of a maid is her name; and no legacy is so rich as honesty" (3.5.11–13).

But despite the productive honor of the older generation, there is a problem with the succession of virtue in France. The times are said to be retrograde, "going backward" in degeneration (1.2.48). The young lords lack the very thing that made the Old Count and Gerard de Narbonne paradigms of integrity, an honor born of virtue. Instead, their

> apprehensive senses
> All but new things disdain; whose judgments are
> Mere fathers of their garments; whose constancies
> Expire before their fashions. (1.2.60–63)

Inconstancy—disdain for all but the most recent fashions—is characteristic of the French youth. It also testifies to an alignment of the "times" with appearance rather than substance. Like their counterparts in the other problem plays, those who labor under this misperception both undervalue the worthy and overvalue the worthless. Their skewed perspective makes them contemptible to the King:

> They may jest
> Till their own scorn return to them unnoted
> Ere they can hide their levity in honour. (1.2.33–35)[6]

Nevertheless, these are the "times" in France. The repositories of true honor have died, and the legacies left to their successors have been squandered.

But this is so only in part, most notably in the case of Bertram. In the case of Helena, the legacy of honor has made a successful transmission, and through her its generative capacity can find a proper channel. The two differ in the degree to which they observe their duties to posterity. A comparison will highlight the difference.

Both Helena and Bertram, having lost their fathers, are bequeathed to others: Bertram to the King, who will be "a father" (1.1.7) to his ward, and hold his "son no dearer" (1.2.76). Likewise, Helena is bequeathed to the Countess, who becomes her second mother (1.1.35). These wardship arrangements had their own historical rights and duties. Traditionally, the guardian swore an oath:

> [C]orporally touching the Holy Gospels that they would in good faith keep and preserve the goods and persons of the said children during the time of their administration to the use and profit of the children and [that they] would do whatever was beneficial for the said children and would avoid what was harmful.[7]

R. H. Helmholz cautions against a dismissal of such oaths, in that the child had a right of action against a misappropriating guardian who did not live up to his pledge.[8]

But while Bertram has succeeded only to his father's "face" (1.2.19), his "shape," but not his "manners"—Helena has inherited all of her father's gifts:

> [H]er dispositions she inherits, which makes fair gifts fairer; for where an unclean mind carries virtuous qualities, there commendations go with pity; they are virtues and traitors too; in her they are the better for their simpleness: she derives her honesty and achieves her goodness. (1.1.37–42)

Helena is a combination of the legacy she has inherited and the goodness she maintains. Using a transactional metaphor that will figure into the play's themes of rights and duties, the Countess speaks of Helena's "lawful title" to love, envisioned as an estate. Her claim is based simply on her essence (principal), without other "advantage" (interest):

> She herself, without other *advantage*, may *lawfully*
> make *title* to as much love as she finds; there is
> more owing her than is paid; and more shall be paid
> her than she'll demand. (1.3.98–101; emphasis added)

Although she is owed much, Helena does not demand all that is rightfully hers. Here the superfluous nature of advantage is analogous to "additions" (in the sense of "titles"), which are castigated later in the play. As the King points out, titles *may* arise from substance, just as honors *should* flow from virtue. But if that is not the case, titles are merely false accretions, yet another sign of the retrograde times. "Advantage" recurs when the honorable Helena banters with the dishonorable Parolles. She accuses him of being born under the sign of Mars, when it was "retrograde":

Parolles:	Why think you so?
Helena:	You go so much backward when you fight.
Parolles:	That's for advantage.
Helena:	So is running away, when fear proposes the safety. (1.1.194–98)

Here, advantage is synonymous with self-interest, a malady affecting Parolles and Bertram.

Many of the early scenes are spent establishing Helena's true worth, a prerequisite to a valid marriage contract. It is not only the Countess who appreciates the virtue the girl has maintained; the King and LaFew testify to her worth as well. She amazes LaFew in her "sex, her years, profession / Wisdom and constancy" (2.1.82–83). And when Helena stakes her life on her word—again, "wagering" herself in sacrifice for marriage—the King accepts her wager precisely because she possesses all that is worthy:

> Thy life is dear; for all that life can rate
> Worth name of life in thee hath estimate:
> Youth, beauty, wisdom, courage, all
> That happiness and prime can happy call. (2.1.178–81)

The King's testament invalidates Bertram's later objection to his marriage on the basis that Helena is "unworthy" (i.e., too low a match). It also calls into question his judgment. As Robert Grams Hunter says, a wedding night with a beautiful, sexually attractive, honorable girl who has won the king's favor should prove—to a reasonable young man—"not the final indignity, but the first consolation."[9] All but Bertram and Parolles see her value, revealing the two's blindness.

In fact, Bertram comes "to woo honour, not to wed it," a pattern of behavior forbidden by the King (2.1.15). This bridal image resonates with his mistreatment of Helena and his attempt to debase Diana. In fact, his conception of honor echoes the alignment of war, sex, and commodity that permeate *Troilus and Cressida*. Disappointed that the King has forbidden him from battle due to his youth and inexperience, Bertram laments that he will have to remain at court: "Till honour be *bought* up and no sword worn / But one to dance with! By heaven, I'll steal away!" (2.1.32–33; emphasis added). With this misunderstanding of how honor is gained, he eventually barters away his heirloom,[10] even though it is "an honour 'longing to our house, / Bequeathed down from many ancestors" (4.2.42–43), in order to fulfill his lust for Diana:

> Here, take my ring:
> My house, mine honour, yea my life be thine,
> And I'll be bid by thee. (4.2.51–53)

In another similarity with the Trojan play, Bertram exhibits his immaturity by allying himself with a "go-between" (5.3.253) and a "ring-carrier" (3.5.91). The foppish Parolles, the personification of the empty words and fashion-mad inconstancy deplored by the King, is Bertram's choice for emulation. And even Parolles testifies to Bertram's inconstancy; when Bertram decides to flee from marriage to the wars, Parolles wonders "Will this *capriccio* [whim] hold in thee? art sure?" (2.3.289).

Still, Helena's imagination "carries no favour in it but Bertram's" (1.1.81), and she proves her devotion by never wavering in her affections. She is aware of the problem that the difference in their estates poses, but after an exchange with Parolles she acquires a more determined outlook. Significantly, their conversation involves playful banter using war and sex as metaphors. Helena asks how women may "barricado" against men who "assail" their virginity (1.1.111). Parolles denies the wisdom of a defense, based on virginity's unnaturalness:

> It is not politic in the commonwealth of nature to preserve virginity. Loss of virginity is rational increase and there was never virgin got till virginity was first lost. That you were made of is mettle to make virgins. Virginity, by being once lost, may be ten times found; by being ever kept it is ever lost. 'Tis too cold a companion. Away with 't! (1.1.123–30)

He continues his rail by pitting virginity against nature: it is a "breeder of mites," "full of self-love," which "murders" and "consumes" itself (1.1.133–40), consistent with the unnatural self-consumption so prominent in *The Merchant of Venice*. He then turns to language of productive commerce, also used in that play: "within the year it [sex] will make itself two, which is a goodly increase; and the principal itself not much the worse. Away with 't [virginity]!" (1.1.144–46).

The generative purposes of nature here find an unlikely spokesman, especially since Parolles will later pander for both himself and Bertram. And as the aim of lust is not generation, but satisfaction, its effects are just as opposed to fruitfulness as those of a resolved virginity.[11] By contrast, Parolles's jokes articulate a naturalness in productivity that is normative for the play. Helena agrees in principle, and the rest of their conversation is merely a debate over the proper context for "goodly increase." In response to how a virgin might lose her virginity "to her own liking," Parolles gives her the answer, albeit unintentionally: "Let me see. *Marry*, ill, to like him that ne'er it likes" (1.1.148).[12] When he leaves, Helena rallies her hopes with an appeal to nature—"The mightiest space in fortune nature brings / To join like likes, and kiss like native things" (1.1.218–19)—and hopes to prove her worth by striving to show her "merit" (1.1.223). The juncture of nature and generation finds further support in the next scene, in which the clown LaVatch begs permission to marry, "because service [with sexual implications] is no heritage." He doubts God will bless him until he has children, "for they say bairns are blessings" (1.3.21–24).

At this point, the play begins to resemble *The Merchant of Venice*, in both the contract achieved in the love quest and in the bonds and sureties that eventually enable it. Like Bassanio's bond with Antonio, which wins him the means to Belmont, Helena reveals her love to the Countess, which wins her the means to Paris. Helena has her leave and love, "Means and attendants, and my loving greetings / To those of mine in court" (1.3.246-48).[13] There, like Bassanio's "hazarding" for Portia's hand at the price of perpetual bachelorhood, Helena will "venture" for Bassanio's hand by curing the King at the cost of her "well-lost life" (1.3.242). And as Bassanio's solving of Portia's father's riddle will free Portia from her entombment in the lead "cere-cloth," and thereby win her hand, so Helena's working of the cure will free the King—Bertram's "father"—from death, and thereby win Bertram's hand. All this is accomplished by virtue of Helena's life-giving legacy, the "prescriptions of rare proved effects" that her father has willed her (1.3.216–17). Helena's father's will provides for his daughter, just as Portia's father's will does for his own. The gift inherited by Helena—her "third eye"—has a productive, life-giving function.

The similarities with *The Merchant of Venice* continue in the way LaFew, Helena, and the King bargain over the terms of the cure. They use not only the language of land transactions in their exchanges, but also the generative imagery associated with marriage. These words often carry double meanings, associating concepts in a way that deepens the significance of both. LaFew, coming from Rossillion with Helena, kneels before the King and asks for his pardon:

King: I'll *fee* thee to stand up.

LaFew [rising]:   Then here's a man stands that has *brought his pardon*. I
                    would you had kneeled, my lord, to ask me mercy, And
                    that at my bidding you could so stand up. (2.1.61–64;
                    emphasis added)

"Bringing" a pardon in "fee," that is, an unencumbered right to absolute possession, carries both the idea of paying for the pardon, as well as the absolute
nature of the pardon so purchased.[14] There is a cost, but the cost accomplishes
all. LaFew's desire to do the same for the King—that is, in "fee"—also implies
the largesse in his wishes for the sovereign. And the cure he brings shows him
to be as good in deed as he is in intention. He states the life-giving qualities
of the medicine in terms of nature, with a subtext of sexual imagery:

> I have seen a medicine
> That's able to breathe life into a stone,
> Quicken a rock, and make you dance canary
> With sprightly fire and motion; whose simple touch
> Is powerful to araise King Pepin, nay,
> To give great Charlemagne a pen in's hand
> And write to her a love-line. (2.1.71–77)

This is Helena's cure, revitalizing ("breathe life into a stone") the manhood
of a failing King.

LaFew then secures the King's permission to know Helena's business. He
leaves the two alone with a joke alluding to Troilus and Cressida: "I am Cressid's uncle / That dare leave two together" (2.1.96–97). But unlike Pandarus,
LaFew brings his friend a girl capable of restoring life, rather than perpetuating loss. The revitalizing nature of Helena's legacy carries over into her own
characterization—her father's "dearest issue" is stored in her "triple eye / Safer
than mine own two, more dear" (2.1.106–7). Finally, she picks up the language
of bargain, "tendering" her cure to him in "all bound humbleness": both an
expression of her compassion, and an offer to enter into an agreement.

But the despairing King portrays the offer in a different light. He will not

> So stain our judgment or *corrupt our hope*
> To *prostitute* our past-cure malady
> To empirics, or to dissever so

> Our great self and our *credit*, to esteem
> A senseless help, when help past sense we deem.
>   (2.1.119-23; emphasis added)

Having noted that his are times in which judgments go by garments, and words are scattered without substance, he is wary of claims at miracle working. His opinion has a foundation in experience: "What at full I know, thou know'st no part / I knowing all my peril, thou no art" (2.1.133-34). To him, claims of cure are illegitimate, and their characterization as such is fitting. In a meeting of the minds, Helena does not object. In fact, she agrees with his premise, and seeks to diffuse his fears of disingenuousness by claiming integrity:

> I am not an impostor that proclaim
> Myself against the level of mine aim;
> But know I think, and think I know most sure
> My art is not past power, nor you past cure.
>   (2.1.154-57)

Rather than deny the King's portrayal of empty promises as corrupt and harlotrous, she endorses it. If Helena is not as good as her word, she ventures the

> Tax of impudence,
> A strumpet's boldness, a divulged shame
> Traduced by odious ballads: my maiden's name
> Sear'd otherwise; nay worse of worst, extended
> With vildest torture, let my life be ended. (2.1.169-73)

For further assurance, she returns to the bargain, promising her performance in certain terms of time and manner. She lists the consequences of breach, then demands consideration from the King in return:

Helena: If I break time, or flinch in *property*
           Of what I spoke, unpitied let me die,
           And well deserved; Not helping, death's my *fee*;
           But if I help, what do you promise me?

King: *Make thy demand.*

Helena: But will you make it *even?*

King:	Ay, by my sceptre and my hopes of heaven.

Helena:	Then shalt thou *give me with thy kingly hand* What husband in thy power I will command. Exempted be from me the arrogance To choose from forth the royal blood of France *My low and humble name to propagate* With any branch or image of thy state; But such a one, thy vassal, whom I know Is free for me to ask, thee to bestow.

King:	*Here is my hand*; the *premises observ'd*, Thy will by my *performance* shall be serv'd;

· ·

If thou proceed
As high as word, *my deed shall match thy deed.*
(2.1.186–202; 208–9; emphasis added)

The language works on two levels: first, on the level of transaction, striking a deal by creating obligations and duties; second, on the level of nature, implying essences, causes, and effects. Helena's "property" is both her side of the bargain, from which she will not "flinch," and the qualities or attributes that she claims for herself. The "fee" she demands is both her payment, as well as the absolute, unencumbered right to what she will be "entitled." The "deed" that will match Helena's is not only the act of performance, but full ownership to what has been bargained for. Also, layers of images—nature, land sale, and marriage—that surround Mariana's "just title" to Angelo, "performed" under a "pre-contract" that is to be "sown" and "tilled," recur here in *All's Well That Ends Well*. From "observing the premises" (satisfying the contractual conditions), the King will perform Helena's will, which is to propagate her name with a man of her choosing.[15]

Also, the similarity of imagery in *The Merchant of Venice* between the bond and the marriage contract, especially Shylock's "merry" bond with Antonio, recurs in this scene. For the agreement makes the King Helena's "surety," as both of them claim in the rest of the play (4.4.3; 5.3.83–87), and borrows the elements that solidify the marriage contract: Helena and the King join hands and make vows; Helena promises not to "break" time, similar to "breaking faith"; the consideration between them is mutual—"even"; and the agreement satisfactorily "performed." Also, integrity is demanded— her "words" must "match" her "deeds (2.1.208–9) (just as Bassanio's meaning must "match" Portia's father's); and integrity is promised in return—the King's "deed" will "match" Helena's own. (2.1.209). Finally, Helena agrees to restore the King's "sound parts" before "twice the horses of the sun shall bring / Their fiery coacher his diurnal *ring*" (2.1.160–61; emphasis added). Like the friendship bond that enables the marriage contract in *The Merchant of Venice*, the suretyship here enables Helena's contract with Bertram.

In a final parallel between the play and *The Merchant of Venice*, Helena must convince the King to trust in her cure, rather than despair at dire appearances. The King's physicians have abandoned hope, and he will not "corrupt" that virtue by believing in Helena's cure. His despair is so complete he "must not hear" Helena's news (2.1.144), denying her "art" and its "labours," which "can never ransom nature from her inaidable estate" (2.1.117–18; 132). Like Bassanio, who by reason chooses the "hazard" of faith over appearances, Helena convinces the King to have hope even when things look bleakest:

> Oft expectation fails and most oft there
> Where most it promises, and oft it hits
> Where hope is coldest and despair most fits.
>   (2.1.141–43)

and

> Inspired merit so by breath is barr'd:
> It is not so with Him that all things knows
> As 'tis with us that square our guess by shows.
>   (2.1.147–49)

That the appearance of the gold and silver caskets is attractive, while the prospects of the King's recovery are not, is a distinction without a difference. In both plays the appearances are deceptive, and require a willingness to trust in something larger than the naked eye reveals.

Helena's achievement is a special one, marking her as an "earthly actor" who shows "heavenly effects" (2.3.22–23). With regard to her charge, the Countess remarks, "Adoption strives with nature, and choice breeds / A native slip to us from foreign seeds" (1.3.140–41). This grafting image applies to both the lowborn Helena's marriage to the highborn Bertram and to the fruitfulness that results when art strives with nature. This is similar to the "art/ nature" exchange between Perdita and Polixenes in *The Winter's Tale*. Helena's success both proves that art can work with nature to produce life and achieves the grafting of her "foreign seed" to the "native slip." This last accomplishment has even further generative results at the play's end.

Having satisfied her part of their agreement, and acquired the King as her surety thereby, all that remains is for the King to perform his own obligation. "Lustier" than a dolphin (2.3.26), he leads Helena into court by the hand, in wedding fashion. He reaffirms his duty, and her right, to the bachelors whose "father's voice" he possesses (2.3.54):

> And with this healthful hand whose banished sense
> Thou has repealed, a second time receive
> The confirmation of my promised gift
> Which but attends thy naming. (2.3.48–51)

Some have objected that Helena is not a worthy match for Bertram, and that his objections are due to his fear of "disparagement."[16] However, the King shows that Helena is a worthy match in the true sense of honor, and even makes her monetary and honorific "worth" equal to Bertram's, which takes away the grounds for the objection. Also, Helena is careful to ask only for a vassal, one the King could freely give her. This suggests Shakespeare was aware of wardship's parameters.[17]

Under their bargain, Helena has the right to "name" the "deed" that will match her "deed" for the King (2.1.209). In effect, she is about to "claim lawful title" to love, as the Countess has said she is due (1.3.99). Helena proceeds to overlook the courtiers, referred to collectively as this "youthful *parcel*," which means both a small part, and a portion of land (2.3.52; emphasis added). With the aim to make a son out of her blood (2.3.97), she takes Bertram by the hand (2.3.102–4). But Bertram, who LaFew has discovered to be "an ass" (2.3.100), refuses the gift. Here the play differs from *The Merchant of Venice* and more resembles *Measure for Measure*. For Bertram wants to make his own choice, by "the help of mine own eyes" (2.3.108).

While it is a common objection that Bertram has no choice in his spouse,[18] several points argue against this reading. First, Bertram's unchecked choice would be at odds with reason. Helena's attractiveness and vitality are even reflected in her name, one she shares with St. Helena, the mother of Constantine, who recovered Holy Land shrines and was patroness of the parish in which Shakespeare lived while in London. Bertram, on the other hand, is drawn as a character who is too immature, and whose vision is too skewed, to choose properly for himself. Bertram, like Angelo in *Measure for Measure*, is at this point unappreciative of what is truly worthy. It is doubtful that his personal choice would better this deficiency in character.

Second, Bertram *is* in fact free to refuse; he simply must bear the consequences. If he insists on his freedom—that he is not obliged to marry Helena on the King's account—the King is likewise under no obligation to provide for Bertram any longer. But the young lord will not bear these consequences, as principle is not his strong point. After his charade, he finances his trip to the wars with his wedding gift. It seems fear of the King is not so strong to dissuade Bertram from gross disobedience, nor is the King's anger so lasting that he will not forgive the young Count in spite of it.

In addition to choosing with his eyes, he will "never hope to know why I should marry her" (2.3.110). Choosing appearances and discounting hope are the very errors Helena has counseled the King against, to his great benefit. But Bertram knows Helena's breeding; he says disdain will corrupt him forever if he marries her. In short, like Angelo in *Measure for Measure*, Bertram questions the worth of his consideration under the contract. And like Angelo, he is not only wrong in his appraisal, but also compounds his mistake by frustrating the contract's performance.

Before Bertram mistakenly undervalues the worthy Helena, the King attempts to change the youth's perspective, that is, to convince him what he receives is truly honorable despite appearances. The King himself has just learned to trust in the hope offered by the physician's daughter, despite the grim forecasts of his doctors. He has good proof of "what she has done" for him (2.3.108):

> 'Tis only title thou disdain'st in her, the which
> I can build up
>
> . . . .
>
>   If she be
> All that is virtuous, save what thou dislik'st—
> A poor physician's daughter—thou dislik'st
> Of virtue for the name. (2.3.117–18; 121–24)

His lesson, aimed at Bertram, is a particular application of the speech he has made regarding the young lords in general, those who judge by appearances and know nothing of honor but its garments. Honor's substance, says the King, is born of virtue and needs no title—"great additions"—to prove its authenticity; rather, it proves itself in deeds. This is reminiscent of the Countess' claim that Helena herself is worthy of the lawful title of love, in principle alone, with no need for further "advantage" (1.3.98). As is often the case when the characters want to convey the meaning of reality, the King resorts to language of title, with double entendre: "The property [both "quality" and "estate"] by what it is should go, not by the "title" [both "name" and "legal ownership"]. And again, images of nature and legacy are related to honor:

> She is young, wise, fair;
> In these to nature she's *immediate heir,*
> And these *breed honour;* That is honour's scorn,
> Which challenges itself as *honour's born*
> And is not like the sire. (2.3.131–35; emphasis added)

The legitimacy images applied to what the King had feared were Helena's empty promises recur here with respect to empty honor. This further delineates the difference between Bertram's position and Helena's. Helena, like the constant Mariana and the virtuous Cordelia, is worthy in and of herself. The King sums up the consideration passing to Bertram under the contract: "Virtue and she is her own dower" (2.3.143-44). The additions of "honour"—in the sense of "titles," as Bertram understands it—and "wealth" are superfluous in the King's eyes. *They* are the accretions added to the principal, not the principal itself.

Like the picture drawn in relation to the Old Count and Gerard de Narbonne, Helena is the vessel of honor. And it is with Helena as his referent that the King draws honor's fullest portrait: it is born of virtue, shows through deeds, and is bred from nature. It is also thoroughly productive. It is as likely to occur in the lowborn as in the highborn, whose mingled blood would lack distinction (2.3.118-20). Against true honor lie its opposites, familiar from the other plays: a deceit that travels under a guise, appeals to the appetite, breeds sickness and disease (e.g., "dropsied honour" [2.3.128], "sick desires" [4.2.35]) and results in a divorce of word from matter. Helena is the repository of honor, and the direct opposite of the empty repository of *Troilus and Cressida,* the similarly named Helen of Troy.

The King points out that he can as easily take Bertram's "honour"—again, in the facile sense Bertram understands—as he can bestow such "honour" on Helena, adding his own worth to Helena's side (2.3.150-51). But despite the King's urging Bertram to throw off his "disdain" (2.3.159), a feat Helena was able to accomplish with regard to the King himself, Bertram chooses wrongly. Rather than submit his will to the King's good judgment, he submits his "fancy" to the King's "eyes" (2.3.167-68), revealing a misunderstanding of which faculties are used when making a wise choice.[19] And even this unwilling submission comes only after the threat of disinheritance; the King warns that chaos of outer darkness will be the end result of Bertram's youth and ignorance (2.3.162–66). Rather than suffer it, he pretends to comply, taking Helena by the hand. The King expresses contentment at what appears to be a contract's formation:

> Good fortune and the favour of the king ·
> Smile upon this *contract*; whose ceremony
> Shall seem expedient on the now-born brief,
> *And be perform'd tonight*. The solemn feast
> Shall more attend upon the coming space,
> Expecting absent friends. As thou lov'st her
> Thy love's to me religious; else, does err. (2.3.177–83;
>   emphasis added)

The King, as Helena's surety, includes himself in the match—"as thou lovest her, Thy love's to me religious"—an act similar to the conflation of community achieved by the bond and contract in *The Merchant of Venice*. He also adds sacrality to the match, which LaFew picks up on when he styles Bertram's change of position a "recantation" (2.3.186). In light of this, Bertram's disobedience is all the more egregious.[20]

An intermediate scene involves the "exposure" of his ally, Parolles, to further illustrate the depth of Bertram's mistake. After one or two meals with him, LaFew discovers the fop's foolish nature, hidden beneath "scarfs and bannerets" (2.3.202). He contrasts his own integrity with that of the insubstantial Parolles: "I write 'Man' to which title age cannot bring thee" (2.3.197–98). Parolles can only reply, privately, "Good, very good, let it be *concealed* awhile" (2.3.261–62). Later, LaVatch also uncovers Parolles nature: "[T]o say nothing, to do nothing, to know nothing, and to have nothing, is to be a great part of your title; which is within a very little of nothing" (2.4.23–26). When Parolles says he's "found" Lavatch to be a fool, Lavatch retorts, "Did you find me in yourself, sir, or were you taught to find me? . . . The search, sir, was profitable, and much fool may you find in you, even to the world's pleasure and the increase of laughter" (2.4.32–35). Following Parolles's disgrace, Bertram reenters, newly married, and consults his ally. His plans have already taken shape: "Although before the solemn priest I have sworn, I will not bed her" (2.3.265–66); and "Oh my Parolles, they have married me. I'll to the Tuscan wars and never bed her" (2.3.268–69). Parolles counsels disdain of marriage and home—"A young man married is a man that's marred" (2.3.294)—and a preference for war:

> To th' wars, my boy, to th' wars!
> He wears his honour in a box unseen,
> That hugs his kicky-wicky here at home,
> Spending his manly marrow in her arms,
> Which should sustain the bound and high curvet
> Of Mars's fiery steed. To other regions!
> France is a stable; we that dwell in't jades;
> Therefore, to the war! (2.3.274–81)

Bertram responds:

> It shall be so. I'll send her to my house
>
> . . . .
>
> Wars is no strife
> To the dark house and the detested wife. (2.3.282–87)

And instead of a marital union resulting in the pain of separation, Bertram bemoans a separation from his fellow soldiers: "I grow to you, and our parting is a tortured body" (2.1.36–37). Later, the King will marvel that wives are such "monsters" to Bertram that he must flee from them (5.3.154–56). In *All's Well That Ends Well*, the youth come to the war as a "physic," after surfeiting on their ease (3.1.18–19). And in an image combining war, birth, and death, the confrontation serves as "[a] *nursery* to our gentry, who are sick / For breathing and exploit" (1.2.15–17; emphasis added). This is the same perverse pairing of marital and generative imagery seen in the "war contract" of *Troilus and Cressida*. Of course, Helena offers a different cure for sickness, intent on life. She will later work a change regarding this preference.

Bertram plots to frustrate the contract by keeping it perpetually unrealized: a marriage with no substance beneath the form. Having pocketed the King's wedding gift to furnish him to the wars, Bertram reveals his plan:

> I have writ my letters, casketed my treasure
> Given orders for our horses; and tonight,
> When I should take *possession* of the bride,
> End ere I do begin. (2.5.23–26)

Just as the King and Countess use the language of transaction and title to convey essential meanings, Bertram uses it to illustrate his nonperformance. A man lawfully entitled takes possession of his estate, a right that Bertram will permanently forego. In some circumstances, failure to "enter" an estate within a year of transfer could result in the loss of title altogether. Possession was thought to "perfect" or "solidify" the transfer, says S. E. Thorne, which explains why Henry de Bracton can speak of a nonpossessory transferee as *in* seisin, "but not yet seised." [21]

This is Bertram's plan, and he carries it out despite acknowledging that the "time" for performance is "due" to Helena under the "great prerogative and rite of love" (2.4.39–40). Here again, the "rite" carries the double meaning of ceremony and entitlement ("right"), both accruing to Helena. But envisioning his wife as a "clog," a restraint that binds him to his contract, he denies her what she is owed by refusing possession.

In a complaint that exemplifies a path she must later take, Helena begs for a parting kiss:

> I am not worthy of the wealth I owe,
> Nor dare I say 'tis mine—and yet it is;
> But, like a timorous thief, most fain would steal
> What law does vouch mine own. (2.5.79–82)

Instead, Bertram sends her home without observing even this most innocent form of affection. His words substantiate the King's doubts about youth and about the "retrograde" times. After he sends Helena away, Bertram throws a taunt in her direction:

> Go thou toward home, where I will never come
> Whilst I can shake my sword or hear the drum.
> Away, and for our flight. (2.5.90–92)

Again, the foolishness of his choice is underscored in the next scene by the clown Lavatch, who abandons his plans to marry after a turn at court. He says the brains of his "Cupid" have been knocked out by the trip, and he has no "mind to Isbel now" (3.2.12–16). But even Lavatch sees the cowardly cast of Bertram's flight:

Lavatch: Your son will not be killed so soon as I thought he
                  would.

Countess: Why should he be kill'd?

Lavatch: So say I , madam—if he run away, as I hear he does. The danger is in standing to't [marriage; sex]; that's the loss of men, though it be the getting of children. (3.2.36–41)

As the Countess later predicts, Bertram's sword will never win the amount of honor he loses by abandoning Helena (3.2.93–94).

Critics from Dr. Johnson forward have criticized Helena for loving an unworthy man.[22] But as Linda Anderson has pointed out, few object that Bassanio is unworthy of Portia, or Orlando of Rosalind.[23] Orsino could be added to the list, as Viola loves him from the outset, despite his irrational love for the state of love. Florizel, when compared to the captivating Perdita, also fares poorly, as does Posthumus when compared to Imogen, or Ferdinand to Miranda. Few comic heroes in Shakespeare match the comic heroines. It may be the disparity in charm is never so pronounced as between Bertram and Helena, but such a disparity is not rare.

In choosing the insubstantial "honor" won by titles, Bertram confirms his alliance with all that is set against nature, reality, and life. He becomes an "unbridled boy" (3.2.26) who scoffs at the good King's command in order to become the "general of the horse" in the Florentine cavalry (3.3.1). He is also the "lover of thy [Mars's] drum, hater of love" (3.3.11), revealing both a perverted enthrallment with the hollow symbol of war and an unnatural aversion to the essential state of devotion. However nobly he fights, his domestic cowardice is a debit to his character.

Similar to the plot development of the other plays, at this point the forces of death have apparently triumphed. But Helena's virtues include not only constancy, but hope. It was by this theological virtue that she succeeded in bringing life to the King, and with it she will rise to Bertram's challenge, inspiring her troops with its aid:

Diana: I am yours,
Upon your will to suffer.

Helena: Yet, I pray you;
But with the word: "the time will bring on summer"—
When briers shall have leaves as well as thorns,
And be as sweet as sharp. (4.4.28–33)

and

> All's well that ends well yet;
> Though time seem so adverse and means unfit.
>   (5.1.25–26)

Just as the Duke deals with Angelo, and Portia deals with Shylock, Helena encourages perseverance until she can deal with Bertram on his own terms. And like those protagonists, she transforms the meaning of those terms by virtue of her contract. Because of this, the terms of the defiance and the aims they are meant to frustrate have heightened importance.

Bertam has frustrated the marriage contract by leaving it inchoate. Although it has been duly and publicly celebrated, it is a marriage in name only. He abandons Helena without taking possession of her, and flaunts the perpetuity of their unrealized marriage in a letter to his mother: "I have sent you a daughter-in-law: she hath recovered the King, and undone me. I have wedded her, not bedded her, and sworn to make the 'not' eternal" (3.2.19–21); and in a letter to Helena:

> When thou canst get the ring upon my finger, which
> never shall come off, and show me a child begotten
> of thy body that I am father to, then call me
> husband; but in such a "then" I write a "never."
>   (3.2.56–60)

Most bitter of all is his final defiance of Helena: "Till I have no wife I have nothing in France" (3.2.73). But like Portia, Helena will make "something" come of "nothing," a metaphysical transformation that will be achieved by contractual performance.

The challenges meant to frustrate performance act as "conditions subsequent" to the contract, requiring certain acts be fulfilled before the instrument can be termed fully executed. Conditions of a certain nature could be placed on a contract, so that the marriage amounted to a contingency until the conditions were accomplished. In medieval times, a classification scheme helped canonists make a determination of what contractual conditions were valid, and prevented marriage from forming immediately, and what conditions were invalid. Helmholz relates the 1351 case of *Roll v. Bullock*, in which the plaintiff sought to upset a man's second marriage because he had promised: "If I taken any woman as my wife, I will take you."[24] Other cases involved contingencies on parental consent being given: "If my father agrees, I take you as my wife"; and on conception of a child: "If I conceive a child by you this night."[25]

The difference is that these are all conditions precedent to the marriage's formation, not *subsequent* to its ceremony, as is the case in Bertram and Helena's contract. Bertram's conditions, like the conditions precedent in *The Merchant of Venice*, do revolve around the proving of worth: Bertram is disdainful of Helena's value, and denies her contractual fulfillment until she can "prove" herself, a requirement he repeats at play's end:

> If you shall *prove*
> This ring was ever hers, you shall as easy
> Prove that I husbanded her bed in Florence,
> Where yet she never was. (5.3.124–27; emphasis added)

Bertram's conditions are illegitimate, as the contract did not anticipate them. It deserves execution on its face.[26] But as is often said in the play, Helena is owed more than she is paid, and gives more than she demands. It is characteristic of her to meet conditions she need not fulfill in order to prove her love.

Like Shylock, who betrays his murderous motives by the smallness of his meanings, Bertram betrays his aversion to reality by his vows to make the "not" eternal. By denying the consequences of a marriage, he effectively denies life. But the specificity of his challenge will work to hoist him on his own petard. For his terms have made Helena's task clear: she will take his meaning—the "not" eternal—and transform it into an eternal "knot," that is, take his denial and turn it into affirmation. In this, she is like Portia, who turns a slave "bond" into a "bond" of community, and like Duke Vincentio, who turns an "execution" into a "performance." The deadly orientation will be rectified, and integrity will follow absence.

Helena will accomplish the task by the vital powers that she has inherited: the "third eye" that has saved the King will save Bertram. She must take on a disguise, perform a trick by use of a double, and become a "pilgrim" (3.5.30), like Bassanio, in order to satisfy the conditions. That the pilgrimage to prove her worth by deeds is to St. James (3.4.4), whose epistle includes the maxim "faith without works is dead," is especially appropriate under the circumstances.

Throughout the play, Bertram's foolish alliance with Parolles testifies to his bad choices; what befalls Parolles is a bellwether of what will befall Bertram. When the Dumaines conspire to expose Parolles, they hope Bertram will benefit by the example:

> I would gladly have him [Bertram] see
> his company anatomiz'd, that he might take a *measure*

> of his own judgments, wherein so curiously he had
> set this counterfeit. (4.3.30–34; emphasis added)

Parolles, whose vacuousness is established by his being called a "bubble" (3.6.5) and a "light nut" without a kernel (2.5.43), is sent after a drum lost in battle. To prompt Parolles's self-betrayal, the Dumaines capture and blindfold him, pretending to be foreign enemies. Denying him the use of his eyes, which penetrate no further than appearances, the men speak an incomprehensible language: "[S]peak what terrible language you will: though you understand it not yourselves, *no matter*; for we must not seem to understand him" (4.1.2–5; emphasis added). Here again, words that do not match meanings trap the dissembler.

Terrified, Parolles betrays his army at the same time he betrays his opinion of Bertram: "a dangerous and lascivious boy, who is a whale to virginity, and devours up all the fry it finds" (4.3.212–13). Further, he says Bertram does not pay what he owes (4.3.218). And in an accidental indictment of the young lord's integrity, he uses language revolving around the law, entitlement, and, most tellingly, inheritance:

> Sir, for a cardecue he [Dumaine] will sell the *fee-simple*
> of his salvation, the *inheritance* of it; and *cut th'*
> *entail from all remainders*, and a *perpetual*
> *succession for it perpetually.* (4.3.269–72; emphasis
> added)

What is slanderous of Dumaine is applicable to Bertram, who has just bartered away his family's "honour," the ring that has passed from "son to son" for generations (3.7.24). In effect, his actions have worked to "cut the entail" (limit the line of inheritance)[27] from all "remainders" (those who would succeed to the limited estate)[28] forever ("perpetually").[29] This refers not only to the ring, but by leaving his marriage unconsummated, and showing a disdain for even the children born of lust, he also "cuts off" the line of succession itself. Significantly, upon arriving to witness Parolles's trial, Bertram brags of his recent conquest in the same transactional language: "By an abstract"—the written outline of property dimensions for the purposes of identifying it in the event of sale—he has effected his "main *parcels* of dispatch" (4.3.83–89; emphasis added), which include the bedding of his wife, unawares.

The irony of Bertram's comments at Parolles's exposure—calling the fop "a counterfeit module," who has deceived "me, like a double-meaning prophesier" (4.3.95–96)—is heightened by the fact that he has just left Diana's bed, darkened at her insistence. Like Parolles, he has been tricked, and in a way that transforms the nature of an act meant to satisfy his appetite. But Bertram's exposure awaits his return to France. There he will meet Parolles in his new role as a clown. For his part, Parolles is grateful at his unmasking. By virtue of it, he finds integrity. And from that integrity flows the possibility of life:

> Yet am I thankful: if my heart were great,
> 'Twould burst at this.
>
> . . . .
>
> Simply the thing I am
> Shall make me live.
>
> . . . .
>
> There's place and means for every man alive.
> I'll after them. (4.3.319–20; 322–23; 328–29)

As Parolles is Bertram's chosen pattern, the pattern of Parolles's exposure is similar to Bertram's own; for Bertram believes himself to be doing one thing, while in fact he is doing another. To his mind, he "fleshes his will" in the "spoil" of a girl's honor (4.3.15). Having given her "his monumental ring," he "thinks himself made in the unchaste composition" (4.3.16–18). The nature of his composition, and of the way in which Bertram thinks himself "made," further illustrates that it is his substance that is at stake. He considers himself composed and made by that which can only discredit him, the dishonor of a maiden and the winning of empty titles. The Dumaines lament this rebellion of the self: "And as in the common course of all treasons we still see them reveal themselves till they attain to their abhorr'd ends; so he that in this action contrives against his own nobility, in his proper stream o'erflows himself" (4.3.20–24). The mix of war, treason, and lust is here portrayed as the ultimate self-betrayal, working to destroy Bertram's nobility.

What has actually transpired is something quite different. Helena has learned that he wages war on Diana's honor in the "unlawful purpose" (3.5.69–73) and would "buy his will" with his legacy (3.7.27). She finds in Diana and her widowed mother allies of a different stripe, ones who pity the "hard bondage" of the wife of a detesting lord (3.5.64–65), and are aware that soldiers' promises and tokens are deceitful "engines of lust" (3.5.19). Helena reveals her identity secretly, but would not "lose the grounds" (both the basis of her argument and Bertram himself) she works on by revealing her identity further (3.7.3).

Still, the Widow worries over her own fallen, but still honorable, "estate." Like the Duke's assurances to Mariana in *Measure for Measure*, Helena must persuade her that the bed-trick will be no sin, since Helena has a lawful claim: Widow: "Now I see to the bottom of your purpose" / Helena: "You see it lawful then" (3.7.29–30). Having won her confidence, yet another bargain is struck: in exchange for Diana's assignment of her obligations to Bertram, Helena will provide a rich dowry for Diana's marriage. This parallels Antonio's assumption of Bassanio's debt in order to finance the youth's marriage, and the assignment of Isabella's obligations to Mariana in exchange for Claudio's life. In each case, the assignment of duties and assumption of obligations provides either for life or for a means to generation through marriage. And again, as in *Measure for Measure* and *The Merchant of Venice*, the deceit that the antagonist has practiced will be practiced upon him, but in order to achieve integrity, not in order to flesh the will:

Helena: Let us *assay our plot*; which, if it speed
                 Is wicked meaning in a *lawful deed*
                 And *lawful meaning* in a lawful act,
                 Where both not sin, and yet a sinful fact. (3.7.44–47; emphasis added)

The "deed" to Helena's "plot" is legitimate, although she must obtain it by trickery.[30]

The plot turns to specifics of time, place, and manner, as they are crucial to satisfying the conditions of Bertram's letter. Time and place will cohere with the lawful claim, working to execute the contract (3.7.37–38). Diana, "'ere she seems won," is to desire Bertram's ring, arrange a meeting, and then "deliver" Helena "to *fill the time*, herself [Diana] most chastely absent" (3.7.31–34). The empty midnight tryst to which Bertram's appetite is "dieted" (4.3.29) will then be transformed, as Helena fills the time with significance. The marriage in form only will acquire substance. As with *Measure for Measure*'s Angelo, this transformation will take place at midnight, as the hour turns from night to day.

At her assigned meeting, Diana tells the insistent Bertram that her mother did her duty toward her father, a duty that Bertram owes his wife (4.2.12–13). She says Bertram would simply have her "serve him," taking her roses and leaving her with the thorns of barrenness, an image of a fruitlessness (4.2.17–19). Finally, she informs Bertram, who cannot distinguish the authentic from the dissembling, that a multiplicity of oaths are not worth a single oath, vowed true

(4.2.23–25). This disjunction between words and deeds makes his many vows worthless, like contracts without the validating "seal":

> Therefore your oaths
> Are words and poor *conditions* but *unseal'd*. (4.2.29–30;
> emphasis added)

A seal could be grandly or commonly impressed, but it was essential to authenticity of the instrument.[31] The purpose of the bed-trick is to help Helena gain access to Bertram's bed, secure his ring, and conceive his son, a purpose that will, under Bertram's own conditions, validate their marriage contract. The child conceived by the trick will in effect "seal" a contract that has lain inchoate. Diana's image of the contractual seal, which leaves an impression or imprint, is similar to the images of man's own creation by God, and of the father's imprint on his child. The idea occurs in both *Measure for Measure*, with regard to Angelo's "forbidden stamps" (2.4.46), and in another play where the value of a marriage partner is debated, *A Midsummer Night's Dream*. Theseus warns Hermia she must obey her father's wishes to marry Demetrius:

> To you your father should be as a god,
> One that composed your beauties, yea, and one
> To whom you but as a form in *wax*,
> By him *imprinted*, and within his power
> To leave the figure or disfigure it. (1.1.47–52)[32]

After explaining her "honour" (chastity) to be a "ring" of equivalent value to Bertram's "honour" (legacy) (4.2.45–51)—a comparison lost on the young lord—she secures his ring in exchange for her own (4.2.55–66). Bertram's offenses are doubled here, as they extend beyond himself and into his posterity. But upon conquering the "maiden bed," he will receive another ring, one that, unbeknownst to Bertram, signifies the King's surety of Helena. Speaking as Helena's proxy, Diana tells him he has "won / A wife of me, though there my hope be done" (4.2.65–66).

Of course, Helena's hopes are indeed "done" in the satisfaction of the contract. For it is she who meets Bertram and consummates the marriage.[33] In this, she also satisfies Bertram's conditions to proving her worth by conceiving his child and winning his ring, the legacy of honor he had meant to squander in fulfillment of his lust. By Helena's agency, the act intended to flesh his "will" actually enfleshes his posterity. For in a bounty of graces to come, not only will Bertam receive the honorable Helena, but he will also retrieve the emblem of his legacy in the form of his ring, and the assurance of that legacy's succession in the person of his child.

But before this resolution can be achieved, Helena must prove the contract. And when Bertram comes to court, that contract is in grave jeopardy. Helena is thought dead, and Bertram is about to enter into another marriage with LaFew's daughter Maudlin (5.3.68).[34] In short, Bertram's characteristic duplicity is about to infringe upon rights that are exclusively Helena's. Her method of exposing Bertram exposes—to him and to all—the effects of that duplicity.[35] By running afoul of unity and integrity, the consequences are as threatening as the death that confronts Bertram.

Proof of Helena's rights converge upon the two rings. Their significance has already been changed, since they are now fused with marriage through the act of consummation. When the King, as Helena's surety, challenges Bertram's possession of the ring he has given her, he does so on the basis that Bertram has wrongfully dispossessed her of it:

> The ring was mine, and when I gave it Helen
> I bade her, if her fortunes ever stood
> Necessitated to help, that by this token
> I would relieve her. (5.3.83–86)

The King's inclusion in this contract, like Antonio's inclusion in that of Portia and Bassanio, implies the size of the community interested in, and under the impact of, the marriage. As the succession of his community comes under his protection, providing for it is his foremost concern (5.3.39–43). The pressing business of providing for posterity intensifies the importance of the marriage contract's purpose. More than Bertram and Helena are at stake, and therefore Bertram's barterings have larger implications than he knows.

This is a characteristic of all the plays discussed here. Society as a whole, not just the relationship between a particular man and woman, hangs in the balance. Threats against its perpetuation are more realistic in these plays than in the festive comedies, where the revels in the green world rectify a more lighthearted discord. In *All's Well That Ends Well*, societal death and desuetude must be overcome; in *Measure for Measure*, social and political corruption; and in *The Merchant of Venice*, the perversion of law itself. In the parody *Troilus and Cressida*, society loses a fight against the powers of the appetite and illusion. This larger perspective may go some way toward answering criticisms that the plays are not satisfactorily resolved. Although the communities include Angelo, Bertram, and Shylock (however unwillingly, in the latter case) at the end of the plays—socializing their asocial personalities—there is more at stake in these dramas than these characters' personal happiness. Societal health is restored by a reorientation toward generation, a feat accomplished via the legal instruments.

For most of the scene, the chaos Bertram has wrought flourishes. Ownership is confused: what was Helena's seems to have been taken from her: "Had you that craft to reave her / Of what should stead her most" (5.3.86–87); what was Diana's seems to have been denied: "He stole from Florence, taking no leave, and I follow him to his country for justice" (5.3.142–44). Bertram seems to have bartered away all legacies, his own and those of others, in service to his will. His mendacity only draws him in deeper. Parolles testifies Bertram loved as gentlemen love: "[H]e lov'd her, sir, and lov'd her not" (5.3.245). Bertram has no "deeds" to gain the King's friendship (5.3.182–83). Death threatens:

> Unless thou tell'st me where thou hadst this ring,
> Thou diest within this hour. (5.3.277–78)

Of course, Bertram cannot tell because he does not know. His deliverer possesses that knowledge, the "surety" (5.3.292) for the ring who will redeem both Bertram and Diana. Bertram's hope is resurrected when the "jeweler that owes the ring" is sent for: "Dead though she be she feels her young one kick" (5.3.290; 296). Helena appears, bearing all that had seemed lost, and redeeming all that had seemed wasted. Ring, writing, witnesses, and child testify to the validity of a claim she has won not once, but twice:

> O my good lord, when I was like this maid, [Diana]
> I found you wondrous kind. There is your ring;
> And, look you, here's your letter; this it says:
> *When from my finger you can get this ring*
> *And are by me with child, et cetera.* This is done;
> Will you be mine now you are doubly won? (5.3.303–8)

By performing the contract, she has transformed the meaning of the ring from death to life. After the contract is proved, the play ends anticipating the delivery of a child to Bertram, which signals unity and prospects for the future. This is an orientation wholly different from that at the play's beginning, where the metaphoric "delivery" of a child—Bertram himself—signals separation and death (1.1.1).

The ring also acts, as Diana says in Helena's behalf, as a "token to the future of our past deeds" (4.2.63). Here the performance of the contract speaks to the issue of time, correcting a disorder as to its observance. For while Bertram's lust-driven appetite concerns itself only with the present—a disposition that makes the time "retrograde"—the duly performed contract establishes rights and duties that encompass all facets of time. It can be called on at any point in the present to testify to obligations avowed in the past, made with regard to obligations owed in the future.

Several times the play's action seems to be done. For example, the King announces "All is whole" just as the contract and its parties are at their furthest point from resolution. (5.3.37). And even though Helena has put forth her proofs, Bertram must confirm their union. The disruption has caused a rift, a quasi state that challenges reality. Diana, speaking in Helena's behalf, explains the gravity of Bertram's unfaithfulness:

> If you shall marry
> You give away this hand and that is mine,
> You give away heaven's vows and those are mine,
> You give away myself which is known mine;
> For I by vow am so embodied yours
> That she which marries you must marry me,
> Either both or none. (5.3.168–74)

In a play in which substance and name are at odds, the unity of the two forms marital integrity. And until the "titled" Bertram claims her, the proven Helena says she is "but the shadow of a wife you see, / The name and not the thing" (5.3.301–2). Bertram declares that she is "both," then promises to love her awaiting the proof of her deeds (5.3.303; 310). In effect, Helena awaits Bertram's acceptance of her suit, just as the Epilogue—in a metadramatic turn that itself rests on the theme of debts, obligations, and marriage—says the players' "ends" await the acceptance of the audience, by the "*lending*" of their "*hands*," and the "*taking*" of "*our hearts*" (Epilogue 1–6; emphasis added).

Finally, the role that Helena takes vis-à-vis the contract is similar to that taken by Duke Vincentio, Portia, and Antonio—and to a certain extent, also by Portia's father, the Countess, the King, and the Widow. As agents, they make sure that the perverted and unrealized instruments are rectified and fulfilled.[36] Sometimes the agent acts for herself, as in the case of Helena, or for others, as in the case of the Duke, Antonio, Portia, and the rest. But the principals and parties to the instruments are not the sole beneficiaries. In fact, because the instruments in these plays concern marriage, fellowship, and life, the integrity they achieve ultimately serves the generative aims of nature. In providing for the union of *res* and *verba*, from the words of a bond to the particulars of a marriage, the instruments ensure a sustainable reality. Upon that reality, society can flourish, generating and perpetuating itself through marriage and fellowship. The consequence, as Duke Vincentio explains to Angelo, is a world in which nature is given "her due." The alternative is a disjunction in reality, a disorder resulting from deception and ending in death. It too has agents in the plays: Pandarus, the broker of the will, as well as Parolles, Ulysses, and the Viennese bawds.

With this understanding of nature's interest in the contract, Helena's accomplishments are all the more impressive. For in her bed-trick, the contract's performance is fused with its generative ends. This makes her agency in nature's behalf unique. The "getting" of both the ring and the child has a double effect, achieved in one act. The "sealing" of the contract is made one with its purpose, integrity and productivity are accomplished in the same deed. In place of fracture, Helena has provided wholeness, and the very ends of the marriage are achieved in its realization; the ends are "well" because they are, finally, "all."

CHAPTER 6

Nature's Double Name

Beyond the Problem Plays

In the plays discussed, unrealized contracts reflect and exacerbate a societal disjunction between *res* and *verba*. They compromise marriage, justice, and legacies for the future. When contractual deficiencies are rectified, societal integrity is restored. Nature can then flourish. *Measure for Measure* is, in many ways, the most complete realization of this idea, and has served as a pattern when looking at the other three plays.

In the Viennese society of *Measure for Measure*, appetitiveness and dissemblance characterize the life of the antagonist, Angelo, and also, to different degrees, the lives of the protagonists, Claudio and Isabella. People are not what they seem, and the institutions meant to provide order in their lives are no better. Justice is a charade; marriage is either formless, in the case of Claudio's true contract, or without substance, in the case of Angelo's precontract. This lack of integrity manifests itself in a world diseased and bawd-ridden on the one hand, cold and unproductive on the other hand. In such a world, life is threatened, and nature is slighted.

It is nature's agent, Duke Vincentio, who restores the integrity necessary for a reorientation. By means of a trick, which uses terms supplied by Angelo himself—*performance, satisfaction, execution*—the Duke transforms the meaning of the legal instrument. That transformation results in a full realization of the inchoate marriage contract, bringing together the elements of publicity, value, performance, and tokens. What would have been Angelo's secret act to satisfy his appetite, and Isabella's vain attempt to stop an execution, is transformed into the ratification of Angelo and Mariana's marriage contract, which redeems the many lives at stake. Angelo and Mariana are brought together to "perform" the "old contract," but on a more fundamental level, the substance of "marriage" is brought together with its name, providing an essential integrity. The Duke also assures that Claudio and Juliet's "true contract" is publicly formalized, thereby providing the missing element with its full realization as well. Rectifying the disjunction between seeming and being restores integrity. Nature is provided for in the process, and consequently, life and hope return to the Viennese community.

Although all elements of a fully realized marriage contract are present in all of the plays, each play emphasizes different aspects. Publicity of the marriage always plays a key role, and for an important reason. If the parties' intentions are honorable, there should be no need for secrecy; making the contract a public affair provides assurance of integrity. In *Measure for Measure*, the clandestine marriage of Claudio and Juliet causes problems because there is no public witness. The two must rely on their own, postfacto testimony to establish its existence, which proves inadequate. And no matter how honorable Claudio's intentions toward Juliet, that he speaks of "restraint" being appropriate for "immoderate use" calls into question his own belief regarding the "truth" of his contract. The private marriage can seem a ready-made excuse. This mask for lust is also exemplified by Bertram's desire for Diana in *All's Well That Ends Well*. The young Count furthers his dishonorable objectives with false promises and bartered legacies; once satisfied, he ends the relationship with lies and abandonment. That their private meeting has been transformed, and has acquired a different significance, only becomes apparent once Bertram's mendacity is exposed in a public forum.

The best illustration of privacy serving to mask lust is the secret, mock ceremony of *Troilus and Cressida*. In the Trojan play, the appetite has been given full rein. The private union of the couple never achieves a status more dignified than a sexual coupling, overseen by a panderer. The effects are profound. Sexual lust, and lust for empty honor, characterize both Greeks and Trojans, and reign at both ends of the drama.

Since such needs are often satisfied privately, they must pass under disguises. In fact, Angelo's lust and Shylock's hate pass under the form of the law itself. *The Merchant of Venice* best illustrates how the private use of a public good, the commercial law of bonds in this case, can threaten a society it is meant to protect. Portia's achievement partly lies in her revealing this fact to Shylock, by showing him the effects of meanings so small that they lie outside "the realm of charity." Like Angelo's, Shylock's experience reveals that the private pursuit of the appetite risks eventual self-destruction. As the plays warn in various ways, the appetite is always in danger of "eating up" itself.

The role of value is also central to the contracts and to the plays that feature them so prominently. But questions regarding value do not merely revolve around an ability to *perceive* value, for example, the true worth of a Mariana in *Measure for Measure*, or a Helena in *All's Well That Ends Well*, or for that matter, the false worth of a Helen of Troy in *Troilus and Cressida*. This is a subcategory of the disjunction between appearance and reality. A separate function of value revolves around the sense of "consideration," which underlies the legal instruments. The underlying consideration illustrates the two disparate orientations toward nature in the plays, and the roles that the law has in their dramatization. The case is most dramatically illustrated in *The Merchant of Venice*, where greed and vengeance underlie one bond and friendship underlies the other. The marriage at Belmont and the expanding community are made possible via the contract and friendship bond. And the surety that Antonio in *The Merchant of Venice*, like the King and Helena in *All's Well That Ends Well*, is willing to provide to others shows a communal involvement in marriage. This disposition toward life and community precedes enacted, or positive, law. It is what the community brings to that law, and is what that law is oriented toward.

Portia's father's will is another example of this disposition toward life and community. The will is based in reason and requires good faith. When that is not the case, as it is not with Shylock's "will," the law is perverted. Shylock brings his personal, vindictive, and esoteric meanings to the law and employs them to exact his revenge. In his hands, the law is no more than a codified system of retaliation. The play develops the idea that laws can either work in concert with, or in contradiction to, life.

In addition to publicity and value, the importance of performance as an element of the marriage contract is also stressed in *Measure for Measure* and *All's Well That Ends Well*. In the former, the meaning of *performance* is transformed: Angelo's purely sexual "performance" and the "performance" of Claudio's execution at his instance are transformed into the "performance" of the marriage contract. In the latter, Bertram leaves his marriage contract unperformed and subsequently places conditions on it. He effectively challenges Helena to transform an impossibility into a reality, to turn a "not" and a "never" into an eternal marriage "knot." By means of the "bed-trick," she brings the contract to performance. In *The Merchant of Venice*, the "performance" of the newly celebrated marriages of Portia and Bassanio and Nerissa and Gratiano must be postponed until Shylock's threat is removed. Once that is accomplished, the play ends with the characters anticipating, and for the first time fully understanding, the union about to take place. In *Troilus and*

Cressida, of course, "performance" is kept at the purely sexual level and joked about in terms of Troilus's potency. No contractual relationship forms by virtue of this "performance"; none is intended.

Finally, the importance of contractual tokens and their attendant ceremonies has a major role in the fulfillment of the contract. The exchanging of rings and the clasping of hands are more than mere formalities. Like the transactional ceremonies commemorated throughout English history, the relationship between the parties is both ratified by, and at one with, these tokens. The characters testify to the fact by objecting to the giving away of "my hand," as Diana complains on Helena's behalf; or by insisting on the ring being fused with the flesh, as Portia complains to Bassanio. Mariana moans in the same way of Angelo's abandonment despite the clasping of hands and despite their night in the ringed-wall garden. The idea of marriage as a holy rite is expressed most fully in this depiction of union. The two have become one, and to barter away "half" of that union is to compromise the whole. Again, the power of *Troilus and Cressida* as a parody of the contract is most felt when Cressida uses Troilus's love token as a surety to pledge a purely sexual future with Diomedes. Whereas the other tokens become one with the ceremony, "binding" it, the token in *Troilus and Cressida* is freely given and swapped, just as Cressida herself has been.

The full realization of the contracts is necessary in disordered realms where appetite triumphs over reason. Characters dominated by their appetites populate all four plays. Angelo throws out all reason to satisfy his "blood." Shylock uses reason, perversely, to argue that he needs no "reason" to satisfy his will toward Antonio. Bertram, although constantly reminded of his duty to posterity, irrationally casts it away for a single night of lust. And reason is ridiculed in *Troilus and Cressida*, mocked along with every other institution. Characters chase the illusions that their appetites present to them and constantly erode what little substance exists in their world. The incessant question—"What's the matter?"—is never answered. This lack of existential and metaphysical integrity in the play is solemnized, blackly, in the mock contract, where the handclasping and token exchanging are parodied with a biting force. A real absence—void, rather than union—is "celebrated" here, if "celebration" is the appropriate word in such a context.

The appetite picks what is attractive to it, whether or not the object is substantial. Illusion is often more attractive than reality. But it is also transitory. There is no thought for past or future legacies; all is sacrificed to the present. The lust of Troilus, Cressida, Bertram, the Viennese bawds, and the special "greed/lust" of Shylock expresses itself in a demand for the immediate. This highlights another dimension of the valid contract, for it commemorates more than mere union; it commemorates a union in *time*. And the contractual union respects time in all its phases. Indeed, the characters that rely on the contract, such as Helena, Mariana, and Portia, do so because they can call on their contracts to prove past, present, and future rights and duties. They memorialize a dateless understanding. In contrast, the extracontractual unions anticipate only the immediate satisfaction of an appetitive need.

With integrity restored to society via the contracts, the orientation toward life and generation becomes possible again. When marriage, friendship, and a community oriented toward life are reestablished, nature's largesse toward the characters is returned. But nature needs help in these plays. The theophanies of the Romances, with appearances by Hymen, Jupiter, and Juno, do not occur here. In *Troilus and Cressida*, nature is never helped, and the "laws of nature" that call for respecting the marriage contract are ignored. Pandarus and Ulysses, as the agents of lust and war, further exacerbate the orientation that leads to the destruction of the Trojan world. In the other plays, however, Duke Vincentio, Portia, Helena, and others bring the contracts to resolution through tricks that produce transformations. In these plays, marital union, enlarged communities, and the prospects of children all return to nature, as the Duke says, both "thanks and use."

To revisit C. L. Barber's idea regarding the effect of revelry in the festive comedies—"release to clarification"—there is indeed no equivalent "release" in the plays examined here. Even in *The Merchant of Venice*, Belmont is matched, and arguably overshadowed, by the Venetian complications. The realism of these plays can be attributed in part to their depiction of institutions: marriage and law. In the festive comedies, it is "revelry" that brings about clarification vis-à-vis nature. But in the four works discussed here, the contract as an instrument of society brings about "integrity through transformation." Nature is a focus of both categories, but she is reached by different means: revelry in the festive comedies, law in the problem plays. In the latter, legal means are employed to generate reality; the contracts make certain that things are as they seem. Unions replace both temporary couplings and perpetual abstention, dispositions equally indifferent to the perpetuation of life. With the achievement of lasting unions, the contracts establish a foundation from which nature's graces can be returned. The reality inherent in these transformations gives these four plays a quality more metaphysical than problematic in nature.

Although integrity by means of transformation is the principal theme of the four plays discussed here, as a theme it is not limited to them exclusively. It is present in other dramas, which can be understood better when seen against this imaginative backdrop. In fact, these four metaphysical plays have often been linked with the great romances and tragedies.[1] Whether *Troilus and Cressida* is comedy or tragedy is a question that stretches back as far as its placement in the First Folio. Some modern views would have *The Merchant of Venice* as a comedy for the Christians and a tragedy for Shylock.[2] The similarities between *Hamlet* and *All's Well That Ends Well* have often been noted.[3] And the magical and allegorical elements in *All's Well That Ends Well* and *Measure for Measure* have caused the two to be coupled with the Romances by some. The comparisons are valid because both the great tragedies and romances continue the relation of law and nature. However, in the plays that fall into these categories, nature's role is both stronger and more active. In *Cymbeline* and *The Winter's Tale*, humans are still the primary agents, but in *Twelfth Night*, nature is not only reached through the law, but also helps order events so that the players may find her. In an out-and-out contrast with the other dramas, however, *King Lear* shows nature in a different light, and with a very different face. Finally, *The Tempest* provides moments that are emblematic of the union sought in other plays.

CYMBELINE AND *THE WINTER'S TALE*

A striking difference between these two plays and the four previously discussed works is the theme of banishment. The other works contain characters who are penalized or ostracized through societal mechanisms, for example, Claudio and Shylock, by way of the judicial system; or through the mechanisms of war, for example, Cressida, by way of trade. But to the extent they are "removed" from society altogether, that removal is most often self-imposed: for example, Angelo, Duke Vincentio, Achilles, and all who cloister their own virtues. But in *Cymbeline* and *The Winter's Tale*, the banishment is involuntary, and the accused are innocent. Further, the innocent are not merely honest and true servants, or even faithful wives. The rolls of the banished innocent also include children, the very fruits of nature's generative scheme. Just as significant, their banishment stems from a wrongheaded refusal to recognize their legitimacy, their genuineness. In these works, Shakespeare again uses the contract to heal societal disjunction, but he focuses on a different point in the rupture. In *Measure for Measure*, *The Merchant of Venice*, and *All's Well That Ends Well*, fecundity is a promise of resolution, a result of the integrity struggled for. *Cymbeline* and *The Winter's Tale* show us the vigilance with which that integrity must be maintained. For lies and dissemblance never cease to be societal threats, and even when one generation is born to another, the living legacy can be lost by failing to recognize it as true.

In *Cymbeline*, the King demonstrates a failure of perspicacity quite familiar by now: not only has he married a vicious queen, but he has also rated her odious son, Cloten, as a worthy, even equal, match for his own daughter, Imogen.[4] This is merely the latest consequence of his failed vision. Twenty years before, he believed the lies and false oaths made by two villains against a trusted servant, Belarius. Outraged at his unjust exile, Belarius stole Cymbeline's two infant sons and raised them in the wilds of nature. Imogen, as Cymbeline's only known child, becomes his heir. But as the play opens, the foolish King is in the process of severing the girl's attachment to a man of real worth, Posthumus, in order to marry her to the worthless Cloten. His designs are foiled, however, because Imogen and Posthumus have been secretly married. The arrogant Cloten characterizes the quality of their marriage in recognizable terms:

> The *contract* you pretend with that base wretch,
> One bred of alms, and foster'd with cold dishes,
> With scraps o'th' court, it is no *contract*, none;
> And though it be allow'd in meaner parties
> (Yet who than he more mean?) to knit their souls,
> (On whom there is no more dependency
> But brats and beggary) in *self-figur'd* [self-contracted]
>   knot,
> Yet you are curb'd from that enlargement, by
> The consequence o'th' crown, and must not foil
> The precious note of it. (2.3.114–23; emphasis added)[5]

Once again, a clandestine marriage complicates the plot, but with a real difference this time. The parties here are worthy of each other, and despite their different stations, recognize each other as intrinsically valuable. It is their society who does not approve, owing to its own corruption. Although it is said of Posthumus that in all the earth "so fair an outward, and such stuff within / Endows a man, but he" (1.1.23–24), Cymbeline's opinion of him is much like Cloten's. Imogen counters with the argument that Posthumus is indeed her equal in worth—that there is no lack of "consideration"—since he is "a man worth any woman, over-buys me / Almost the sum he pays" (1.2.77–78). Still, the King banishes Posthumus.

The issue of value receives further attention when Imogen tells Cloten that he is not worth the suit on Posthumus's back. The news so mystifies Cloten that he builds the idea into his revenge against her. Wearing Posthumus's clothing as he tries to intercept Imogen's escape, Cloten marvels:

The lines of my body are as well drawn as his: no less young, more strong, not beneath him in fortunes, beyond him in the advantage of the time, above him in birth, alike conversant in general services, and more remarkable in single oppositions; yet this imperceiverant thing [Imogen] loves him in my despite. (4.1.9–14)

But Imogen is not "imperceiverant"; unlike her father, she can see real differences between men, and can recognize the false from the true. She is also capable of a larger observation, that "man and man" should consider each other brothers. Social distinction complicates that awareness:

Arviragus: Are we not brothers?

Imogen: So man and man should be,
                 But clay and clay differs in dignity,
                 Whose dust is both alike. (4.2.3–5)

Her argument for equal value in her marriage contract is based on this understanding: man-made distinctions of rank belong to the passing material world, whereas the real value of personal integrity, which Posthumus possesses, makes him her equal. This same note rings throughout the King of France's speech to Bertram, when he attempts to impress the young Count with an understanding of true value.

Ironically, it is Imogen's value that is unfairly maligned in the balance of the play, and by Posthumus of all people, whose value she has sacrificed so much in defending. Her similarities with Helena are never so striking as when the man she loves begins to abuse her honor. In Rome, Posthumus contends that he would abate nothing as to Imogen's peerless price (1.5.64). Iachimo says this is a kind of "hand-in-hand comparison," which claims equality only, not superiority, and puns upon the "hand-fast" ceremony at betrothal (1.5.70–71).

This use of "hand" imagery is of great importance in the play, as is that of the "rings." Iachimo brags that he can capture Imogen's virtue, and Posthumus wagers the ring that Imogen gave him at their parting (1.5.134). They put their "wager," with the etymological history of that word's association to marriage in the background, in "hand-writing," mentioning it several times within twenty lines. So the handfast ceremony solemnizing the couple's union is here put to the test by a wager, solemnized in handwriting and handclasping, and staked by the token of fertility, sexuality, and eternity: the marriage ring. Although Imogen proves her worth by repulsing Iachimo's overtures (1.7.141–55), the bracelet Posthumus gave her at their last meeting is stolen by Iachimo, who secretly gains access to her room at midnight—the transformational hour so common in these plays—to claim a symbol of lustful conquest. Upon taking the bracelet from the sleeping girl's arm, he says, with sexual implications, "Come off, come off; /As slippery as the Gordian knot was hard" (2.2.33–34).

Hands, central to the commemoration of friendships, agreements, and marriages, as well as rings, the embodiments of marriage themselves, help to unskein the secrets, lies, and misconceptions. In the final scene, Imogen's faithfulness and value is proven, just as Helena's was, and the parties recognize that the rightful owners have been faithful to their contracts. It is an event similar to the return of the necklace in *The Comedy of Errors*, and the rings in *All's Well That Ends Well* and *The Merchant of Venice*.

With the restoration of the marriage comes the healing of a fundamental breach in society, the recognition of the valid union between worthy parties. And when the maligned Imogen is proven true and recognized by her husband, the reconciliation harbingers further news, and precipitates its telling. For Imogen must explain the story of her flight from Cloten, which occasions the testimony of others, including the wronged Belarius. He in turn must disclose the identity of his supposed sons, the true princes of England, one of which stands under the King's death sentence for killing Cloten.

Throughout the play, nature "sparks" out in the two boys (3.3.79). She is said to "blazon" in their compositions, framing them to royalty (4.2.170, 178). They are "worthy" of her, being a "breed of greatness" (4.2.25). Nature somehow "prompts" the boys to their rightful character, though raised in mean conditions (3.3.84). Nature in a real sense testifies through their legitimacy, and through them her claims are made. There has been a vacuum in society, owing to the dislodgment of the princes from their rightful place. That dislodgement follows from Cymbeline's failure to see rightly, and from his allegiance with liars and villains at the expense of the worthy. With a final threat of death coming from the King himself, the hole in society is about to become permanent. But through proofs of the boys' legitimacy, which comes about through the witness of their natures, they reassume their rightful places. The breech is filled.

Recognitions of kin are hard won in *Cymbeline*, but they eventually restore a society divided for twenty years. They even heal the wounds of war, as England reacknowledges its tribute to Rome. Once the marriage contract is reaffirmed, children, thought long dead, are returned to a society that sorely needs them. Both they and the kingdom find a new life. There is perhaps no better means of expressing nature's purpose in seeing life realized than the lines: "Nature doth abhor to make his bed / With the defunct, or sleep upon the dead" (4.2.357–58). In *Cymbeline*, nature is patient in realizing her aims.

Another years-long breach in society occurs in *The Winter's Tale*. Again, children are among those wrongfully banished, and again the banishment rises from a failure to distinguish the real from the apparent. Leontes madly embellishes on a false inference and accuses his wife of adultery with his friend Polixenes. This leads to other false inferences: doubts about, and downright denials of, his own children's legitimacy, despite nature's testimony to their integrity in the "mould and frame of hand, nail, finger" (2.3.102). Convinced she is a bastard, Leontes orders his newborn daughter to be exposed to the elements, to nature.

Predictably, that is when things take a turn. Nature is not so easily defeated, and can use even these inauspicious means to prove Perdita's legitimacy, Hermione's faithfulness, Leontes's foolishness, and to restore both the rift within Sicilia and that between Sicilia and Bohemia. The point is made in Perdita's famous and important exchange with the disguised Polixenes: "Nature is made better by no mean / But nature makes that mean" (4.4.89–90). All devices are within her purview; most tellingly, even art.

Leontes's affront to nature is particularly egregious, for he disclaims a living, breathing stamp of his own nature, his own child. In this act, a real integrity is challenged by its own author, a man who has no reason to doubt its authenticity and every reason to admit it. This self-wound is matched by his de facto divorcement from a faithful wife, whose observance of her marital contract has the imprimatur of the gods (3.2.131). But Leontes indulges his will, led on by false images. The product of his folly proves devastating; losses follow upon losses, and years of penance are necessary to effect the wrenching change.

Leontes's faults, though most dramatic, are not the only ones in the play. Failure to recognize kinship bonds runs both ways; fathers may fail to recognize sons and daughters, but sons fail to recognize fathers, and the duties owed to them, as well. An example of the latter occurs, once again, in the familiar context of the secret marriage contract.

The disguised King witnesses his son Florizel take Perdita's hand and ask the Old Shepherd to "contract us fore these witnesses" (4.4.392). An astonished Polixenes asks whether the boy even has a father (4.4.396–98). Upon Florizel's assurances that his father lives, is reasonable, and in good health, Polixenes insists that the boy's father should attend:

> You offer him, if this be so, a wrong
> Something unfilial: reason my son
> Should choose himself a wife, but as good reason
> The father (all whose joy is nothing else
> But fair prosperity) should hold some counsel
> In such a business. (4.4.408–12)

Polixenes states the generative aim of both the father and the society at large: "fair prosperity" of the marriage. But Florizel denies him no less than five times, and asks that Polixenes simply "mark our [his and Perdita's] contract" instead. (4.4.418). Only then does Polixenes reveal himself, his anger, and his intention to disinherit Florizel (4.4.119). Although the King's intentions were to spy on his son at the feast, prior to Florizel's disownment of his father's role in his wedding, the King had been nothing but captivated by Perdita.

While questions of mutual value or sexual frustration often complicate the marriage contract, the secret marriage creates a set of recurring and consistent problems. All of society is invested in the fruitfulness that flows from the unions, another reason for the public celebration. Certainly, many of the comedic lovers' problems would be suffered regardless of their marriages' publicity, but since so much bad history is remedied by public celebration, privacy merely postpones the cure. Even in a tragedy such as *Romeo and Juliet*, the star-crossed lovers would have likely suffered their families' wrath for marrying, but its secrecy in no way lessens their trial. Juliet rightly fears the haste of their contract (2.2.117). Despite Friar Laurence's best intentions, the secret marriage causes misunderstandings that contribute to the tragic end.

In *The Winter's Tale*, Florizel and Perdita must disguise themselves to flee Bohemia, where Perdita fears "the heaven sets spies upon us / will not have our contract celebrated" (5.1.202–3). Heaven's collusion is for a good reason, since secrecy and disguise are at cross-purposes with resolution. Breaking family alliance has caused the play's problems, and that pattern must end. Only the full participation of society through the ceremony can achieve this, so among the series of unveilings and revelations at the end of the play, the public celebration of the contract is put into process (5.3.135–55). On one level, Florizel and Perdita, Camillo and Paulina, and Leontes and Hermione are drawn together by the contract's public observance; on a larger level, the sixteen-year disjunction between the societies of Sicilia and Bohemia is also ended. Being romances, *Cymbeline* and *The Winter's Tale* are struck through with the supernatural, with the idea that the characters' good is being schemed for by larger forces. But nature plays an even larger role in two late plays, one a quasi romance, *Twelfth Night*, and the other a tragedy, *King Lear*. In these works, nature's presence is felt, with beneficent consequences for the Illyrians, and ominous ones for the ancients of Lear's kingdom.

TWELFTH NIGHT AND KING LEAR

Nature's interest in providing for herself through the valid contract is most forcefully exhibited in *Twelfth Night*. There, the same themes occur as in *All's Well That Ends Well*, and the plot unfolds in a similar way. The play opens with Orsino luxuriating in the music of love:

> If music be the food of love, play on,
> Give me excess of it, that, surfeiting;
> The appetite may sicken, and so die. (1.1.1–3)

But within four lines the strain that was so sweet has begun to fail him; he calls for its end. Then, while extolling the "spirit of love," he reverses and says love devalues whatever it receives, like the encompassing and voracious sea (1.1.9–11). The skittish Orsino, however poetic his opening lines, leaves one less convinced of his love, and more convinced of his infatuation with the state of being in love.

For her part, the object of his affections, Olivia, renounces love in favor of mourning. Death, not love, has its own attractions, consistently pondered in these plays. Like Mariana in *Measure for Measure*, Olivia has lost a brother and lives apart. But unlike Mariana, she has exiled herself. She takes on the mantle of melancholy, veiling herself like a cloistress and abjuring the company of men. Although she is upbraided for refusing to leave a copy of her beauty, she perversely inventories her features and consigns them to the grave (1.5.235–37). The state of affairs in Illyria lies between these two unnatural extremes: a Duke mistakes lust for love, and a Countess refuses love altogether. A union of any permanence is frustrated by one, any union at all is frustrated by the other. Nature cannot flourish here, and into this world comes Viola, disguised.

Washed up on the shores of a strange land, she knows the importance of being able to trust that things are as they seem. Rightly, she gives her allegiance to the sea captain because his mind seems to match his outward character (1.2.50–51). And yet her first business is to employ this man to conceal her from the world. She even takes the guise of a eunuch, a being incapable of generation: "Conceal me what I am, and be my aid" (1.2.53). The disguised heroine further complicates matters by falling in love with the Duke, whose love she cannot pursue because of her disguise. She also unintentionally wins the love of the Countess, whose "knot" is too hard for her to "untie" (2.2.40–41). Caught in the snare of her own deceits, well-intentioned though they may be, her futile protest to the Countess's affections is revealing: "I am not what I am," she says (3.1.142). The power of these very same words Shakespeare uses to different effect in another play, and in a different context, but the phrase bodes the same unsettling future: Iago speaks them in an aside, as he plots to ruin Othello. *Res* and *verba* are never so far apart as here, in an expression that is the nadir of the disingenuous. That they are also the opposite of the expression of pure being, God's name: "I am that I am" (a performative utterance of the highest complexity) is perhaps more than mere coincidence.

The difference between *Twelfth Night* and the other plays is that an agent of nature does not accomplish the resolution. While in the other plays the agents of nature must disguise themselves to trick the antagonists on their own terms, in *Twelfth Night* all of the characters are disguised, either by intention or by self-deception. When Viola speaks of men proving "much in our vows, but little in our love," her eloquence springs from her earlier epiphany regarding dissemblance. It is humankind's plight not to be what it says it is. "Disguise," says Viola, is the wicked means by which the "pregnant enemy" can do much (2.2.27–28). The Illyrians have made a muddle of their own world, and no one is outside the self-engendered trap.

Without an agent, nature must do her own work. Like the other plays, doubling figures into the redemptive trick, but the doubles in *Twelfth Night* are of nature's own making. They take the shape of the twins, Viola and Sebastian, who are doubly virtuous. By her devices, nature sends the double, Sebastian, to Illyria. The unraveling of deception makes for a larger community, and none too soon, as the confusion is at its peak. Olivia expresses the cry for authenticity. Confused by the supposed Cesario's unwonted receptiveness toward her, oblivious to the fact that it is Sebastian, not Cesario, who is so agreeable, Olivia insists on a contract of betrothal to assuage her fears:

> If you mean well
> Now go with me, and with this holy man,
> Into the chantry by: there before him
> And underneath that consecrated roof,
> Plight me the full assurance of your faith,
> That my most jealous and too doubtful soul
> May live at peace. (4.3.22–28)

And toward the end of the play, Olivia calls on the "contract of eternal bond of love"—celebrated with the "joinder of hands," "close of lips," and "interchangement of rings," and "sealed" with the testimony of the priest's function (5.1.153–58)—to publicly proclaim her marriage with Sebastian. Of course, she thinks she has married Cesario, but the disordered alignment that frustrates nature is changed when true identities are revealed. Nature shows her hand, as it were. Sebastian can reassure Olivia that her marriage has satisfied nature because of the role nature herself has played in the contract's execution:

> So comes it, lady,
> you have been mistook.
> *But nature to her bias drew in that.*
> *You would have been contracted to a maid,*
> Nor are you therein, by my life, deceiv'd.
> You are betroth'd both to a maid and a man.
>   (5.1.255–59; emphasis added)

Questions about the validity of the union between Olivia and Sebastian are made moot by the fact that Olivia ratifies the contract she has celebrated with her new husband, regardless of her mistake (5.1.310–12). Similarly, Bertram ratifies the contract with Helena, despite all of his earlier efforts to thwart it. Olivia turns her affections toward Sebastian, and Orsino toward Viola. The proposed unions will effect a "solemn combination" of their souls (5.1.375–76), and will have a double effect in the virtue, and happiness, of an—almost—unified Illyria. Malvolio's treatment leaves him in the position of a troubling outsider, but the action of the play at least recognizes his wrongs, and it ends with overtures to bring him back within the fold.

Nature's largesse to those who comply with her ends is a constant in these plays, but is by no means a universal. The world of disorder portrayed, and commemorated, in *Troilus and Cressida*, has its equivalent in *King Lear*. In *King Lear*, however, nature is not slighted or perverted. Instead, nature has a harsher visage when she appears on the heath and makes her own unfathomable demands. The foolish, the scheming, the treacherous, the blind, all suffer here, but so do the noble, the honorable, and the true. As in *Twelfth Night*, no one escapes the deceitful trap that is the common trick of the human condition. But in *King Lear*, nature does not come to the rescue. We are unsure whether nature could be appeased on the heath, and whether what happens is the result of the law's neglect,[6] or its impotence, in the face of a universe unstrung. Here, we see the chaos only prophesied in Troy.

In Lear's tragedy, the legitimate world and its rule are assaulted by the illegitimate world of unruly nature. Rather than working in concert, with law as a means to help nature fulfill her goals, nature and law are at odds, especially to the extent that characters betray their "natural" loyalties. The legitimate son, Edgar, is besieged by the illegitimate child of nature, Edmund; the child of the marriage contract is besieged by the child born outside the contract:

> Thou, Nature, art my goddess; to thy law
> my services are bound.
>
> . . . .
>
>   Well, then,
> Legitimate Edgar, I must have your land.
> Our father's love is to the bastard Edmund
> As to the legitimate. Fine word "legitimate."
> Well, my legitimate, if this letter speed,
> and my invention thrive, Edmund the base
> shall top the legitimate. I grow. I prosper. (1.2.1–22)

With deft wordplay, Edmund sees no difference between himself, the "illegitimate," and the "legitimate" Edgar. There is indeed barely a letter—the letter "i"—between the two words. When he asks his false "letter" to speed his fortunes, he expects its falsity to help him top the "legitimate" son.

The image of Edmund "growing" wild, overtaking his culture as a vine chokes a tree, hints at the ominous quality nature assumes here. Edmund takes on the semblance of the legitimate son, discredits him, replaces him, and destroys the world order. Whereas substitution tricks—the real for the false, the wife for the object of lust—are means of redemption in *All's Well That Ends Well* and *Measure for Measure*, in *King Lear*, the bastard substitutes himself for the lawful child. The substitution trick is as destructive as the ones in *Troilus and Cressida* (Ajax for Achilles, Antenor for Cressida) are fruitless.

Rather than work redemption, Edmund brings disorder. As Edgar says to Edmund:

> Our pleasant vices [adultery]
> make instruments to plague us.
> The dark and vicious place where thee he [Gloucester] got
> Cost him his eyes. (5.3.168–71)

Edmund, begotten in a dark, vicious, secret place, costs his father his "eyes," both literally and figuratively. The same can be said for Lear, his two older daughters, and his world. All is so disordered that the legitimate children forsake their "natural loyalty" and side with the illegitimate Edmund. Mystified at his treatment, Lear must ask Goneril "Are you our daughter?" (1.4.209), and when refused a satisfactory answer, brands her a "degenerate bastard" [generation going backward] (1.4.245). He even calls upon nature to curse her with deformed offspring: "[I]f she must child, let it be disnatured" (1.4.275). Like the "retrograde times" in *All's Well That Ends Well*, nature in *King Lear* is in a state of reversion.

Not recognizing the child—the kinship bond by which nature has set her seal—is the greatest of affronts. Indeed, failing to recognize the bond of kinship is a fundamental error, epic in origin; kinship binds human to human and acts as the glue that makes society cohere. Either those bonds are observed, or their neglect leads to destruction. While in *Cymbeline* and *The Winter's Tale* that observance is eventually the case, in *King Lear*, the refusal to recognize the bond is flagrant, sweeping, permanent.

Unnatural allegiances are common in the play, including attempts to form illegal marriage contracts. Before she dies, Regan hastily tries to accomplish a kind of "performative" marriage with Edmund, to thwart her sister's designs on the bastard:

> General,
> Take thou my soldiers, prisoners, patrimony:
> Dispose of them, of me; the walls are thine.
> Witness the world, that I create thee here my lord and
>   master. (5.3.75–79).

But Albany is aware of the menage à trois between the two sisters and Edmund and makes an objection:

> For your claim, fair sister,
> I bar it in the interest of my wife [Goneril];
> Tis she is *sub-contracted* to this lord,
> And I, her husband, contradict your banns [marriage
>   announcement]
> If you will marry, make your love to me. My lady is
>   bespoke. (5.3.85–89; emphasis added)

Like the unrealized marriage contracts in other plays, this subcontract is tainted, here with a bigamous intent. Bigamy, adultery, incest, rape, and other extracontractual sex are means of bypassing the marital contract.

While in the other plays a reorientation toward nature and life takes place, establishing integrity, the initial rift in nature only worsens in *King Lear*. Characters who might triumph through transformation elsewhere are defeated here by an ever-widening gap between the true and the untrue. Edgar can dispatch his bastard brother from the world, but not in time to save the world. Cordelia cannot expose her sisters, whose true selves she "knows" full well (1.1.271). "Time" does not unfold their "plighted cunning" (1.1.282), at least not before existence unravels. In the end, we are left with Lear himself, fumbling at a mirror, trying to see something—life—when there is none, trying to find the spark of fire in his child's breath as though he were Adam searching for the breath of God. But none comes, and the stock of reality is ultimately depleted. In *King Lear*, humankind shatters the contract. Perhaps the power of the play is in the centrifugal force one feels as chaos begins to wax.

THE TEMPEST

What is often considered to be Shakespeare's last play, and what is certainly considered his most metaphysical poem, provides fine examples of the law and nature relationship examined here. In both instances, certain emblematic moments encapsulate what the characters in the other plays work so hard to achieve.

In *The Tempest*, the sacred nature of the marriage is observed ceremonially and intentionally. Ferdinand and Miranda, after exchanging praise for each other, and professing their unworthiness as objects of affection, perform what amounts to a clandestine marriage:

Miranda:	I am your wife if you will marry me; If not, I'll die your maid: to be your fellow You may deny me; but I'll be your servant, Whether you will or no.
Ferdinand:	My mistress, dearest, And I thus humble ever.
Miranda:	My husband, then?

Ferdinand: Ay, with a heart as willing
                       As bondage e'er of freedom: here's my hand.

Miranda: And mine, with my heart in 't. (3.1.83–90)

The couple make their pledge in the same fashion as Portia and Bassanio, sacrificing the self to the other. The ubiquitous Prospero witnesses the exchange, and although it takes him unexpectedly, he approves. After all, as the agent of nature, he has orchestrated their meeting. In fact, by arranging the marriage, Prospero makes a step toward working with nature and ending his manipulation of her.

But Prospero's approval comes with a fundamental caveat: if the two do not wait for all "sanctimonious ceremonies," ministered with "full and holy rite," dire consequences will follow:

> But if thou break her virgin-knot before
> All sanctimonious ceremonies may
> With full and holy rite be ministr'd,
> No sweet aspersion shall the heavens let fall
> To make this contract grow. (4.1.15–19)

He goes on to warn them that instead of happiness, they will experience hate, disdain, and discord. After Ferdinand vows not to let his honor melt into lust, the celebration of "a contract of true love" (4.1.84) can continue, performed by the goddesses of Nature, Childbirth, and the Rainbow (significant as marking the "covenant" between God and man). Like the reunion between Bohemia and Sicilia in *The Winter's Tale*, the contract between the children of Alonso and Prospero reunites—"contracts"—a long-separated society. "Contract" in this sense stresses not only the binding and resolving instrument, but also what the contract actually does, the binding of the characters and the resolving of their fractured world. It rings with the same note of metaphysical soundness as Helena's achievement in *All's Well That Ends Well*.

⚜

The marriage contract is an example of the law acting as an ordering principle. It does not merely prevent people from committing infractions, but acts as a safeguard of integrity, a pillar of any healthy society. It also sets society on a path toward self-perpetuation. In addition, when the positive law has this meliorative effect, it works in conjunction with the divine order to "be fruitful and multiply." But this generative goal is not without its prerequisite: the integrity of a true and lasting union between two people. In these plays, the contracts, bonds, and sureties—instruments of the law—function as dramatic conceits by which societal and marital integrity is achieved. The union established by this integrity is sought by, and most fiercely maintained by, the Marianas and Helenas of these plays. It has much in common with the strange, paradoxical union implied in Shakespeare's *The Phoenix and Turtle*:

> Property was thus appalled.
> That the self was not the same.
> Single nature's double name
> Neither two nor one was called. (Lines 37–40)[7]

The mystery of this most metaphysical of poems echoes something of the integrity so earnestly worked for in the metaphysical plays. Here, being is not lost in another, but somehow fulfilled in conjunction *with* another.

What lies at the core of these plays' "busyness," which has garnered no scarcity of criticism, is a depiction of authenticity's achievement. It is an accomplishment so simple it can be overlooked, but so essential it cannot be ignored, at least not at the expense of reality. Indeed, in all of Shakespeare, integrity, or the lack thereof, is a fundamental concept. Characters may or may not learn to be patient (another great Shakespearean virtue) with their lots; prosperity, even existence, is at risk: Macbeth suspects he should be content with his station in life, his own place of being, but cannot; neither can many a Shakespearean king, be he York or Lancaster or Caesar. Conversely, some rulers, like Vincentio, commit the opposite affront to "being" by abdicating their responsibilities. But unlike the Duke, they do not take them up again: Richard II, for all his eloquence, learns too late.

Abdication and usurpation, striving for a greater or a lesser place than one has, yearning for more or less than one is, provides dramatic friction in so many of the great plays that we know. And a character's learning to break that cycle leads to some of those plays' most powerful discoveries. Like Edgar, who teaches his impatient father about contentment ("the ripeness is all"), the tormented Hamlet, in his own highest moment, comes to learn that "the readiness is all," that he must simply "let be." Unlikely as it may seem, their epiphanies are not too far from that of Parolles, when he finds joy in merely being "the thing I am." Human fulfillment shines most brightly at such times, when sheer contentment in a genuine existence is world enough.

Much has been written to explain the strange qualities of these works, or to justify their being called problematic and dark. Critics have argued that their plots are unresolved, their endings less than happy, their tones less than joyful. But as the plays deal with an "everyday world" so pervasively, what is achieved in the end is an "everyday" solution. By helping institutions and individuals find integrity, the legal instruments provide for societal cohesion, and the perpetuation of a world always in danger of death. In *Troilus and Cressida*, that death seems assured. But in the other three plays, although the resolution may not be so complete that audiences feel that all is—and will ever hereafter be—well, things have at least been set on a generative path. A future for the characters and their world becomes a prospect again. Hope is the defining virtue of such dramas, where the characters and their societies have been given one more chance, as Duke Vincentio says, to provide for better times to come.

Notes

CHAPTER I. THE SEMBLANCE OF VIRTUE

1. Frank Kermode, "Justice and Mercy in Shakespeare," *Houston Law Review* 33 (1996): 1155–74, esp. 1159.

2. Ibid. 1163–4.

3. Histories of this area include Michael Jamieson's "The Problem Plays, 1920–1970: A Retrospect," *Aspects of Shakespeare's Problem Plays: Articles Reprinted from Shakespeare Survey*, ed. Kenneth Muir and Stanley Wells (Cambridge: Cambridge UP, 1982); and Robert Ornstein's introduction to *Discussions of Shakespeare's Problem Comedies*, ed. Robert Ornstein (Boston: Heath, 1961) vii–viii.

4. For an overview, see George W. Keeton, *Shakespeare's Legal and Political Background* (London: Pitman, 1967); and O. Hood Phillips, *Shakespeare and the Lawyers* (London: Methuen, 1972).

5. James Boyd White, *The Legal Imagination* (Boston: Little, 1973) xx.

6. Scholarship in this area includes that of Sir Arthur Underhill, "Shakespeare's Law," *Shakespeare's England*, vol. 1 (Oxford: Clarendon, 1916) 381–412; E. W. Ives, "The Law and the Lawyers," *Shakespeare Survey* 17 (1964): 73–86; and Ronald Berman, "Shakespeare and the Law," *Shakespeare Quarterly* 18 (1967): 141–50.

7. Thomas Aquinas, *Summa Theologica*, quoted in Keeton 72.

8. Ibid.

9. Ibid. 73. Further, R. S. White contends that "the supremacy of Right Reason was not to be undermined until after the Restoration, although obviously the roots of the dislodging forces were evident very much earlier" (*Natural Law in English Renaissance Literature* [Cambridge: Cambridge UP, 1996] xiv).

10. Keeton 74, quoting Richard Hooker in *Of the Laws of Ecclesiastical Polity*, 4 vols., ed. W. Speed Hill (Cambridge: Belknap/Harvard UP, 1977–98).

11. R. S. White xi.

12. Ibid. xiv. John S. Wilks is also of the opinion that Shakespeare's works betray a scholastic, precisely Thomistic, worldview (*The Idea of Conscience in Renaissance Tragedy* [London: Routledge, 1990], 6).

13. R. S. White 3.

14. Kermode 1172.

15. William Shakespeare, *Hamlet*, Arden edition, ed. Harold Jenkins (Walton-on-Thames: Nelson, 1982) 2.2.306, 308.

16. C. L. Barber, *Shakespeare's Festive Comedy: A Study of Dramatic Form and Its Relation to Social Custom* (Princeton: Princeton UP, 1959) 6–8. Barber comments that this "saturnalian" pattern came to Shakespeare from many sources, both in social and artistic tradition (5).

17. Ibid. 8.

18. Ibid. 3. Although Barber includes *The Merchant of Venice* in his festive comedies, he says it is not shaped by festivity, and is qualified in his characterization (166). He discusses the dynamic between Shylock and the Christians, emphasizing the same troublesome qualities as problem play critics do (189–91).

19. R. S. White 8. White also holds that "doing what is necessary for survival is at the heart of the moral programme," and that most theorists of the Natural Law posit some form of communitarianism as essential to human survival (4).

20. William Shakespeare, *Troilus and Cressida*, Arden edition, ed. David Bevington (Walton-on-Thames: Nelson, 1999) 1.3.120–24.

21. Barber 6.

22. Sir Frederick Pollock and F. W. Maitland, *The History of English Law before Edward I*, vol. 2 (Cambridge: Cambridge UP, 1898) 186.

23. William Shakespeare, *Othello*, Arden edition, ed. E. A. J. Honigman (Walton-on-Thames: Nelson, 1997) 3.3.116.

24. *Timon of Athens* 1.1.253 (William Shakespeare, *The Arden Shakespeare Complete Works*, ed. Richard Proudfoot, Ann Thompson, and David Scott Kastan [Walton-on-Thames: Nelson, 1998]).

25. *Hamlet* 5.1.61.

26. Davies P. Harding notes that when Shakespeare uses the word, there is no doubt of betrothal. ("The Elizabethan Betrothals and *Measure for Measure*," *Journal of English and Germanic Philosophy* 49 [1950]: 139–58, esp. 150n. 36). Linda Boose describes a "comic contract" between playwright and audience, and contends that Shakespeare used the marriage bond to fulfill his duty of providing pleasure to the audience, while at the same time problematizing the contract itself ("The Comic Contract and Portia's Golden Ring," *Shakespeare Studies* 20 [1988]: 241–54).

27. A. W. B. Simpson, *Legal Theory and Legal History: Essays on the Common Law* (London: Hambledon, 1987) 111. In another work, Simpson explains the nature of assumpsit

as "an undertaking, in the sense of an assurance, and for many purposes this is no doubt accurate enough to catch the sense of the word in the early cases." However, he goes on to deepen that meaning and elaborate on it (*A History of the Common Law of Contract* [Oxford: Clarendon, 1975] 215).

28. To a certain degree, judges have refined the issue. One party makes an "offer," and the other party makes an "acceptance" of that offer.

29. Harold Potter sets out the leading theories in academic dispute as to the derivation of the doctrine. Notably, Justice Oliver Wendell Holmes contended that it came from the old requirement of quid pro quo in the action of 'Debt' (*Historical Introduction to English Law* [London: Sweet, 1943] 407).

30. Simpson, *Contract* 424.

31. J. H. Baker, *The Legal Profession and the Common Law: Historical Essays* (London: Hambledon, 1986) 372.

32. Potter 409. This is not so much similar to quid pro quo as it is to the doctrine of detrimental reliance, which Simpson points out appears in St. Germain's *Doctor and Student*: "What is most significant in *Doctor and Student* is the appearance of an alternative to *quid pro quo*—the idea that there should be liability because there has been induced reliance upon the promise." Though St. Germain was in all probability considering the action of debt in the passage quoted, his "charge" doctrine never replaced or supplemented quid pro quo in the field sur contract; in *Jordan's Case* (1535), where the idea could have been used, it was never mentioned" (*Contract* 159).

33. Simpson, *Contract* 419–21. The case of *Lever v. Heys* (1598) decided, controversially, that a third party who would have benefited from the marriage—in this situation, the father—could not bring suit (ibid. 477).

34. Then, as now, the courts were not inclined to delve into the "adequacy" of consideration. Bad bargains were the business of the contracting parties; if a man pledged a day's worth of labor for a mere shilling, he was nevertheless bound. See Baker, *Common Law* 375.

35. Pollock and Maitland 188.

36. Pollock and Maitland are qualified in their comparison between Germanic handclasp and the act of homage or supplication, but note that the feudal contract is a formal contract (ibid. 189).

37. Thomas Littleton, *Tenures*, sec. 91, quoted in P. S. Clarkson and C. T. Warren, *The Law of Property in Shakespearean and Elizabethan Drama* (Baltimore: Hopkins UP, 1942) 20.

38. Clarkson and Warren 18. A. W. B. Simpson elaborates on the dual character of the feudal bond: "What was involved was both a personal relationship between superior and inferior, lord and vassal, marked by reciprocal duties of protection and service, and the granting of a benefice, that is, a parcel of landed estate to be enjoyed upon favorable terms,

so long as the service due was faithfully performed" (*A History of the Land Law* [Oxford: Clarendon, 1986] 2).

39. Clarkson and Warren say that a writing, though not obligatory, was nevertheless desirable because it perpetuated testimony (114). S. E. Thorne is of the same opinion, emphasizing the importance of the transfer, not its memorialization in writing: "Actual or symbolic change of possession as an objective fact must take place. . . . But the document will serve to retain the extent of the gift" (*Essays in Legal History* [London: Hambledon, 1985] 35–36). Sir William Holdsworth noted that in Germanic law, there was a tendency to confuse symbolic livery with actual livery, which was not the case in England (cited in ibid. 33n. 10). During the reign of the Stuart kings, the Statute of Frauds required certain transactions be transferred by written instrument.

40. Thorne 204.

41. Henry de Bracton gives this description, and says a staff or wand could also be used, if there was no building on the land (see ibid. 48).

42. Ibid. 37.

43. Ibid. 39.

44. Ibid. 34.

45. Pollock and Maitland, 34.

46. Simpson explains these formal necessities in his *Legal History* 112–18.

47. Although he frowns on the "rationalization," Potter relates that in later law, it was said, "a seal imputes consideration" (385).

48. Simpson, *Contract* 95.

49. Pollock and Maitland 117.

50. The images associated with early legal concepts belie the cold, unimaginative character often attributed to the law. An example is the idea of a mortgage. Pollack and Maitland explain the varying senses of the word: the property pledged for the debt was considered "dead"—*mort*—to the debtor until the debt was paid. As the debt was a kind of usury, it was a sin; if the debtor died owing the money, his property was confiscated by the King (ibid. 119; 119n. 3). However, if the arrangement was that the profits of the land should go to diminish the debt, then the gage was *vivum vadium*, a living pledge, and an honorable transaction (Simpson, *Land Law* 141).

51. Ives 73.

52. Margaret Loftus Ranald, *Shakespeare and His Social Context* (New York: AMS, 1987), xi. She goes on to make the point that of the many Elizabethan dramatists who used the law extensively in their works, only John Webster was known to have legal training. The plays, Ranald suggests, would have failed with a lay audience if the words, concepts, and so forth were not known on some common level (3).

53. Kermode 1162.

54. See, for example, *Nuuel v. Wilstrop* (1218-19), as reported in J. H. Baker and S. F. C. Milson, *Sources of English Legal History: Private Law to 1750* (London: Butterworths, 1986) 39.

55. Luke Wilson, *Theaters of Intention* (Stanford: Stanford UP, 2000) 4.

56. See Daniel J. Kornstein, *Kill All the Lawyers?: Shakespeare's Legal Appeal* (Princeton: Princeton UP, 1994) 16-17.

57. John Maxcy Zane, *The Story of the* Law (Indianapolis: Liberty Fund, 1927) 238.

58. Marjorie Garber, *Coming of Age in Shakespeare* (New York: Methuen, 1981) 117. Ranald notes Shakespearean use of the "prohibitive" and "diriment" impediments to marriage. The prohibitive impediments obstructed marriage, while the diriment voided it altogether. Prohibitive included premarital sex and lack of parental consent; diriment included mistake, disparity of religion, marriage between unbaptized and baptized persons, criminality, threats, reverential fear, compulsion, prior marriage, and consanguinity (6).

59. Ranald 10.

60. George Elliott Howard, *A History of Matrimonial Institutions*, vol. 1, (Chicago: U of Chicago P, 1904. Littleton, CO: Rothman, 1994) 306.

61. R. H. Helmholz, *Marriage Litigation in Medieval England* (Cambridge: Cambridge UP, 1974) 36.

62. Ibid. 31. The Church's theological reasoning arose from Lombard's critique of Gratian's view. See B. J. Sokol and Mary Sokol, *Shakespeare's Legal Language* (London: Athlone, 2000) 291.

63. Henry Swinburne, *A Treatise on Spousals* (London: Roycroft, 1686) 6-7. Pollock and Maitland comment that the one contract that should have been the most formal was ironically made the most informal of all (369).

64. James A. Brundage, *Law, Sex and Christian Society in Medieval Europe* (Chicago: U of Chicago P, 1987) 114, 190. In addition to Brundage's work on Christian marriage in Europe, see Kenneth Stevenson, *Nuptial Blessing: A Study of Christian Marriage Rites* (New York: Oxford UP, 1983); and on dowries, see Sokol and Sokol 91-103.

65. John 3:29; Mark 2:19 (King James Version).

66. In their chapters on the two "Venetian" plays, *The Merchant of Venice* and *Othello*, Allan Bloom and Harry Jaffa explain that "[m]arriage is a part of political life, of civil society. One cannot purify it of its political element without depriving it of its substance" (*Shakespeare's Politics* [New York: Basic, 1964] 62).

67. Harding relates that out of seventeen such cases in the court records of Chester, ten showed men trying to sneak out of their contracts after they had slept with the women (145n. 21).

68. Other legal consequences included the disallowarnce of a woman's right to dower or to administer her deceased husband's estate unless the marriage was solemnized (Ranald 9).

69. Helmholz, *Marriage* 57. To underscore the gravity of the problem, Helmholz notes that in Lichfield between 1465 and 1468, suits to establish marriage validity outnumbered suits for divorce by a margin of thirty to fifteen (25). The courts dealing with marital and sexual problems were known as "bawdy courts" (Sokol and Sokol 290).

70. Richard Whytford, *A Werke for Housholders*, published 1530 by Wynkyne de worde and reprinted in 1537, quoted in Harding 145 (Harding states that Whytford's book has not been seen, and the passage comes from Howard's *A History of Matrimonial Institutions* 350).

71. Session 24, cap. 1., *De Reformatione Matrimoni*.

72. John A. McHugh, O.P., and Charles J. Callan, O.P., trans., *Cathechism of the Council of Trent for Parish Priests* (New York: Wagner, 1923) 338.

73. Ibid. 338–39, 342.

74. Ibid. 353.

75. Brundage 552–53.

76. Margaret Scott, "Our City's Institutions: Some Further Reflections on the Marriage Contracts in *Measure for Measure*," *English Literary History* 49 (1982): 790–804, esp. 796–97. Garber (118) lists the Anglican canon law of 1604, which tried to make weddings even more public. They had to take place between eight o'clock and noon in a parish of one of the partners, presumably to ensure that there was no prior marriage. Other marriages, at night, or in inns, received censure. Garber goes on to cite Sir Oliver Martext in *As You Like It* as an example of the kind of "hedge-priest" who would perform irregular marriages. Jacques tells Touchstone and Audrey to get to a church and be married by a priest who knows what marriage is. Taking this advice, their marriage is blessed at the end of the play by Hymen.

77. *Tametsi* was not actually published in England until the nineteenth century. See Brundage 565.

CHAPTER 2. THINGS SEEN AND UNSEEN

1. All references are to William Shakespeare, *Measure for Measure*, Arden edition, ed. J. W. Lever (New York: Routledge, 1965).

2. See Harriet Hawkins, "What Kind of Pre-Contract had Angelo? A Note on Some Non-Problems in Elizabethan Drama," *College English* 36 (1974): 173–79.

3. Scott 792.

4. Ibid. 796–97. For my purposes, it is unnecessary to inquire whether Shakespeare meant to support the Anglican or Catholic position on spousals. Scholars have argued both sides. See Daryll Gless, *Measure for Measure, the Law and the Convent* (Princeton: Princeton UP, 1979) for the argument that the play is antimonastic satire. D. J. McGinn, on the other

hand, contends that the play propounds a Catholic view ("The Precise Angelo," in *Joseph Quincy Adams Memorial Studies*, ed. James G. McManaway, Giles E. Dawson, and Edwin E. Willoughby [Washington, DC: Folger Shakespeare Library, 1948] 129–39.

5. The idea of the child as an imprint of his father, and of the seal as symbolic of conception, is also central to the contract in *All's Well That Ends Well*.

6. A recent recounting of the argument is in Sokol and Sokol's *Shakespeare's Legal Language* (303).

7. Garber says that economic considerations were "the most visible, if not necessarily most important, among the great families and nobilities," and that the norm would probably be represented more nearly by Angelo's and Bertram's rejection of their brides (121).

8. William Shakespeare, *King Lear*, Arden edition, ed. R. A. Foakes (London: Nelson, 1997) 1.1.243.

9. See the exchange between Bertram and the King in *All's Well That Ends Well* (2.3.117–44) and between Imogen and the King in *Cymbeline* (1.2.70–82). All references to *All's Well That Ends Well* are to the Arden edition, ed. G. K. Hunter (Walton-on-Thames: Nelson, 1997). All references to *Cymbeline* are to Shakespeare, *Complete Works*.

10. The Duke tells the newly married Mariana he will "instate and widow" her with all of Angelo's property, effectively rectifying her poverty (5.1.422). Clarkson and Warren explain that a felon's property was confiscate to the state, and Mariana would have lost her dower under ordinary circumstances (205). But Mariana exhibits a different understanding of value when she "craves no better husband" than Angelo, though she now has "worth" enough to "buy herself a better husband" (5.1.424–25).

11. The use of clothing in comparisons is also in *All's Well That Ends Well*, in reference to the poseur Parolles (2.3.202), and in *Cymbeline*, in reference to the contemptible Cloten (2.3.133–37).

12. See Muriel C. Bradbrook, "Authority, Truth, and Justice in *Measure for Measure*," *Review of English Studies* 17 (1941): 385–99; Richard L. Levin, "Duke Vincentio and Angelo: Would 'A Feather Turn the Scale,'" *Studies in English Literature* 22 (1982): 257–70; and N. W. Bawcutt, "'He Who the Sword of Heaven Will Bear': The Duke versus Angelo in *Measure for Measure*," *Shakespeare Survey* 37 (1984): 89–97.

13. James Black explains another type of disjunction between *res* and *verba* in the comic scene between Pompey and Elbow, where the very words upon which the system of law rests are joke material ("The Unfolding of *Measure for Measure*," *Aspects of Shakespeare's Problem Plays: Articles Reprinted from Shakespeare Survey*, ed. Kenneth Muir and Stanley Wells [Cambridge: Cambridge UP, 1982] 78–86, esp. 80).

14. Although J. W. Lever's Arden edition defines *acknowledge* as "come to be known," some scholars interpret the Duke as implying hopes that Mariana will become pregnant. See William Shakespeare, *Measure for Measure*, Oxford edition, ed. N. W. Bawcutt (Oxford: Clarendon, 1991), note to 3.1.253 on 162. If so, her similarity with Helena in *All's Well That Ends Well* and the similarity between the two bed-tricks is all the closer.

15. *Oxford English Dictionary*, 2nd ed., s.v. "perform."

16. Garber, 163-65. See Luke 1:26-27.

17. St. Thomas Aquinas, *Summa Theologica*, vol. 12, trans. Fathers of the English Dominican Province, (New York: Benziger, 1947) 100.

18. See Gless 73.

19. As Black points out, "words must find enactment," lest God's name be simply, as in Angelo's case, chewed in the mouth (82). Also, the Duke's plans are nothing if not busy, a quality so pronounced that modern critics consider him a schemer. See Hal Gelb, "Duke Vincentio and the Illusion of Comedy; or All's Not Well that Ends Well," *Shakespeare Quarterly* 22 (1971): 25-34.

20. Legal scholars are quick to point out that the fornication statute that Angelo enforces has, presumably, also lain fallow for fourteen years. A general legal principle is that laws can become repealed by desuetude, which makes Angelo's actions even more despotic. See Keeton 392-93.

21. Some have argued that Isabella shows monasticism in a sorry light, which would have appealed to the Elizabethans. See Gless 78-79. However, this position does not account for the unscathed friars in the play, including the Duke when acting as a friar. Also, it seems Isabella's mistakes could grow as easily from Puritanism as monasticism. But I do agree that Isabella's excesses in the cloister establish a similarity between her and Angelo's "angelism." A more defensible position would aim at *cloistered* monasticism as a foe to Nature. But even that conclusion may be going too far. Isabella's trial novitiate, both as nun and as sibling, reveals an immaturity she does not outgrow until the end of the play.

22. Michael Goldman says "scope" suggests not only a prescribed arena of movement, but also control and balance (*Shakespeare and the Energies of the Drama* [Princeton: Univ. Press, 1972], 166). The scope marriage provides to the sexual appetite gives the appetite control and balance.

23. All four plays rehearse this theme: *All's Well That Ends Well* and *Troilus and Cressida* demonstrate unrestrained appetites for war, and *The Merchant of Venice*, for greed and revenge.

24. Ernst Kantorowicz, *The King's Two Bodies: A Study in Mediaeval Political Theology* (Princeton: Princeton UP, 1957). Also see Elizabeth Marie Pope, "The Renaissance Background of *Measure for Measure*," *Aspects of Shakespeare's Problem Plays: Articles Reprinted from Shakespeare Survey*, ed. Kenneth Muir and Stanley Wells (Cambridge: Cambridge UP, 1982) 57-73, for explanations of the analogy between God and man in the play.

25. Shakespeare, *Complete Works*.

26. On the many levels of substitution in the play, see Alexander Leggatt, "Substitution in *Measure for Measure*," *Shakespeare Quarterly* 39 (1988): 342-59.

27. *Oxford English Dictionary*, 2nd ed., s.v. "execution"; s.v. "satisfaction."

28. Robert Grams Hunter, *Shakespeare and the Comedy of Forgiveness* (New York: Columbia UP, 1965) 204-8.

29. Kermode 1168.

30. *The Comedy of Errors*, Shakespeare *Complete Works*, 2.2.118-45; *Cymbeline* 3.4.128-30.

31. Ranald explains that physical consummation of the marriage was necessary for an indissoluble union, a *martrimonium ratum* (37).

32. Hunter 204.

33. R. J. Kauffman, "Bond Slaves and Counterfeits: Shakespeare's *Measure for Measure*," *Shakespeare Studies* 3 (1967): 85-97, esp. 95-96.

34. *Twelfth Night*, Shakespeare, *Complete Works*, 5.1.375.

35. See Amy Lechter-Siegel, "Isabella's Silence; The Consolidation of Power in *Measure for Measure*," *Reconsidering the Renaissance*, ed. Mario Di Cesare (Binghamton, NY: Medieval and Renaissance Texts and Studies, 1992) 371-80.

36. Black points out that the play is largely set in places removed—prisons, cloisters, and retreats—and illustrates that a fugitive and cloistered virtue is of equal uselessness to a "buried talent" (78).

37. Justice as a means of reminding transgressors of their "kinship" to society has particular application here and in *The Merchant of Venice*. Rudolf Stammler and Mohandas Gandhi are two articulators of this as the proper role for justice. See Raymond B. Marcin, "Justice and Love," *The Catholic University of America Law Review* 33.2 (1984): 363-91.

38. As Kauffman explains, children are seen as either legal, or as made from forbidden stamps, a concept that underscores the legal metaphors in the play (91).

39. Garber 131.

40. Erasmus, quoted in Thomas Wilson, *Art of Rhetoric*, ed. Peter E. Medine (University Park: Pennsylvania State UP, 1994). See Shakespeare, *Measure for Measure* (ed. Lever) 24n. 41-44.

41. The corn to be reaped and the "tilth" to be sown alludes to the children who can spring from the belated consummation. J. W. Lever, among other editors, prefers "tithe" to "tilth" because it accentuates the idea that "sowing" is "due" from the marriage partners. Lever mentions Dr. Johnson's suggestion that "tithe" in conjunction with the Duke as friar implied the dues owed to the Church. Lever appreciates the remark, since corn tithes were often paid to the Church (100n. 76). But since the Duke began the play with what Angelo owes nature, nature seems the better referent. Other editions use "tilth" for Lucio's husbandry (1.4.44).

42. Berman suggests that Paul's letter to the Romans sheds light on the sensuality and righteousness of the characters. He also contends that Shakespeare's concept of lust is that of Luther, an expression of self-love in the pursuit of sensuality (142). If so, it is the flip side of the charge of selfishness with which the young man of the sonnets is upbraided for in his

coldness, and the analogy proves that Angelo only changes from one type of selfishness to another.

43. J. A. Bryant, Jr., *Shakespeare and the Uses of Comedy* (Lexington: UP of Kentucky, 1986) 218.

44. Barber 185.

45. See R. S. White on Aquinas and other natural law thinkers regarding unjust civil laws (34).

46. See for example Baker, *Common Law* 460–76; Thorne 187–210.

CHAPTER 3. PERFECTION IN REVERSION

1. The "problem" with *Troilus and Cressida* has often concerned its genre. Whether comedy, history, or tragedy, it was for some time thought to have been performed at the Inns of Court. One of the first proponents of this view was Peter Alexander, who makes his observation in *Shakespeare's Life and Art* (London: Nisbet, 1939) 195. For a different view, see Alfred Harbage's work that relates the play to the Elizabethan war of the theaters (*Shakespeare and the Rival Traditions* [New York: Macmillan, 1952] 119).

2. All references are to Shakespeare, *Troilus and Cressida*.

3. Hector may allude here to the "law of nations," a concept drawn from Italian legal scholar Alberico Gentili's work, *De Jure Belli*, published in 1591. See O. J. Campbell, *Comical Satyre and Shakespeare's Troilus and Cressida* (San Marino, CA: Huntington Library, 1959) 191–92, 207. On medieval distinctions between the law of nations and the natural law, see R. S. White 28.

4. *Oxford English Dictionary*, 2nd ed., s.v. "secrecy"

5. For an overview of Girard's theory as it relates to culture, and particularly literature, see Rene Girard, *Violence and the Sacred* (Baltimore: Johns Hopkins UP, 1972).

6. Rene Girard, *A Theater of Envy: William Shakespeare* (New York: Oxford UP, 1991) 123.

7. A. P. Rossiter, *Angels with Horns*, ed. Graham Storey (London: Longmans, 1961) 142.

8. Linda Anderson comments that the ostensible reason for the war, Helen's rape, is presented as below contempt. Predictably, only Paris and Menelaus pay it much attention. The Greeks are concerned with degree, and the Trojans, honor (*A Kind of Wild Justice: Revenge in Shakespeare's Comedies* [Newark: U of Delaware P, 1987] 133).

9. Campbell summarizes what is known as Hector's volte-face: "[H]e thereby yields his rational leadership to a democracy of passions and takes the fatal step that ends in the ruin of himself and of his cause (207).

10. See Clarkson and Warren 79–80.

11. Simpson, *Land Law* 108.

12. In Sonnet 94, line 14, the sonneteer, disgusted with sex and his faithless lover, says "Lilies that fester smell far worse than weeds."

13. The statute of *Quia Emptores* (1290) put an end to this type of tenure, making the use here more important for its imaginative relationship to Cressida as property—a farm upon which Troilus will "build." Also see Clarkson and Warren 15; and Sokol and Sokol 120.

14. Clarkson and Warren 125-26n. 114. Sokol and Sokol explain this to be the language of indentures (148-49).

15. A change in tone in the use of agricultural metaphors is not limited to the sex theme, but extends to the war theme. Vivian Thomas points out that Nestor describes Hector as mower (a pastoral image), whose swath fells the "strawy Greeks" (5.5.24-25) (*The Moral Universe of Shakespeare's Problem Plays* [Totowa, NJ: Barnes, 1987] 127). The image is life-destroying, not life-enhancing.

16. Clarkson and Warren explain that when a lesser estate granted comes to an end, the possession reverts to the grantor: "An estate in reversion then is the residue of an estate continuing in a grantor after a smaller particular estate has been conveyed away, and which commences in possession after the determination of the latter" (73). Shakespeare also uses the term in *Richard II*, when the Queen fears she possesses her future, unnamed grief in "reversion" (2.2.35-38) (*Richard II*, Shakespeare, *Complete Works*).

17. Sokol and Sokol note that "reversion" here is related to the language of sexuality (325).

18. The constancy of the Turtledove to her mate, the Phoenix, is the theme of Shakespeare's poem *The Phoenix and Turtle*. The similarity between the idea of marriage there and the idea as expressed in *Measure for Measure* was mentioned in the last chapter. Of course, in the context of the mock marriage here, the reference is ironic.

19. See Thorne 39.

20. Campbell sees this as a satirization of the "aubaude," or ode to morning, with the ribald crows waking the two sensualists (213). Garber makes a similar observation regarding *Romeo and Juliet* (143).

21. Questions without answers are a hallmark of Troilus and Cressida, accentuating its metaphysical tone. Thomas reports that there are around four hundred questions in the play, more than any other Shakespearean drama (102).

22. Bryant thinks Ulysses does not intend to restore the chain of command, but to restore Achilles to the Greek effort (181). Considering his enterprise, it may be that Ulysses is tacitly referring to Achilles, not Agamemnon, as the missing head of the chain.

23. To the Greeks, Achilles is caught in the image of his self-worth, another instance of imitation: "Pride is his own glass, his own trumpet, his own chronicle—and whatever praises itself but in the deed devours the deed in the praise" (2.3.153-55). Achilles's

"pageants" are among other metadramatic references that reinforce the theme of foolish imitation.

24. Girard, *Violence and the Sacred* 50–51. He continues by placing Ulysses's dire predictions within a tradition found in literature, one that eventually erupts in violence and sacrifice. The play's great theme, in Girard's opinion, is the threat of primordial chaos.

25. Campbell 226. G. Wilson Knight's view is that reason triumphs over intuition in the play, with Troilus as the spokesman for intuition and the tragic philosophy (*The Wheel of Fire* [London: Methuen, 1949], 48). I prefer Campbell's explanation, seeing the tension in the play as between reason and appetite, not reason and intuition. I do not believe it follows that simply because Troilus is defeated, and because Troilus scoffs at reason, therefore it is reason that defeats him. To my understanding, he is defeated because he rejects reason and prefers his appetite.

26. Girard, *Theater of Envy* 146–47.

27. Girard sees Ulysses's strategy to win Achilles as similar to Cressida's strategy to win Troilus. At first, Cressida plays hard to get, increasing her worth; she loses value when she gives in to Troilus, only to regain it when Diomedes appears to want her. Conversely, under Ulysses plan, the Greeks pretend to want Ajax more than Achilles, then pretend they are not interested in Achilles at all (*Theater of Envy*, 143–47).

28. Further evidence lies in Paris's calling the "*generation* of love" a "*generation* of vipers" (3.1.126–28; emphasis added). Even natural generation is tainted; Diomedes says Paris is like a lecher, pleased to "breed his inheritors" out of "whorish loins" (4.1.65–66).

29. Richard Hillman says this passage suggests the equivalent of a poetic device, the male *blazon* of female beauty. Here it is implied perversely, for purposes of deciding where to inflict the fatal wound (*William Shakespeare: The Problem Plays* [New York: Twayne, 1993] 25).

30. Girard, *Theater of Envy* 150.

31. Rossiter comments that Hector's honoring his vow "because he said he would" is the same logic Troilus used in the council, when debating whether to keep the stolen Helen. Rossiter calls this "thieves' honor" (143n. 1).

32. Campbell notes that at the end of the play, Pandarus's final address includes a promise that his "will" is to be made *here* in two months time, referring to the Inns, where lawyers assembled (192).

33. Oxford English Dictionary, 2nd ed., s.v. "clap."

CHAPTER 4. MATCHING MEANINGS

1. All references are to William Shakespeare, *The Merchant of Venice*, Arden edition, ed. John Russell Brown (Walton-on-Thames: Nelson, 1997).

2. In the case of *Brett v. J.S. and Wife.* Potter 410.

3. Baker 376. Plowden argued for "natural causes" as sufficient consideration, and Dyer was, according to reports, of two minds (ibid. See also Simpson, *Land Law* 178).

4. *A Midsummer Night's Dream,* Shakespeare, *Complete Works* 1.1.41.

5. *Pericles,* Shakespeare, *Complete Works* scene 1, line 34.

6. Barber 171.

7. In Launcelot's comment is one example of the many Christian allusions found throughout the play. In Romans 2:14–15 (King James Version), St. Paul writes, "For when the Gentiles, who have not the law, do by nature the things contained in the law, these, having not the law, are a law unto themselves; Who show the work of the law written in their hearts, their conscience also bearing witness, and their thoughts accusing or else excusing one another." This idea of God's law written on the hearts of men accords with the classical conception of the natural law as the eternal law inscribed on men's souls. See Heinrich Rommen, *The Natural Law* (Indianapolis: Liberty Fund, 1998) 31, 117.

8. In a comment that touches on the *res/verba* question so central to the problem plays, Bloom and Jaffa contrast Morocco, who chooses images by his senses, to Arragon, who chooses deserts by written texts: "True civilization implies a mixture of developed understanding and reflecting with a full capacity to perceive; one must both see things as they are and react to them appropriately. Texts and images must go together as a natural unity." Bassanio, say the authors, puts text and image together (26).

9. *Measure for Measure* 1.3.20.

10. This tempering image recurs when Jessica says she is never merry when she hears sweet music, and Lorenzo explains the tempering effect of music on the spirit, imagined as "unhandled colts" (3.1.68–78).

11. Bloom and Jaffa 26. Barber says Portia does not warn Bassanio off gold and silver, and to suggest otherwise is a "busy-body emendation that eliminates the dramatic by seeking to elaborate it" (174). However, with regard to the trial scene, Barber later says Portia—though emphatic about not putting the moral machinery of life aside—does not allow it to get in the way of life (186). This is especially so when Shylock perverts the law to his private ends.

12. For an influential work on Christian themes, see Barbara Lewalski's "Biblical Allusion and Allegory in *The Merchant of Venice,*" *Shakespeare Quarterly* 13 (1962): 327–43.

13. See chapter 2, note 28.

14. The balcony scene is yet another late comedy allusion to *Romeo and Juliet,* in line with the mock alba scene in *Troilus and Cressida,* the counsel between the Friar/Duke and Juliet in *Measure for Measure,* the "Capilets" in *All's Well That Ends Well,* and the spousal questions in all three.

15. William Kerrigan says the metaphor implies that written promises are more binding than others, a distinction that echoes through the trial scene, where the written bond

is alluded to repeatedly (*Shakespeare's Promises* [Baltimore: Johns Hopkins UP, 1999] 122–23).

16. *Measure for Measure* 1.1.36–40.

17. Clarkson and Warren 119–20. Shakespeare also uses "indenture" in *Hamlet* (5.1.119) and in *I Henry IV*, Shakespeare, *Complete Works* 3.1.76. See Sokol and Sokol 148–49.

18. Clayton Koelb remarks that the "flesh and blood" bonds of kinship are more important to the characters in the play than the legal bond Shylock secures with Antonio's flesh ("'The Bond of Flesh and Blood': Having It Both Ways in *The Merchant of Venice*," *Cardozo Studies in Law and Literature* 5.1 [1993]: 107–13, esp. 108).

19. Frederick Turner, *Shakespeare's Twenty-First Century Economics: The Morality of Love and Money* (New York: Oxford UP, 1999) 34. Charles Spinosa makes a similar comment, contrasting two views of commercial exchange: a "contract culture," which insists that everything be spelled out, and an older approach, a "customary culture," where transactions grow out of the relationship developed between vendor and purchaser. Spinosa concludes that Shylock is the communitarian and the Christians are the contractualists ("Shylock and Debt and Contract in *The Merchant of Venice*," *Cardozo Studies in Law and Literature* 5.1 [1993]: 65–85, esp. 69–74). See Wilson, 78. While it is arguable that Shylock wants to be included, Portia insists as she does because Shylock has made that response necessary. I would reverse Spinosa's assignments: the friendship bond reveals the dispensation toward nature that Turner talks of, while up until his defeat, Shylock's commercial bond insists on the "letter."

20. Issues "at law" were of two kinds, law and fact. In the first, called *demurrers*, the parties agreed upon the facts, but each claimed that "by lawe" [*sic*] (i.e., according to the law) he should win. Issues of fact were disputes over, naturally enough, facts (Ives 84). By "confessing the bond," Antonio does not dispute he owes the sum; he does not even dispute he should be let off "at law." His willingness to pay is complete. ·

21. Kerrigan 136.

22. Shylock's association of his bond with the appetite is echoed in the song that links "appearances" with the "appetite": "fancy" is "*en'gendered* in the *eyes*," is "fed" by "*gazing*," and dies where it is "en'gendered." This repeats the association of appetite and death used in the stillborn imagery of *Troilus and Cressida* (4.4.36–37).

23. Antonio's question about the breeding of barren metal echoes Aristotle's comparison in *Politics*, and the same question raised by Aquinas in the *Summa*. See Lewalski 332.

24. In *Measure for Measure*, when Claudio speaks of postponing both his marriage and the legitimizing of his child until they can "propagate" Juliet's dower (1.2.139), the same unnatural connotations arise. The fruits of marriage cannot depend on the fruits of money.

25. On "single bonds," see Simpson, *Legal History* 114.

26. Ibid.

27. This relief brought about a distinction between penalties and liquidated damages. See Simpson, *Contract* 118.

28. Coke's Reports in *Burton's Case* (1591) (5 Co. Rep. 69a) makes this argument (see ibid. 115). Canonists distinguished between usury and "interesse," which could be charged legally to compensate for the loss suffered by forfeiture (ibid. 114).

29. The reasons for usury's unnaturalness were many. One of the most ingenious was that usury was the sale of time; only God owns time (see ibid. 510–511).

30. See ibid. 321.

31. According to Richard Posner, Portia understands that a measure of impersonality in the administration of laws, and thus a willingness to provide justice to aliens, is necessary to preserve Venice's commercial position (*Law and Literature: A Misunderstood Relationship* [Cambridge: Harvard UP, 1988] 110). The point highlights a breadth in Venetian alien law that critics overlook: aliens are afforded the same property rights as citizens *until* they conspire against the lives of citizens, whereupon they stand to lose those rights.

32. See Phillips for an interesting alternative source for the "pound of flesh" story. It is found in Gregorio Leti's *The Life of Pope Sixtus the Fifth*, trans. Ellis Farnsworth (1754) 100–102. A Jew, Ceneda, and a merchant, Secchi, wagered a pound of flesh on the veracity of a story that Santo Domingo had been plundered. Ceneda lost, and Secchi appealed to Sixtus to take his winnings. The pontiff agreed that all contracts must be enforced, but told Secchi that if he took more or less than a pound, he would hang. The merchant declined. He was then imprisoned for attempting murder, as was Ceneda for wagering his body in a way that amounted to suicide. In the end, Sixtus allowed friends to bail them out. Pope Sixtus V (1585–90) was involved in sending the Armada against Elizabeth, so it is likely that the English knew of him.

33. *Troilus and Cressida* 5.3.107.

34. Conscience was added to the Natural law equation by Aquinas and St. Germain. Grotius argued that conscience is simply reason applied to ethical dilemmas (R. S. White 2; see also, Wilks 9–23).

35. *Measure for Measure* 3.2.248.

36. Ibid. 4.4.24.

37. Ibid. 3.2.254–69.

38. Whenever the integrity of one of the legal instruments or concepts is at stake, Shakespeare employs a trial to resolve it. In *Measure for Measure*, the pseudocontracts require a trial for their resolution. In *The Merchant of Venice*, the interpretation of the bond is at stake. In *All's Well That Ends Well*, the marriage contract must prove itself by means of a trial. In *Troilus and Cressida*, where there is only a mock contract, there is no trial except for the Trojan council's debate over Helen.

39. Charles J. Fillmore, "Frame Semantics and the Nature of Language," *Annals of the New York Academy of Sciences: Conference on the Origin and Development of Language and*

Speech 280 (1976): 20-32. In a similar observation, Black says the Pompey-Elbow exchange in *Measure for Measure*, with its haze of "misplaced words and irrelevancies," illustrates how judging becomes impossible when neither prosecutor nor defendant can, or will, stay within the logical bounds of words, where law can work (80).

40. Posner 38. For accounts of legal conjecturing, see Keeton 147-50; and Phillips 91-118.

41. A recent history of the scholarship regarding the trial can be found in R. S. White's work (160). Ranald sums it up best when she says audiences must suspend disbelief as to Portia's legal "cram course" and as to Antonio's failure to buy marine insurance (60).

42. Hunter 204-8. What Kermode calls the "iconographic habit" of the English mind is illustrated in this scene, where characters' positions interchange as a tableau of justice and mercy. He makes an interesting observation in terms of unified form and matter, which I contend is so central to understanding these plays: "Equity may be thought of as matter to which Justice gives form," much as human conception was thought to depend on the male seed imposing form on the female matter (1170-71).

43. On the "use" and the English law of wills, see R. H. Helmholz, "The English Law of Wills and the *Ius Commune*, 1450-1640," *Marriage, Property, and Succession*, ed. Lloyd Bonfield (Berlin: Duncker, 1992) 309-326. Keeton explains that a "use" under the Statue of Uses of 1535 will vest a legal life estate in Shylock, with a vested remainder to Jessica and Lorenzo. He adds that trusts were formerly known as "uses," and that Antonio is not necessarily holding the money at interest (146). Clarkson and Warren say that Shylock could have only transferred what he had at the time in his deed of gift, not all "after-acquired property" (183). Sokol and Sokol give a history of this confusing issue (384-87). It seems to me that Antonio is implying something in the manner of a will, by which Shylock would provide for his daughter in a selfless way, just as Portia's father's will has done.

44. A. D. Moody, "The Letter of the Law," *The Merchant of Venice: Critical Essays*, ed. Thomas Wheeler (New York: Garland, 1991) 79-101.

45. See Girard, *Theater of Envy* 252; and Kornstein 76-79.

46. The alternative title, *The Jew of Venice*, was entered on the Stationer's Register in 1598.

47. Explaining the ribaldry of the jests, Garber says that the image of the ring placed upon the outstretched finger is an old symbol of intercourse in folklore, and is repeated in the jeweled circlets of both *Cymbeline* and *The Comedy of Errors* (160-62). The rings in *All's Well That Ends Well* could be added to the list, as could Cressida's "glove," insofar as it is a parody of the convention.

48. This is Bertram's threat in *All's Well That Ends Well*, although meant there to frustrate the act of consummation. The statement underscores the association of the ring with marital rights.

49. Sigurd Burckhardt says the play is circular in nature, a symbol of the "gentle bond" that Portia makes by transforming the vicious circle into a ring of love ("*The Merchant of*

Venice: 'The Gentle Bond,'" Shakespearean Meanings [Princeton: Princeton UP, 1968] 206-236). The ring as the emblem of integrity finds further support in the play's circular structure: Antonio, to help Bassanio, provides the means by which Bassanio can travel to Belmont and free Portia from the casket; once freed, Portia, to help Bassanio, provides the means by which Bassanio can travel to Venice and free Antonio from death's threat. The circularity implies a unity here, as opposed to the circularity of meaninglessness in *Troilus and Cressida.*

50. Bloom and Jaffa 17.

CHAPTER 5. LAWFUL TITLE

1. W. W. Lawrence, *Shakespeare's Problem Comedies* (New York: MacMillan, 1931) 33.

2. See Peter Ure, *Shakespeare: The Problem Plays* (London: Longmans, 1961); and E. M. W. Tillyard, *Shakespeare's Problem Plays* (London: Chatto & Windus, 1950).

3. Shakespeare, *All's Well That Ends Well*, xxix. All references are to this edition.

4. *The Merchant of Venice* 3.2.68-69.

5. *Troilus and Cressida* 4.4.36-37.

6. Parolles can be counted among these scoffers. It is said he corrupts Bertram's "well-derived nature" (3.2.87-89), and gives him the "scornful perspective" that skews his appreciation of Helena's value (5.3.48).

7. York Act book M2(1)c, f. 7r. (1372), quoted in R. H. Helmholz, "The Roman Law of Guardianship in England, 1300-1600." *Tulane Law Review* 52.2 (1978): 223-57, esp. 244.

8. Ibid. 245.

9. Hunter 118.

10. Heirlooms were not proper subjects of testation in the Renaissance. They generally passed by family tradition (Clarkson and Warren 240n. 60).

11. After performing his "business" with Diana (in actuality, Helena), he fears to "hear of it hereafter" (4.3.93-94), that is, fears that she will become pregnant. In this way, frigidity and lust are equally set against procreation.

12. Peggy Munoz Simonds suggests an Erasmian colloquy, "Proci et Puellae," or "The Wooer and the Maiden," as a possible source for the virginity debate. It concerns the value of virginity and the necessity of losing it in a fruitful marriage. It is the maiden who makes the rational case for marriage, seeking a changed relationship, rather than a temporary union ("Sacred and Sexual Motifs in *All's Well That Ends Well*," *Renaissance Quarterly* 42.1 [1989]: 33-59, esp. 47). G. K. Hunter also makes reference to this colloquy in his edition (12n. 148).

13. Like Bassanio, Helena has been considered a profiteer by some scholars, another reason for considering the play problematic. See Clifford Leech, "The Theme of Ambition in *All's Well That Ends Well*," *Discussions of Shakespeare's Problem Comedies*, ed. Robert

Ornstein (Boston: Heath, 1961) 56–63, esp. 62. This position is not convincing, since Helena never mentions Bertram's titles and wealth in her love. Her ambition is to win Bertram, not his additions.

14. Clarkson and Warren observe that Shakespeare uses *fee* to convey the absolute nature of the estate. The authors go on to explain that in Shakespeare's day, it would not have been sufficient to make a conveyance to a man "forever" or even "in *fee* simple." Without the word *heirs* in the conveyance, the estate conveyed was limited to the life of the grantee (52). Thus, when *fee* is used in *All's Well That Ends Well*, in which themes of legacy, inheritance, and generation are threatened, the word has particular significance.

15. In a comment that expresses the way in which Helena works to reunify *res* and *verba* in the play, G. K. Hunter says Helena is virtue—the real thing—"seeking the name," but not knowing how to acquire it. For a time, she is defeated by *mere* name, Parolles (xli).

16. See Phillips 134.

17. The right of the master to dispose of his ward in marriage was proprietary in nature. There were strong monetary disincentives to a ward's refusing a suitable match (Clarkson and Warren 31; and Simpson, *Land Law* 18). Shakespeare's patron, the Earl of Southampton, was under a wardship arrangement. The playwright could have gained an understanding of such problems by being privy to them.

18. See R. B. Parker, "War and Sex in *All's Well That Ends Well*," *Shakespeare Survey* 37 (1984): 99–113, esp. 101; and Carol Thomas Neely, *Broken Nuptials in Shakespeare's Plays* (New Haven: Yale UP, 1985) 62.

19. G. K. Hunter points out that it is Bertram's fancy, not his judgment that he submits to the King (59n. 168). He also notes (60n. 176) that Bertram only half complies with the King's command; he takes Helena by the hand but refuses to carry out the rest of the order—"tell her she is thine" (2.3.174).

20. Simonds' critique of the religious analogies in the scene adds a different kind of culpability to Bertram's behavior. To Renaissance Christians, marriage was analogous to the mystical union between Christ and his people, the Church. The implied theological analogy would have been clear to an audience: a count who refuses to give new life to his family and society—at the King's command, no less—is refusing to imitate Christ's promise to provide new life to the world (50–53).

21. Thorne 43, 48. Simpson states it this way: "[T]he law favored holders of estates who were prompt in claiming seisin; their right began as a right of entry and in time would become a mere right of action, and eventually be destroyed entirely by the rules as to limitation of actions" (*Land Law* 88).

22. Rossiter says the disagreeable Bertram shakes the fairy-tale foundations and makes us choose between saying Shakespeare is inept, cynical, or "aware of what he had done, even if it was the best he could do" (92).

23. Anderson 145. Richard Wheeler's Freudian approach considers the psychological determinants in the plays to "overburden" Helena; the "maternal dimension" to the girl, which he says makes Bertram react against her, is better realized in *The Winter Tale*'s Hermione; like-

wise, the young heroine dimension is better as Perdita, and the priestess-like manipulator of the plot better as Paulina (*Shakespeare's Development and the Problem Comedies: Turn and Counter-Turn* [Los Angeles: U of California P, 1981] 91).

24. Helmholz, *Marriage Litigation* 35–45. The case's final disposition went unrecorded, but the last report before appeal had decided the marriage was conditional only.

25. Ibid. 47, 51.

26. The insertion of a condition to marriage after a pause was allowed, but only if it followed very closely (ibid. 49). Even so, this caveat applied at the formation stage, not subsequent to the marriage ceremony.

27. Clarkson and Warren 62, 132.

28. See Sokol and Sokol 110, 256–57. A grantor could convey away an interest in land that, if retained, would be a reversion. If this interest was disposed of at the same time, and by the same conveyance as the smaller estate, it was called a "remainder." The person holding was a "remainder-man" (Clarkson and Warren 75–76).

29. Phillips says this may be a topical allusion to *Chudliegh's Case*, decided in 1595, which contains the first use of the word *perpetuity* in the law books. This case stopped the practice of creating successive contingent remainders, which inhibited the free conveyance of land (82).

30. An agent could receive possession in behalf of a transferee of land (see Thorne 49). Here, Diana is Helena's agent for part of her task, obtaining the ring.

31. Simpson, *Legal History* 113–14.

32. William Shakespeare, *A Midsummer Night's Dream*, ed. Harold F. Brooks (London: Thomas Learning, 1979).

33. Objections to the propriety of the bed-trick include G. K. Hunter's, who finds it "irrelevant and tasteless" (xliv). In an argument against finding any indelicacy in the bed-trick, Simonds says that the bed-trick is a respectable convention in Judeo-Christian history: Tamar tricks Judah into sleeping with her to make him fulfill his duty to provide an heir to Israel. She also refers to the bed-tricks in the Arthurian cycle that give us Galahad and Arthur. The bed-trick, says Simonds, was meant to be seen as necessary, not immoral, since "certain children must be born into the world" (55–56). Finally, William Toole cites precedent for deceit in crucial circumstances. According to Gregory of Nyssa, God deceived Satan by taking human form to ransom mankind (*Shakespeare's Problem Plays* [The Hague: Mouton, 1966] 151–54).

34. Bertram's nascent penitence for his behavior may be further intimated in his proposed marriage to "Maudlin," the vernacular form of Magdalene. Mary Magdalene is the traditional penitent, turning from harlotry to rectitude after great penance (see Neely 85).

35. In Shakespeare's day, bridegrooms often gave a bond that no precontract existed, a fact that is pertinent to Bertram's situation. Shakespeare gave one upon his marriage to Anne Hathaway (see Underhill 408).

36. Helena's association with Nature is well noted. Mark Van Doren says that Helena's favorite words include *nature*, and she naturally speaks of Bertram in metaphysical language (*Shakespeare* [New York: Holt, 1939] 215–16). Robert Hunter says that although Fortuna has slighted Helena, "Natura" raises her fortunes. G. Wilson Knight sees her as a divine miracle worker ("Helena," *Shakespeare: The Comedies, A Collection of Critical Essays*, ed. Kenneth Muir [Englewood Cliffs: Prentice, 1965] 133–51). Heaven and nature work toward the same goal, as the nature-blessed Helena works in heaven's behalf.

CHAPTER 6. NATURE'S DOUBLE NAME

1. G.K. Hunter, lv.

2. See Girard, *Envy* 252.

3. See Hillman 55–56.

4. Constance Jordan explains an aspect regarding rulers in Shakespeare's romances that is applicable to the Duke in *Measure for Measure*:

> Removed from the seat of their authority and power, they also become alienated in mind. They think not as heads of state, but in ways that take them from their principal business. The agencies responsible for their return to a proper government are various and in some cases ambiguous. . . . The work of return cannot, it seems, be encompassed only by equitable judgments; it also requires patience and suffering.

(*Shakespeare's Monarchies: Ruler and Subject in the Romances* [Ithaca: Cornell UP, 1997] 5). The same observation could apply by extension to those who have "removed themselves" from society or abdicated their responsibility, such as Angelo, Shylock, or Bertram.

5. All references to *Cymbeline, The Winter's Tale, King Lear, Twelfth Night,* and *The Tempest* are to Shakespeare, *Complete Works*.

6. George C. Herndl is of the opinion that the "rack" Lear is on is not nature, but the perversion of what the law requires, that is, it is the "unnaturalness" of his daughters that tortures him. Man's will, such as Edmund's conflation of his appetite with nature, is what engineers the kingdom's fall (*The High Design, English Renaissance Tragedy and the Natural Law* [Lexington: U of Kentucky P, 1970] 13).

7. Shakespeare, *Complete Works*.

Works Cited

Alexander, Peter. *Shakespeare's Life and Art*. London: Nisbet, 1939.

Anderson, Linda. *A Kind of Wild Justice: Revenge in Shakespeare's Comedies*. Newark: U of Delaware P, 1987.

Aquinas, Thomas. *Summa Theologica*. Vol. 12. Trans. Fathers of the English Dominican Province. New York: Benziger, 1947.

Baker, J. H. The Legal Profession and the Common Law: Historical Essays. London: Hambledon, 1986.

Baker, J. H., and S. F. C. Milson. *Sources of English Legal History: Private Law to 1750*. London: Butterworths, 1986.

Barber, C. L. *Shakespeare's Festive Comedy: A Study of Dramatic Form and Its Relation to Social Custom*. Princeton: Princeton UP, 1959.

Bawcutt, N. W. "'He Who the Sword of Heaven Will Bear': The Duke versus Angelo in *Measure for Measure*." *Shakespeare Survey* 37 (1984): 89–97.

Berman, Ronald. "Shakespeare and the Law." *Shakespeare Quarterly* 18 (1967): 141–50.

Black, James. "The Unfolding of *Measure for Measure*." *Aspects of Shakespeare's Problem Plays: Articles Reprinted from Shakespeare Survey*. Ed. Kenneth Muir and Stanley Wells. Cambridge: Cambridge UP, 1982. 78-86.

Bloom, Allan, and Harry Jaffa. *Shakespeare's Politics*. New York: Basic, 1964.

Boose, Linda E. "The Comic Contract and Portia's Golden Ring." *Shakespeare Studies* 20 (1988): 241–54.

Bradbrook, Muriel C. "Authority, Truth, and Justice in *Measure for Measure*." *Review of English Studies* 17 (1941): 385–99.

Brundage, James A. *Law, Sex, and Christian Society in Medieval Europe*. Chicago: U of Chicago P, 1987.

Bryant, J. A., Jr., *Shakespeare and the Uses of Comedy*. Lexington: UP of Kentucky, 1986.

Burckhardt, Sigurd. "*The Merchant of Venice*: 'The Gentle Bond.'" *Shakespearean Meanings*. Princeton: Princeton UP, 1968. 206-236.

Campbell, O. J. *Comical Satyre and Shakespeare's Troilus and Cressida*. San Marino, CA: Huntington Library, 1959.

Clarkson, P. S., and C. T. Warren. *The Law of Property in Shakespearean and Elizabethan Drama*. Baltimore: Johns Hopkins UP, 1942.

Fillmore, Charles J. "Frame Semantics and the Nature of Language." *Annals of the New York Academy of Sciences: Conference on the Origin and Development of Language and Speech* 280 (1976): 20-32.

Garber, Marjorie. *Coming of Age in Shakespeare*. New York: Methuen, 1981.

Gelb, Hal. "Duke Vincentio and the Illusion of Comedy; or All's Not Well that Ends Well." *Shakespeare Quarterly* 22 (1971): 25-34.

Girard, Rene. *A Theater of Envy: William Shakespeare*. New York: Oxford UP, 1991.

——. *Violence and the Sacred*. Baltimore: Johns Hopkins UP, 1972.

Gless, Darryl J. *Measure for Measure, the Law and the Convent*. Princeton: Princeton UP, 1979.

Goldman, Michael. *Shakespeare and the Energies of the Drama*. Princeton: Princeton UP, 1972.

Harbage, Alfred. *Shakespeare and the Rival Traditions*. New York: Macmillan, 1952.

Harding, Davies P. "Elizabethan Betrothals and *Measure for Measure*." *Journal of English and Germanic Philology* 49 (1950): 139-58.

Hawkins, Harriet. "What Kind of Pre-Contract Had Angelo? A Note on Some Non-Problems in Elizabethan Drama." *College English* 36 (1974): 173-79.

Helmholz, R. H. "The English Law of Wills and the *Ius Commune*, 1450-1640. *Marriage, Property, and Succession*. Ed. Lloyd Bonfield. Berlin: Duncker, 1992. 309-326.

——. *Marriage Litigation in Medieval England*. Cambridge: Cambridge UP, 1974.

——. "The Roman Law of Guardianship in England, 1300-1600." *Tulane Law Review* 52.2 (1978): 223-57.

Herndl, George C. *The High Design, English Renaissance Tragedy and the Natural Law*. Lexington: U of Kentucky P, 1970.

Hillman, Richard. *William Shakespeare: The Problem Plays*. New York: Twayne, 1993.

Hooker, Richard. *Of the Laws of Ecclesiastical Polity*. 4 vols. Ed. W. Speed Hill. Cambridge: Belknap/Harvard UP, 1977-98.

Howard, George Elliott. *A History of Matrimonial Institutions.* Vol. 1. Chicago: U of Chicago P, 1904. Littleton, CO: Rothman, 1994.

Hunter, Robert Grams. *Shakespeare and the Comedy of Forgiveness.* New York: Columbia UP, 1965.

Ives, E. W. "The Law and the Lawyers." *Shakespeare Survey* 17 (1964): 73–86.

Jamieson, Michael. "The Problem Plays, 1920–1970: A Retrospect." *Aspects of Shakespeare's Problem Plays: Articles Reprinted from Shakespeare Survey.* Ed. Kenneth Muir and Stanley Wells. Cambridge: Cambridge UP, 1982. 126–35.

Jordan, Constance. *Shakespeare's Monarchies: Ruler and Subject in the Romances.* Ithaca: Cornell UP, 1997.

Kantorowicz, Ernst. *The King's Two Bodies: A Study in Mediaeval Political Theology.* Princeton: Princeton UP, 1957.

Kauffman, R. J. "Bond Slaves and Counterfeits: Shakespeare's *Measure for Measure.*" *Shakespeare Studies* 3 (1967): 85–97.

Keeton, George W. *Shakespeare's Legal and Political Background.* London: Pitman, 1967.

Kermode, Frank. "Justice and Mercy in Shakespeare." *Houston Law Review* 33 (1996): 1155–74.

Kerrigan, William. *Shakespeare's Promises.* Baltimore: Johns Hopkins UP, 1999.

Knight, G. Wilson. "Helena." *Shakespeare: The Comedies, A Collection of Critical Essays.* Ed. Kenneth Muir. Englewood Cliffs: Prentice, 1965.

——. *The Wheel of Fire.* London: Methuen, 1949.

Koelb, Clayton. "'The Bonds of Flesh and Blood': Having It Both Ways in *The Merchant of Venice.*" *Cardozo Studies in Law and Literature* 5.1 (1993): 107–13.

Kornstein, Daniel J. *Kill All the Lawyers?: Shakespeare's Legal Appeal.* Princeton: Princeton UP, 1994.

Lawrence, W. W. *Shakespeare's Problem Comedies.* New York: Macmillan, 1931.

Lechter-Seigel, Amy. "Isabella's Silence: The Consolidation of Power in *Measure for Measure.*" *Reconsidering the Renaissance.* Ed. Mario Di Cesare. Binghamton, NY: Medieval and Renaissance Texts and Studies, 1992. 371–80.

Leech, Clifford. "The Theme of Ambition in *All's Well That Ends Well.*" *Discussions of Shakespeare's Problem Comedies.* Ed. Robert Ornstein. Boston: Heath, 1961. 56–63.

Leggatt, Alexander. "Substitution in *Measure for Measure.*" *Shakespeare Quarterly* 39 (1988): 342–59.

Levin, Richard L. "Duke Vincentio and Angelo: Would 'A Feather Turn the Scale'?" *Studies in English Literature* 22 (1982): 257–70.

Lewalski, Barbara. "Biblical Allusion and Allegory in *The Merchant of Venice*." *Shakespeare Quarterly* 13 (1962): 327–43.

Marcin, Raymond B. "Justice and Love." *The Catholic University of America Law Review* 33.2 (1984): 363–91.

McGinn, D. J. "The Precise Angelo." *Joseph Quincy Adams Memorial Studies*. Ed. James G. McManaway, Giles E. Dawson and Edwin E. Willoughby. Washington, DC: Folger Shakespeare Library, 1948. 129–39.

McHugh, John A., O.P., and Charles J. Callan, O.P., trans. *Catechism of the Council of Trent for Parish Priests*. New York: Wagner, 1923.

Moody, A. D. "The Letter of the Law." *The Merchant of Venice: Critical Essays*. Ed. Thomas Wheeler. New York: Garland, 1991. 79–101.

Neely, Carol Thomas. *Broken Nuptials in Shakespeare's Plays*. New Haven: Yale UP, 1985.

Ornstein, Robert. *Discussions of Shakespeare's Problem Comedies*. Ed. Robert Ornstein. Boston: Heath, 1961.

Parker, R. B. "War and Sex in *All's Well That Ends Well*." *Shakespeare Survey* 37 (1984): 99–113.

Phillips, O. Hood. *Shakespeare and the Lawyers*. London: Methuen, 1972.

Pollock, Sir Frederick, and F. W. Maitland. *The History of English Law before Edward I*. Vol. 2. Cambridge: Cambridge UP, 1898.

Pope, Elizabeth Marie. "The Renaissance Background of *Measure for Measure*." *Aspects of Shakespeare's Problem Plays: Articles Reprinted from Shakespeare Survey*, ed. Kenneth Muir and Stanley Wells. Cambridge: Cambridge UP, 1982. 57–76.

Posner, Richard. *Law and Literature: A Misunderstood Relationship*. Cambridge: Harvard UP, 1988.

Potter, Harry. *Historical Introduction to English Law*. London: Sweet, 1943.

Ranald, Margaret Loftus. *Shakespeare and His Social Context*. New York: AMS, 1987.

Rommen, Heinrich. *The Natural Law*. Indianapolis: Liberty Fund, 1998.

Rossiter, A. P. *Angels with Horns*. Ed. Graham Storey. London: Longmans, 1961.

Scott, Margaret. "Our City's Institutions: Some Further Reflections on the Marriage Contracts in *Measure for Measure*." *English Literary History* 49 (1982): 790–804.

Shakespeare, William. *All's Well That Ends Well*. Arden Edition. Ed. G. K. Hunter. Walton-on-Thames: Nelson, 1997.

———. *The Arden Shakespeare Complete Works*. Ed. Richard Proudfoot, Ann Thompson, and David Scott Kastan. Walton-on-Thames: Nelson, 1998.

——. *Hamlet*. Arden Edition. Ed. Harold Jenkins. Walton-on-Thames: Nelson, 1982, reprinted 1997.

——. *King Lear*. Arden Edition. Ed. R. A. Foakes. London: Nelson, 1997.

——. *Measure for Measure*. Arden Edition. Ed. J. W. Lever. New York: Routledge, 1965.

——. *Measure for Measure*, Oxford Edition. Ed. N. W. Bawcutt. Oxford: Clarendon, 1991.

——. *The Merchant of Venice*. Arden Edition. Ed. John Russell Brown. Walton-on-Thames: Nelson, 1997.

——. *A Midsummer Night's Dream*. Ed. Harold F. Brooks. London: Thomas Learning, 1979.

——. *Othello*. Arden Edition. Ed. E. A. J. Honigman. Walton-on-Thames: Nelson, 1997.

——. *Troilus and Cressida*. Arden Edition. Ed. David Bevington. Walton-on-Thames: Nelson, 1999.

Simonds, Peggy Munoz. "Sacred and Sexual Motifs in *All's Well That Ends Well*." *Renaissance Quarterly* 42.1 (1989): 33–59.

Simpson, A. W. B. *A History of the Common Law of Contract*. Oxford: Clarendon, 1975.

——. *A History of the Land Law*. Oxford: Clarendon, 1986.

——. *Legal Theory and Legal History: Essays on the Common Law*. London: Hambledon, 1987.

Sokol, B. J., and Mary Sokol. *Shakespeare's Legal Language*. London: Athlone, 2000.

Spinosa, Charles. "Shylock and Debt and Contract in *The Merchant of Venice*." *Cardozo Studies in Law and Literature* 5.1 (1993): 65–85.

Stevenson, Kenneth. *Nuptial Blessing: A Study of Christian Marriage Rites*. New York: Oxford UP, 1983

Swinburne, Henry. *A Treatise on Spousals*. London: Roycroft, 1686.

Thomas, Vivian. *The Moral Universe of Shakespeare's Problem Plays*. Totowa, NJ: Barnes, 1987.

Thorne, S. E. *Essays in English Legal History*. London: Hambledon, 1985.

Tillyard, E. M. W. *Shakespeare's Problem Plays*. Toronto: Chatto P, 1950.

Toole, William. *Shakespeare's Problem Plays*. The Hague: Mouton, 1966.

Turner, Frederick. *Shakespeare's Twenty-First Century Economics: The Morality of Love and Money*. New York: Oxford UP, 1999.

Underhill, Sir Arthur. "Shakespeare's Law." In *Shakespeare's England*. Vol. 1. Oxford: Clarendon, 1916.

Ure, Peter. *Shakespeare: The Problem Plays*. London: Longmans, 1961.

Van Doren, Mark. *Shakespeare*. New York: Holt, 1939.

Wheeler, Richard. *Shakespeare's Development and the Problem Comedies: Turn and Counter-Turn.* Los Angeles: U of California P, 1981.

White, James Boyd. *The Legal Imagination.* Boston: Little, 1973.

White, R. S. *Natural Law in English Renaissance Literature.* Cambridge: Cambridge UP, 1996.

Wilks, John S. *The Idea of Conscience in Renaissance Tragedy.* London: Routledge, 1990.

Wilson, Luke. *Theaters of Intention.* Stanford: Stanford UP, 2000.

Wilson, Thomas. *Art of Rhetoric.* Ed. Peter E. Medine. University Park: Pennsylvania State UP, 1994.

Zane, John Maxcy. *The Story of Law.* Indianapolis: Liberty Fund, 1927.

Index